PORTFOLIO / PENGUIN

THE SECRET CLUB THAT RUNS THE WORLD

Kate Kelly, author of the *New York Times* bestseller *Street Fighters*, covers Wall Street for CNBC. She spent ten years at the *Wall Street Journal*, where she won the Livingston Award and two Gerald Loeb awards. She lives in Brooklyn with her family.

THE SECRET CLUB THAT RUNS THE WORLD

INSIDE THE FRATERNITY OF
COMMODITY TRADERS

KATE KELLY

PORTFOLIO / PENGUIN

PORTFOLIO / PENGUIN

Published by the Penguin Group
Penguin Group (USA) LLC
375 Hudson Street
New York, New York 10014

USA | Canada | UK | Ireland | Australia | New Zealand | India | South Africa | China
penguin.com
A Penguin Random House Company

First published in the United States of America by Portfolio / Penguin,
a member of Penguin Group (USA) LLC, 2014
This paperback edition published 2015

ISBN 978-1-59184-546-1 (hc.)
ISBN 978-1-59184-713-7 (pbk.)

Printed in the United States of America
10 9 8 7 6 5 4 3 2

Set in ITC New Baskerville Std
Designed by Alissa Rose Theodor

While the author has made every effort to provide accurate telephone numbers, Internet
addresses, and other contact information at the time of publication, neither the publisher nor
the author assumes any responsibility for errors or for changes that occur after publication.
Further, publisher does not have any control over and does not assume any responsibility for
author or third-party Web sites or their content.

For my husband, who makes everything possible.

CONTENTS

CONTENTS

CAST OF CHARACTERS

At BlueGold Capital Management

Pierre Andurand, *chief investment officer*
Dennis Crema, *chief executive officer*
Paul Feldman, *chief financial officer*
Neel Patel, *trader*

At Glencore International

Ivan Glasenberg, *chief executive officer*
Alex Beard, *global head of oil*
Marc Rich, *founder*

At Morgan Stanley

John Mack, *chief executive officer*
John Shapiro, *global head of commodities*
Jennifer Fan, *commodity index trader*

Goran Trapp, *European head of commodities*
Jean Bourlot, *commodity trader*

At the Commodity Futures Trading Commission

Gary Gensler, *chairman*
Bart Chilton, *commissioner*
Michael Dunn, *commissioner*
Dan Berkovitz, *general counsel*
David Meister, *director of enforcement*

At Delta Air Lines

Richard Anderson, *chief executive officer*
Edward Bastian, *president*
Paul Jacobson, *treasurer and, later, chief financial officer*
Jon Ruggles, *vice president of fuel*

At Goldman Sachs

Gary Cohn, *president and chief operating officer*
Brett Olsher, *investment banker*
Jeff Currie, *European cohead of commodities research*
Trey Griggs, *head of U.S. energy risk management*

At Xstrata

Mick Davis, *chief executive officer*

Trevor Reid, *chief financial officer*

Thras Moraitis, *head of strategy and corporate affairs*

At the Qatar Investment Authority

Sheik Hamad bin Jassim bin Jaber Al Thani, *chief executive and prime minister of Qatar*

Ahmad al-Sayed, *chief executive of Qatar Holding, the investment arm of QIA*

Other Key Players

Evgenia Slyusarenko, *Pierre Andurand's wife*

Carl Levin, *Democratic senator and chairman of the Permanent Subcommittee on Investigations*

Sheik Mohammed bin Rashid Al Maktoum, *vice president of the United Arab Emirates and ruler of Dubai*

Jon Corzine, *former head of Goldman Sachs and chief executive officer of MF Global*

Spiro Youakim, *investment banker at Lazard*

Michael Klein, *investment banker and founder of M. Klein & Co.*

Tony Blair, *consultant and former UK prime minister*

Ivonne Ruggles, *Jon Ruggles's wife*

Tony Ward, *cofounder of Armajaro*

PREFACE

A few years ago, a colleague at CNBC turned me on to an interesting topic: natural gas hedging. There was a large driller in Oklahoma City called Chesapeake Energy that had made billions of dollars by buying and selling contracts betting on future prices of gas, he explained—perhaps even more money at times than it had made selling actual gas. Chesapeake's chief executive, Aubrey McClendon, liked to brag about his company's trading prowess, and some investors were becoming antsy about whether he was focused enough on his underlying business.

I flew out to Oklahoma to meet with McClendon, who was unapologetic about his gas trading activities. "If gas prices go to zero in 2011, it's great for customers, it doesn't bother us, it hurts our competitors," he told me in a televised interview. "So once we get hedged, we kind of want lower gas prices."

His sanguineness about potential price declines in his company's central product, which was then trading at unusually low levels, amazed me, and it struck many of CNBC's viewers as strange too. Over time, an investigation by Reuters revealed that McClendon was such an avid trader that he'd operated a hedge fund outside of Chesapeake Energy that handled contracts connected to some of the same products the company produced. Amid this and other revelations of apparent conflicts of interest, he announced his retirement in 2013.

Meanwhile, I'd become hooked on the topic of commodity trading. I'd met a crude-oil trader at a New York–area hedge fund whose withering take on his own business—which he felt was dominated by irrational penchants for risk and a bunch of grown men with emotional issues—had made me want to learn more. I'd traveled to Nebraska to interview a corn farmer whose Tweets about crop yields and planting conditions were being watched by brokers on the Chicago Mercantile Exchange, showing both the interconnectedness of the physical farming business to its futures counterpart and the hunger with which traders searched for clues. And I'd covered the initial public offering of Glencore International, the $60 billion Swiss commodity-trading colossus founded by the longtime American fugitive Marc Rich, which made huge markets in everything from crude oil to cobalt and yet was completely unknown to the public.

As far as I could tell, commodity-contract trading was a black box. It was a business that was both massive and impactful, affecting the day-to-day prices of raw materials like crude oil and wheat, and, in turn, influencing the cost of everything from iPhones to coffee. But the whole market was scantly covered by the media and poorly understood in general. At home, successful commodity hedge-fund traders might be profiled in the newspaper, but how they bet on markets and what motivated them to make such bold moves rarely was. Overseas, commodity giants like Glencore and its counterparts were a complete mystery—even though they dominated the markets for important products universally used.

I wanted answers. Who were these guys, and how did they work? What impact did they have on the price of physical commodities? And who was monitoring them?

This book tells you what I found.

—November 2014

AUTHOR'S NOTE

This book is the product of scores of interviews with people who buy, sell, trade, regulate, or study commodities for a living. Many of them spoke to me on the record, and their quotes appear throughout the text, either as what they said at the time of the events described, or what they have said on more recent reflection.

A number of interviewees, however, spoke on the condition that they not be named as sources. I have used their input, alongside that of named sources, to reconstruct the events of the book. The meetings, trades, thought processes, life events, and professional histories I've covered have in every case come from my own direct observations, relevant documents, a primary source who was involved, secondary sources who were in close proximity to the situations described, or, finally, from prior reporting that I have cited.

Not everyone agrees on the precise details of every interaction. Where documentary or other decisive evidence was not available, I solicited comments from all major parties and reflected their input in the book. The controversies that required additional context are described in further detail, often with suggestions for further reading, in the endnotes.

THE
SECRET CLUB
THAT RUNS THE
WORLD

1

THE BUBBLE

Pierre Andurand was so comfortable with his $8 billion crude-oil position that he spent the first half of his day doing a hard-core workout with his personal trainer, casually reading the news on a Bloomberg computer terminal, and munching on lean protein and toast at his London town house. It was May 5, 2011, Osama bin Laden had just been killed, and political instability in the Middle East seemed guaranteed to raise energy prices.

Andurand made the short walk to his hedge-fund office at midday. Brent crude-oil futures, the commodity market based on petroleum drilled in Europe's North Sea that he followed most closely, had been hovering in the low $120s that morning, which annoyed him. He'd been betting for weeks that oil would trade higher, but prices had not obliged. Still, with the U.S. markets having only recently opened for the day and the amount of trading still a bit light, he kept a previously scheduled meeting with the author of a book series called Market Wizards in a conference room downstairs from his trading desk.

An hour or so into the meeting, Andurand got an urgent e-mail from one of his traders, who had returned from a coffee break to find the Brent market down $2.50. That was a big move for a single afternoon in London, let alone for a fraction of an hour. The trader was baffled.

Andurand wasn't worried. The oil market was a volatile beast, he knew, and such fluctuations weren't unprecedented. He'd always played them to his advantage, even awakening one time from surgery to find that Brent had risen $10, just as he'd predicted. He kept chatting with the writer, telling him about his philosophy on trading and how he'd applied it at his hedge fund, BlueGold Capital Management, which had been celebrated for having predicted both the high point and the low point of the crude-oil market in 2008. It was a call that had established the firm as one of the most successful commodity hedge funds of all time.

E-mails from upstairs began flooding in. The Brent drop had widened another fraction of a dollar, then another dollar. Andurand's team was scouring the trader chat rooms and the Internet for information that would explain the sell-off—a production hike by OPEC? A release of the U.S. Strategic Petroleum Reserve?—but there was none to be found. Meanwhile, BlueGold was losing hundreds of millions of dollars. Andurand couldn't focus. "Why are you looking at your BlackBerry?" the writer finally asked him.

Andurand ended the meeting and rushed upstairs. His two young traders, Neel Patel and Sam Simkin, were sitting at their computers, looking anxious. Brent futures had fallen several dollars in an hour, and their downward spiral was weighing on other parts of the market too. It was a level of distress the thirty-four-year-old Andurand, who had been trading energy products daily for more than a decade, had rarely seen. He called a few other traders to ask what was happening. He instant-messaged a few more. Nobody had a clue.

Whatever it was, it was bad for BlueGold. Andurand and his partners had used complex trades to build a position three times as large on paper as the $2.4 billion in assets they were managing, and it was set to maximize profits as crude oil prices rose. But if crude fell sharply, as it did that day, it could be disastrous for the hedge fund.

Andurand turned to his traders. "Sell a few hundred million worth!" he said. "See how the market takes it."

Clicking their mouse buttons furiously to finalize trades on their computer screens, Patel and Simkin began selling off futures on Brent crude as well as its U.S. counterpart, the West Texas Intermediate, or WTI, oil contract, which was pegged to physical crude oil stored in Oklahoma. Although crude was always subject to its own regional supply and demand issues, jitters about the trajectory of prices tended to play out publicly in the futures markets, where hedge funds like BlueGold made bets on whether prices would stay low or high in the months and years to come.

Unloading a multibillion-dollar set of trades was extremely difficult to do without losing additional money in the process. On a calm day, sale orders comprising large numbers of contracts— each of which was linked to one thousand barrels of actual, physical petroleum—could tip other traders off to the idea that somebody had a lot to sell and prompt them to sell oil contracts themselves. The result was an even further price drop. On a rough day, a large sale could prove an even stronger depressant on prices.

BlueGold's initial sales on May 5 seemed to worsen the markets. Brent continued falling, and the fund's traders perceived an added drop whenever they pressed the sell button. A few hours into the rout, Brent was down $6, then $7, with little sign of settling.

But Andurand couldn't afford to stop. He told the traders to wait twenty minutes before making additional sales, hoping that would let the market calm a bit. It was chaos in their office. Land lines and mobile phones were ringing. Competitors and friends wanted updates and gossip. Was BlueGold collapsing? they asked. Reporters had the same question. Everyone knew of Andurand's appetite for enormous bets—and his reputation for relaxed risk management.

Brent went down, down, another dollar, another fifty cents, another dollar. BlueGold continued selling. By 7:30 that evening in London, as the U.S. markets dwindled to a close, Brent had fallen almost $10.40 per contract, a historic move.

Andurand, finally able to pause, was in a state of shock. Blue-Gold had managed to sell off $3 billion worth of positions, far more than he had expected they could under such duress. But the firm's losses for the day were a half billion dollars, and it still had $5 billion invested in the markets, betting that crude-oil would rise.

■

Andurand's day that May was the sort of experience that would humble any good trader. But in the world of commodity trading, where a relatively small circle of powerful players take enormous risks gambling on the future price of physical raw materials like oil, corn, and copper, huge market moves and the resultant gains and losses are incredibly common.

"Commodity" is an overused word that in colloquial terms applies to things so widely available—toilet paper, milk, dry cleaning—that they are bought and sold almost solely on the basis of price. In the context of the global markets, physical commodities serve a crucial purpose, however: they are the basic building blocks of agriculture, industry, and commerce. The reason Brent crude oil or the widely grown grain known as number two yellow corn are called commodities—a term that brings to mind things that are easily found and not overly valuable—is that their structural, chemical makeup is the same no matter where in the North Sea they are drilled or in what field they are harvested. Like toilet paper and dry cleaning, those commodities also trade on the basis of price. But price in their case is an outgrowth of a long list of what traders call "fundamentals": the cost of actually getting the commodity out of the earth, the cost of moving it from its source to a buyer, how many people want to buy it at a given time, how plentiful it is in other locations, and at what price, at that particular time.

Commodities may sound like an esoteric market, but everyone has heard of at least some of them. Gasoline and crude oil are important ones, and copper, which is used in the wiring of iPhones and air conditioners and maintains a minor presence on the U.S. penny (which at this point is mostly zinc), is another. Corn, wheat, and cotton are consumed or worn by almost everyone. Other commodities, such as the element cerium, referred to as a "rare-earth" commodity because of its elusiveness, are obscure—although cerium too is put to work in mundane products like cigarette lighters and movie-projection bulbs.

The practice of gaming out commodity price changes through financial bets—the subject of this book—is believed to be quite old. More than three thousand years ago, Sumerian farmers promised a portion of their harvests in exchange for silver up front. Those agreements, known to modern traders as "forwards," were memorialized in the first written language, a body of symbols known as cuneiform.

The trading of commodities based on future deliveries persisted for centuries, from ancient Rome to the Italian merchant cities to the Dutch traders who exchanged tulips in the 1630s. Commodity trading came to the U.S. with the British colonists, and was formalized by the opening of the Chicago Board of Trade in 1848, spurring a century and a half of more sophisticated virtual trading by a group of more dedicated practitioners. Eventually, commodity trading became its own dedicated niche. Farmers uncertain of the next year's crop wanted to ensure that they had a reliable amount of income, even in a bad year, and companies dependent on a certain metal for manufacturing wanted to lock in lower prices in advance to guard against a huge price spike that could erase their profit margins. Over time, additional commodity exchanges opened in the cities that most needed them, and entire companies grew up around the need simply to hedge commodities.

During the 2000s, however, commodity trading became the new fad. Volume and volatility in the commodity contract markets exploded, propelled by a massive influx of both everyday and professional investors. In the "listed" markets, where contracts traded at places like the New York Mercantile Exchange and the IntercontinentalExchange in Atlanta, volume shot from roughly 500 million contracts per year in 2002 to nearly 2 billion contracts in 2008.

Meanwhile, in the over-the-counter market for commodity contracts, where an array of exotic financial products connected to physical commodities was traded party-to-party by phone and computer (in other words, off the exchange), the total value on paper of the trades outstanding spiked from about $800 billion to more than $13 trillion over roughly the same period. Suddenly, commodity contracts, once a rounding error in the world of tradable products, were all the rage.

Nonetheless, commodity investing was small compared to stocks, bonds, and currencies. Until the mid-2000s, most investors had never seriously considered adding commodities to their individual portfolios, which tended to favor simple, easily traded things like stocks and U.S. Treasury bonds. But something happened to commodities in the 2000s to change their minds: a huge increase in prices and an especially convincing sales job by Wall Street.

Between the early 2000s and the middle of 2008, before the U.S. financial crisis hit, the contracts tracked by the Goldman Sachs Commodity Index, known as the GSCI for short—the commodity equivalent of the Standard & Poor's 500 Index—nearly tripled in price. (S&P, in fact, bought the index and added its own name to the title in 2007.) Crude oil futures rose three and a half times their earlier levels. Corn futures also tripled. Even gold, an oddball commodity because it often performs better when the stock markets fall—and in this case stocks were on fire—nearly doubled.

It was a period of easy money, and the benefits were felt all around, from state pension funds that had added commodities to their investments in order to mitigate their exposure to other, unrelated markets, to individual investors, who had dipped into commodities as a way to make money off of skyrocketing oil prices even though their gasoline was so much more expensive at the pump. Salesmen for the GSCI and other commodity indexes argued that their products were an important way to diversify investment portfolios. An array of new securities that traded like stocks but tracked precious metals like gold and silver had made commodity investing easier for regular people than ever before, and the commodity market's inexorable upward movement meant that they'd be crazy not to buy in.

"Wall Street did a nice job of marketing the value of having the diversification of commodities in your portfolio," says Jeff Scott, chief investment officer of the $74 billion financial firm Wurts & Associates. "I don't mean that sarcastically. And there is value to having certain commodities in your portfolio. Unfortunately, the return composition changed." In other words, at a certain point the money wagon stopped rolling along.

Until 2008, there were many reasons to like commodities, particularly the torrid pace of demand in India and China and the strength of the U.S. dollar, which, as the standard currency for trading raw materials, benefited prices dramatically. Those economies, which were driving up the price of raw materials around the world, were widely seen as the harbingers of what the buzzier banking analysts referred to as a new "supercycle," a period of sustained world growth the likes of which had not been seen since World War II. There was also a prevalent theory known as "Peak Oil" suggesting that the world's petroleum supplies were well on their way to being tapped out—a situation that would make crude oil, the engine of so many economies, frighteningly scarce. Both hypotheses augured a continuing climb in the price of oil.

But during the second half of 2008, the belief in higher commodity prices vanished. Like stocks and bonds, commodities were roiled by the financial crisis in the U.S. The main commodity index plummeted, and crude-oil contracts sank to a fraction of their record high of $147. Underlying their sudden drops amid volatile times in the market was a broader story line: the whole commodity craze had by then begun to fizzle.

Throughout the bubble in commodities, a core group of traders were siphoning much of the profit. They were industry veterans who, like Pierre Andurand, used a combination of strategy and heft to play the markets to their benefit. Along the way, their bets that commodity prices would rise had the ability to move markets upward, and their bets that prices would fall, the opposite. For the most part, they weren't manipulating prices by hooking up with fellow traders to orchestrate group decisions, nor were they buying physical commodities to constrict supplies while collecting money by betting that the futures prices would go up, a classic commodity swindle known as cornering. But their intimate knowledge of nuanced industries, their access to closely held information, and their enormous resources gave them tremendous advantages that few others had. And even when they bet wrong, they were still so rich and well connected that they could usually return the next day and begin to make their money back.

It was an industry of optimism, peopled by wealthy, focused traders who were not afraid of an occasional setback. Some had absentee fathers whose gaps they longed to fill with power and money, some were simply more comfortable with risk than their counterparts. After all, commodities were an area in which the market swings in a given day could be exponentially greater in size than the typical moves in stock or bond markets.

"When you trade commodities, you realize really quickly that markets can do anything," explained Gary Cohn during an interview in Goldman's sleek New York corporate offices one day in

2012. "So I love when I sit there with guys who say, 'that would be a three-standard-deviation move,'" that is, a shift in market prices that was three times as great as the typical one would be—as if that notion should come as a shock to the listener, he added: "In commodities, we have three standard-deviation moves in a day."

Commodity players can appear pampered, even lazy. Maybe they spend half the summer in Provence or Nantucket, working remotely from a Bloomberg terminal in their home office while their kids are minded by a live-in nanny. They might piddle away a serious investor meeting talking martial arts, move a long-scheduled international appointment just days in advance, refuse to take a view on the markets, or be too busy grouse-hunting in Norway to answer a couple of questions about the crude-oil business. All of the above happened with people interviewed for this book. But when it comes to trading raw materials, they are a shrewd and indomitable lot, and, at least for the moment, the contracts they trade are still so loosely regulated that the correct combination of money and skill creates irresistible opportunity. That's why I am only half-joking when I call them the secret club that runs the world.

In BlueGold's prime, it had several hundred competitors in the hedge-fund business, each of varying size. Commodity hedge funds, typically based in London, Greenwich, or Houston, picked one or more raw materials they understood well, then made a business of trading in the related contract markets. Their investors, usually a combination of larger money-management firms and wealthy individuals, presented them with billions of dollars to trade. There were many winners, but John Arnold, a onetime Enron trader who went into business for himself after it folded, did the best of all; his natural-gas-focused hedge fund, Centaurus

Energy, generated 317 percent returns in 2006. Several years later, Arnold retired, a billionaire at the age of thirty-eight. He became a philanthropist.

Prodigies like Arnold were the superstars of the industry, commanding respect as a result of the enormous sums of money they'd made. Andurand, who generated 209 percent returns in 2008, was in there too. But few hedge-fund traders were quite that accomplished. The rest of the commodity-trading hierarchy was topped by the large, multinational brokers involved in every single aspect of commodity harvesting and trading, from extracting the coal out of Colombian mines to hiring massive cargo ships to move them to Singapore while hedging the future price of coal as it was transported. Those companies, based largely outside of the U.S., had a long and sordid history of doing backroom deals with shady politicians, flouting international trade and human-rights laws, and engaging in tax dodges, pollution, even, allegedly, child labor. The big players in the industry were companies like Glencore and Trafigura, and their founding father was the American fugitive Marc Rich. Other parts of the commodity business feared their aggressive approach to business, given that they transacted with parties with whom the majority of the business community was loath to work.

But their scope and sheer manpower helped them understand tiny regional discrepancies in the price of oil and other goods, allowing them to source commodities more cheaply and sell them at a premium. That process generated tens of billions in profits. "This is off the record," or at least it has to be anonymous, one industry analyst told me, before describing one of the companies, because he didn't want the subject of his comments "to be blowing up my car." Many investors and even other traders had reservations about the international trading houses. But the comprehensive approach taken by Glencore and others, helped by a creative use of corporate regulatory havens, had given them elite status in certain commodity markets and made their executives exceedingly wealthy.

Most hedge-fund traders sat somewhere in the middle of the totem pole. In the larger scheme of commodity trading, they were essentially money changers, pooling other people's cash to try to outmaneuver the markets, placing bets on where prices would go, and skimming profits off the top of whatever they made when they were right—generally 20 percent of a year's earnings and about 2 percent of the money investors gave them. A Frenchman who had socialist influences growing up, Andurand considered the physical oil business to be dirty and distasteful, and told me at one point he would never consider taking delivery of an actual barrel of crude. He was just a trader, and although he had an £11 million house near Harrods in London, a customized Bugatti sports car, and a gorgeous Russian wife, he would never attain the sort of riches and power that his counterparts in the corporate commodity logistics business would. He was a mere millionaire, not a billionaire.

Still, Andurand had something others lacked: fearlessness. He traded billions of dollars' worth of oil contracts in the markets daily, exposing himself to potential losses that many traders couldn't stomach. Commodity hedge-fund traders talked often about their daddy issues and other insecurities and how they had learned to compartmentalize their financial woes without bringing them home at night. "My wife couldn't tell you if I had a good day or a bad day—ever," one Greenwich-based oil trader told me late in 2011. Andurand shared that thinking; he preferred to spend tens of thousands of euros on a bespoke wedding gown for his fiancée than to acknowledge his setbacks to her directly.

The international banks that dabbled in commodities were lower in the pecking order. In better days, Goldman Sachs and Morgan Stanley took in more than $3 billion apiece in revenue from buying and selling oil, gasoline, copper, and other commodities. They arranged elaborate hedging strategies for airlines dependent on cheap jet fuel, charging fees for their advice along the way, and they lent capital to hedge-fund traders, pocketing interest and fees in return. Sometimes they profited from trading directly with those clients, buying a commodity the client was selling, for instance, and making money unexpectedly when markets moved against that client. But the real money was made in trading for the house—turning their commodity traders into mini-Andurands with purses provided by the bank's shareholders. In 2008, for instance, two of the best-paid employees at the Swiss firm Credit Suisse were a pair of commodity traders who took home a combined $35 million after betting correctly on the crude markets. Their role was effectively eradicated in 2010 when a new law in the U.S. barred bank employees from trading for the house, prompting them and many of their counterparts to flee to less regulated parts of the industry. But the banks continued nosing around the regulatory margin, looking for ways to optimize their commodity-trading chops, and the Credit Suisse traders simply quit the bank and started their own oil-focused hedge fund.

Lying miserably at the bottom of the commodity-trading power structure were the individuals and corporations that depended on physical commodities—the Coca-Colas, Starbucks, Delta Air Lines, and small farmers of the world. Those actors were paralyzingly dependent on aluminum, sugar, coffee, and jet fuel for survival, but were, almost without exception, unable to keep up with the commodity traders at banks and hedge funds. Conservative-minded by nature, and loath to use the exotic financial products or fast-moving trading strategies that professional commodity traders employed, they lacked the expertise to game the markets and felt it wasn't their job to try, anyway. After all, they were selling lattes and airline seats, not risky commodity contracts that required multithousand-dollar down payments. Still, with the prices of many commodities climbing, the companies couldn't accommodate price shocks, so they often wound up hiring banks to hedge their vulnerability to volatile product markets. The result could include added fees, bad quarters—even potential bankruptcy, if large demands from banks or other trading counterparts for extra cash or collateral became too much to bear.

And if their limited knowledge and power were not enough of an obstacle, these companies and people were also damaged by sleaze in the brokerage business. Twice in the aftermath of 2008, middleman firms that lent money to commodity-contract buyers and sellers to make trades and then finalized them on exchanges failed due to the mishandling of funds, wiping out customer money in the process. One of them, MF Global, was run by Jon Corzine, a former head of Goldman Sachs in the 1990s and later the governor of New Jersey, who at MF used small investor money to pay debts from a side bet on European bonds that had gone bad. The case against him is still cycling through the courts, and it took more than two years for MF Global's customers to be made whole.

The astonishing wealth of commodity trading's inner circle was created in near-total obscurity. Because it operated within either closely held companies that didn't trade on public exchanges or deep within large banks and corporations, where commodity profits and losses weren't disclosed separately, the commodity-trading power elite has enjoyed utter anonymity. But if the individual participants in the boom went unnoticed, their impact did not. The commodity market's sudden growth in volume, and the parallel surge in commodity prices, along with the entrance of public investors such as the California Public Employees' Retirement System, raised serious questions about whether traders were jacking up the prices paid for commodities by average citizens.

In the United States, where so many people depend on car travel, fuel was an especially charged issue. During the commodity price spikes of 2008, the resultant $4-per-gallon price of gasoline sparked an outcry in the U.S., where members of Congress held forty hearings on the topic in the first half of that year alone. Motorists, trucking companies, and other fuel buyers blamed commodity speculators for driving up prices, and they wanted the government to rein things in. Under intense public pressure, Congress and the Commodity Futures Trading Commission vowed to scrutinize the speculators, who their own records showed were accounting for a much larger portion of the markets. But the brewing financial crisis and an ongoing political struggle between those in Washington who believed speculators affected commodity prices and those who didn't made the CFTC slow to act.

Overseas and in the States, the cost of food was another red flag. Food prices had risen during the market boom of the mid-2000s, but the concurrent inflation of home prices and the availability of cheap credit had blunted the impact on consumer spending. In the years after 2008, the price of staple grains like corn, wheat, and soybeans hit all-time highs, making food products costlier, even unaffordable. Some analysts believed that grain prices were causing revolution in already-stressed places such as Egypt, which played a pivotal role in the 2011 uprising known as the Arab Spring. And while unpredictable weather, poor crop yields, and a rise in demand were certainly influences, some academics also argued that commodity indexes like the GSCI were to blame, saying that the structure of those investments, which was to bet over and over again that prices would rise, actually caused such rises to happen in the physical and futures market.

They had a point, as an academic paper published in 2010 later proved. But the clear evidence of causation was still hard to find; even when a connection appeared obvious, the support for the theory tended to be largely anecdotal. Andurand estimates that during that fateful day in May 2011, BlueGold moved the Brent futures market down an additional $2 or $3—exacerbating by up to 33 percent what was already a huge, $10 down spiral in the crude market. Negative headlines about a lawsuit implicating the hedge-fund manager John Paulson, a large holder of the physically backed gold security known as the GLD, appeared to force gold futures down nearly 2 percent on a single day in 2010—a considerable move in a very large market that is difficult for any single party to affect. The idea that there is a connection in both cases is powerful, and likely accurate. But because the impact of market sentiment is impossible to document, we'll never completely know.

What is clear is that the last decade in commodity trading had a unique impact, both on the market itself and the public's perception of commodities as a compelling investment. The abundance of new speculators, the meteoric growth of the GSCI and other, similar investment vehicles, and the general ebullience about the supercycle and its implicit effect on raw materials all made the market's shifts more dramatic. That volatility created kings in the trading world's empowered class, and drove other people and companies into financial ruin. The commodities bubble of the 2000s is a snapshot of one of the most extraordinary periods in American finance, providing an object lesson on the role of markets, regulators, and how the money world can sometimes lose its connection to the real one.

2

THE SPECULATOR

Over a leisurely lunch one July day a couple of years ago at a sidewalk bistro in Andurand's hometown of Aix-en-Provence, the warm, bustling city near the Mediterranean coast in southern France, I asked him who was the best commodity trader in the world. "I'd like to say it's me," he said, with a small chuckle, then went back to cutting his food.

Medium-height and beefy at the time, with rimless glasses and short blond hair, Andurand was wearing his standard ensemble that day: linen shirt unbuttoned just enough to reveal a plug of chest hair, relaxed-fit jeans, and suede loafers. He'd spent the morning reminiscing about his youth in Aix and Réunion, the island off the coast of Madagascar where he'd lived for a few years, and the nuances of betting on oil prices for a living. He spoke fluent English in a thick French accent, making the occasional word incomprehensible to an American, and glanced at his ever-present BlackBerry every so often for word on a pending merger between several Dutch kickboxing businesses he'd recently bought. He was on hiatus from trading that summer and focused his considerable energies instead on staging live fights that fall in Milan and Tokyo.

Andurand was at first glance the archetypical hedge-fund trader. He was nouveau riche in a loud way, the evidence including his wife (Russian, former model), his house (a 5,000-square-foot residence on one of West London's most charming streets), and his cars (a specially designed $1.5 million Bugatti sports car for cruising around town and a sleek black Porsche Cayenne for family trips). He wintered in Thailand, at an island resort he had bought and was remodeling, invested in movies and real estate, and was summering in a ten-bedroom château in the south of France, even though it was only his immediate family and mother-in-law there. The year before our lunch in Aix, Elton John and the Bolshoi Ballet had performed at his St. Petersburg wedding, and he'd made a film to show back in London for those who couldn't attend.

Despite his self-made hundreds of millions, however, Andurand was flaky in the extreme. He risked scads of money in the markets, but he couldn't remember a doctor's appointment without his wife's help. Successfully scheduling a meeting with him required half a dozen e-mails, a couple of phone calls, a venue change, and a long wait. Sometimes I'd make a trip to London and he wouldn't return my messages at all. He used these passive-aggressive tactics rather than simply saying he was unavailable, no doubt because he liked the publicity, and, ultimately, he did want to get together. But he also dreaded confrontation, which can be tough in a business where the phrase "he got his face ripped off" is about as common as "hello." Rather than upbraiding an employee who was screwing up, he explained, he favored having a "nice chat" about whatever was going on.

He lacked introspection. He was often hard-pressed to explain why he was comfortable taking such large risks; asked what motivated a given trade, he'd shrug and say something like, "I read a lot" or "I just saw that the price action was weird." Then he might turn the subject to kickboxing or home design. It was hard to tell whether he had never given the original question much thought, or if he was just intensely private. He seemed to have an uncanny knack for predicting the markets using a modicum of research combined with gut instinct. A decade in oil trading, which had provided him with an inside look at how banks and physical traders moved money and contracts around, had given him a feel for the cyclical nature of trading and what flashpoints in politics or the economy would trigger price changes in petroleum contracts. As long as he was up on the news and the predominant market theories at work, he could use his horse sense to bet on up or down moves pretty accurately.

This was possible in the oil market because the "fundamentals," or verifiable data on supply and demand, that drove it were constantly buffeted by events that were entirely unpredictable. A trader like Andurand could study world statistics on which countries were producing oil and how much per year. He could also look at global demand figures, broken down by country or even region. But unlike a tech company that had certain fixed costs and certain booked sales, as well as identifiable costs for research and the development of new products, the world crude market could shoot higher at any moment because war broke out in a place like Nigeria or Libya. Demand in the U.S. could soften any month—even months or a year after crisis hit—because of the recession that was pinching consumer spending. Reading up on the macroeconomic factors at play in the key oil-producing and oil-consuming nations gave a trader like Andurand a feel for what was possible. But in the end, trading crude involved much more guesswork than trading shares of Dell Computer.

Andurand had always been competitive. As a baby in Aix, he crawled out of his family's ninth-floor apartment and up a wall on the balcony before his mother pulled him to safety. When he got his first bicycle with training wheels, he threw a fit until she removed them. He begged for fancy shoes and other *accoutrements* that his parents, who worked as a civil engineer for the French government and a teacher, could not afford. Despite having comfortable homes in Aix and in Réunion, his frequent grousing spurred a family joke: that he was Dugommeau, the hero of a popular French comic strip *Les Frustrés*, "The Frustrated."

In elementary school, Andurand's teachers suggested that he skip a grade, saying he had a genius-level intellect. His mother Danielle, obliged, but laughed at the idea nonetheless. "Those tests don't mean anything," she says. Even after the grade-jump, school bored her young son.

Swimming became his obsession. By the time Andurand was in high school in Aix, he was swimming twice a day, six days a week at the suburban *piscine* near his high school. At fifteen, he impressed his coaches with a record-breaking time in the 200-meter freestyle competition; it would become his signature event. By age sixteen, he was the second-fastest swimmer in that race on the continent and had earned a spot on France's junior national team.

Through those interminable laps in the pool, a longer-term objective drove him: to compete in the Olympics. He wanted to test himself against some of the top athletes in the world.

The 1996 summer Olympic Games in Atlanta were a few years away, and his pace was a little short of the mark, but he thought there was time to improve. He enrolled at the National Institute for Applied Science, or Institut National des Sciences Appliquées, in Toulouse, a much larger city in southwestern France near the Pyrénées, where he could train with a superior university swim team while working toward a five-year engineering degree. But almost immediately after arriving, his performance slowed significantly. The pool in Toulouse was shorter than its counterpart in Aix, and the more frequent flip-turns hurt his performance. What had once been his lean athlete's diet also suffered. Instead of eating six thousand calories a day of the low-fat protein and vegetables his mother had always made, he was suddenly piling on pounds from ice cream and pizza binges.

He also spent five hours a day in relative solitude at the pool, where the other guys were standoffish. "In Aix, I was the number one swimmer," Andurand says. "In Toulouse I was one of the group, not one of the very best."

He had hit a mental block. Extra workouts weren't helping, so instead of pushing his body so hard, he relaxed and caught up on lost sleep. His times began to get better, just enough to make a difference. After riding him for weeks, his coach, who had at one point asked if he had used performance-enhancing drugs to speed his times in Aix, backed off. But Andurand's times still weren't what he'd hoped. Atlanta felt like an impossible goal. He could get a bit better, he figured, but he would never be good enough to make an Olympic final. Genetically speaking, he just wasn't built for it.

It was a harsh revelation, and Andurand had no idea how to fill the gap in his life. "He was quite depressed," remembers his mother. "He couldn't imagine a life without passion."

He avoided drugs and alcohol because he didn't like the idea of losing control. He'd observed some of his teammates getting loaded in Toulouse, and found the spectacle terribly sad. But he needed an outlet somewhere.

He was focusing on applied mathematics, the science of solving complex, real-world problems through quantitative means. It was lots of computer programming, lots of modeling, and ultimately only a handful of people in the world could even comprehend the stuff. Andurand imagined himself in five or ten years wearing bottle-cap nerd glasses and toiling in some dull *banlieue* as an engineer for a large corporation. He'd be surrounded by other men, never travel, meet no women, and make a hopelessly middle-class living.

He would have to think of something else.

■

Andurand spent the next several years going through the motions of school, trying to forge a plan. He considered his interests: sports, film. There was no obvious career in either. It would be so nice to have financial freedom, he thought. What about getting a job in the City of London or on Wall Street?

He began studying financial books. The Internet had limited content at the time, but he trolled what was there for ideas. Sales and trading seemed interesting, he thought, tapping into both market psychology and quantitative skills.

Ten years after the movie *Wall Street* had turned the trading industry into heroes and villains, and still in the early stages of a stock-market boom that was popularized by wildly lucrative technology-company initial public offerings, or IPOs, in the U.S., financial services didn't get much attention at a French engineering school like INSA. There was also a cultural bias against the rich. Andurand's father, Claude, a lifelong civil servant, liked to quote Balzac's famous line about how behind every great fortune lay a great crime. Andurand's professors considered trading to be a low calling too. Every time he raised the notion of working in banking or finance with them, they arched their eyebrows as if they thought he was crazy.

"They thought I was selling my soul to the devil," Andurand says.

■

In 1999 Andurand transferred to Paris, to the École des Hautes Études Commerciales de Paris, or HEC Paris, to get a master's degree in international finance.

He also began looking for an entry-level opening at a major bank. He had his heart set on an internship at Goldman Sachs. Not only did it have the most prestige, but the people he met during his interviews were the most welcoming—an ironic first impression coming from what was probably the most cutthroat firm on Wall Street.

Early in 2000, Andurand got an e-mail from Isabelle Ealet, the firm's managing director in charge of commodities. Ealet had reviewed his résumé and liked what she saw. She suggested they meet in Paris.

Sitting in the lobby of the palatial Plaza Athénée, one of Paris's most posh hotels, Ealet ordered tea. "What makes you want to do trading?" she asked, pleasantly, in French.

"It's what drives the world," Andurand said, as if he were able to make grand statements about how the financial system worked without ever having worked in it. "If you understand the flows of money, you understand what's going on in the world.

"I like the game aspect of it," he added, explaining his theory about how trading successfully was a combination of knowing politics, emotion, and math. "Money gives you the score, so it's easy to be measured."

"Why would you be good at it?"

"I have the drive, and I have the competitive spirit, from athletics."

He sensed that Ealet understood him. She, too, had grown up in Provence, and had come a long way from her early environs and the socialist culture. Now she was a wealthy, accomplished trader at an internationally known investment bank.

Ealet, in fact, was an anomaly in her profession, an assertive female executive who had traded physical commodities—crude for the French oil and gas company Total—and was an experienced manager too. In 1992, when a rising Goldman partner named Gary Cohn had relocated to London, she had helped him sort out who was who in the City's commodities circles. He, in turn, became one of her mentors at the firm.

On that day in Paris, Andurand jelled with Ealet. About a month later, after many more interviews and what felt to him like an agonizing wait, Goldman offered him an entry-level trading job in Singapore, its hub for trading energy contracts in Asia.

Singapore was a big oil processing center, where large ships brought raw crude to ports and, using sophisticated refining techniques, altered its chemical composition to churn out more readily usable products, like auto fuel and diesel. The refined oils would then be sold to gas distributors, airlines, logistics companies, and other bulk buyers around the region.

Andurand worked for a team that helped companies who bought or sold either crude oil or refined products in large quantities in order to hedge, or curb, their exposure to significant moves in their price. If a chain of gas stations, for instance, was concerned about a potential spike in the price of unleaded auto fuel, it might hire Goldman to reduce its vulnerability to higher prices by using gasoline contracts that locked in lower future prices in the market. The client would pay Goldman a small fee for arranging the contract trades, and Goldman was also free to use its own money to become directly involved in them, perhaps becoming the seller to a client buyer rather than simply matching that client up with another seller in the market, or using the information gleaned from the client's market position to trade for itself elsewhere in the gasoline markets.

Goldman's commodities business at the time was generating about a half billion dollars in revenue each year. Corporate commodity hedging, the term used to describe the sort of trades Andurand's team was arranging for clients, was becoming more popular. Other market participants were using commodity contracts simply to speculate on where markets would go. That meant there was plenty of room in the markets for Goldman to do a little house trading, known as proprietary, or "prop," trading, as well as whatever it was hired to do by clients.

Once a client trade was completed, Andurand would sometimes end up with leftover market exposure that he couldn't offload right away. He could hang on to those contracts until a buyer arrived, or he could trade them on a speculative basis and try to make a little profit. He liked doing the latter, and was making money at it. But he felt stymied by Goldman, which had strict risk controls that prevented him from making larger bets, and made him share a pool of capital with two other traders, which he regarded as a handicap.

■

After a year and a half, Andurand took a job at Bank of America. The old-fashioned depositor, headquartered in Charlotte, North Carolina, lacked Goldman's track record in the commodities business, but it was willing to give Andurand his own kitty to trade. He thought the opportunity was worth the sacrifice in prestige.

In his first nine months there, he was given a relatively small purse and told he could lose no more than a few million dollars on any given day (a sum that, outside of commodities, was large enough that it could be grounds for firing a young trader in stocks or other products). He managed to turn that capital into gains of $50 million—the single best performance in his department and easily half of the bank's entire commodities profits for that year.

Armed with a $3 million bonus check, Andurand took a triumphant trip home to France. He was learning how the game was played on bank commodities desks, and gaining valuable insight on an important regional energy market in Asia. His confidence was high. He was only twenty-five.

Still, Andurand lived a relatively modest lifestyle at home in Singapore. Now in a much happier head space than he had been after quitting the swim team, he was again working out and eating carefully. He still avoided the party scene. Instead of going out and getting bombed, as many traders in Singapore's expatriate community did, he spent quiet evenings at home with his girlfriend, a junior employee in Morgan Stanley's commodities division.

The risk-taking Andurand did do was all in the markets. He was beginning to understand the ebb and flow of market senti-ment in his corner of the commodity-trading business, and was making considerable money off his price wagers. His instincts soon led to another big win. In the first few months of 2003, his second year at Bank of America, a series of well-timed trades gen-erated another $30 million, an astonishing sum for an inexperi-enced trader.

With his pile of cash and risk limits higher than ever, he went into the second quarter betting that jet fuel prices would trend higher as a result of new flights that Asian airlines were adding to their schedules. Instead he was hit with one of those unexpected, market-changing events: the outbreak of a respiratory flu called SARS, or severe acute respiratory syndrome, that devastated the region's economy. In the wake of the epidemic, people stopped flying, and the price of jet fuel tanked as a result, losing Andurand $40 million in the markets.

The situation arguably could not have been foreseen, so An-durand didn't castigate himself. He was still plenty confident. It was turning into a bad year for commodities at Bank of America overall, and management was under pressure to improve results. The SARS loss was just bad timing, Andurand told himself. He thought he might be better off at a dedicated trading firm that understood risk-taking and provided the money with which to do it, rather than in a small department within a giant bank that had other, more important priorities and would be chastened by a single bad quarter.

It was typical of his mind-set, both then and later. "He fully expects that he will make a huge amount of money and that he's right," says Paul Andersen, who hired Andurand for the Bank of America job and still considers him a friend. "If the trade doesn't go well, then the market doesn't understand."

Whether he was fired or quit wasn't clear. But Andurand hit the job market with his signature attitude—admitting the missteps he'd made, but at the same time blaming the environment and vowing to do better. In an industry that valued traders with both swagger and a desire to change their errant ways, Andurand struck just the right tone, and Vitol Group, the large physical oil trader that operated a 250-man derivatives operation around the world, was impressed.

"There was no attempt to justify himself, and there was a very clear acknowledgement that things had gone wrong," remembers one of the Vitol managers who interviewed Andurand over dinner in London. Andurand told the group that "there were a number of aspects he had not taken into account, had not understood, and he believed he could learn those aspects by coming into maybe a more rounded organization than a bank," the manager adds, "which always takes a rather one-sided look at things. He was willing to reinvent himself to an extent."

Andurand stayed in Singapore during his first year with Vitol. Unlike Bank of America and Goldman, which did a little client hedging and a little house trading, Vitol was a huge dealer in physical oil and refined products and used derivatives to mitigate its exposure to short-term price changes. If Vitol bought crude oil from Nigeria at a fixed price, for instance, it might be a couple of weeks before the crude reached its destination in Europe, during which time the price could drop. It was the job of Vitol's traders to use futures or other contracts to lock in more attractive prices for crude that would smooth out any potential losses from that two-week lag. In so doing, traders like Andurand were made privy to perfectly legal inside information on the world's physical petroleum markets—which former Soviet states were selling for which price, which refiners in the Singapore region were buying which grades at which price—that was invaluable to understanding the developing market trends at any given time. If demand were slowing in a typically hard-core market for crude purchasing, Vitol and its rivals would be the first to know, since they were negotiating deals with crude buyers directly. The minute a good customer reduced their order, the firm's contract traders would be informed so that they could hedge Vitol's exposure to price changes accordingly. Over time, the constellation of data points to which Andurand was exposed added up to a far more nuanced picture of the global petroleum markets than the version a bank trader would have seen.

In addition to receiving a more sophisticated lesson in global physical oil-trading, Andurand was learning patience in the markets. Trading oil sometimes required taking a longer-term view, he realized. It also demanded an analysis of both large, overarching factors, such as central bank policies and their effect on state economies, as well as more market-driven developments, like whether there was a floor price for crude-oil contracts below which the market's traders appeared reluctant to go.

On a personal level, he was almost universally regarded as a sweet, self-effacing guy. When he came into money, he offered to buy his parents a bigger house in Provence and showed up the day after his mother sent him a listing in Beaurecueil, a town just east of Aix, to look at and buy it. He supported his sister and her family, at one point employing her as a secretary in London when she needed work. His friends found him charming, even if he was occasionally a spendthrift. "He's just a smart, good, guy and does it his way," Paul Andersen says.

On the trading desk, however, Andurand was making the occasional enemy. Early in his tenure at Vitol, he was tipped off to a trading opportunity in the jet-fuel market by a social acquaintance at Morgan Stanley who also dealt with commodities. The other trader, a brash fellow Frenchman named Jean Bourlot who got so worked up about his ideas he almost vibrated with intensity, was convinced that the Singapore market for jet fuel was poised for price gains.

Singapore jet fuel at the time was trading at about $40, but Bourlot expected it to move much higher in the months to come. He had good contacts in the small marketplace where the product traded and was positive of it. Bourlot had placed that bet in the markets himself, and wanted to put even more cash into the trade. But he had reached his maximum trade size under Morgan Stanley's policies—which, like Goldman and Bank of America, placed limits on the amount of risk a trader could take—so he offered to sell some of his call options, which were the right to buy jet fuel at predetermined prices, to Andurand. In return, he wanted Andurand to sell those rights back to him when the time was right.

Andurand studied the market in question and quickly agreed to purchase the contracts; Singapore jet fuel also struck him as underpriced. He bought positions from Bourlot, predicting that Singapore jet fuel would trade above $50. The cost of doing so was relatively cheap—about $2 and change per option. Andurand was under no obligation to accommodate Bourlot's wishes in handling the trade afterward, but Bourlot seemed to have the impression that Andurand would sell the contracts when Bourlot told him to.

A few months later, Bourlot's market hunch proved correct. Amid a big surge in the price of crude, a series of demands for additional cash from lenders forced China Aviation Oil (Singapore) Corporation Ltd., which was reportedly Singapore's biggest jet trader, to liquidate its own trading positions in a hurry. The cash demands were such that China Aviation couldn't afford to wait for an attractive price to offload its contracts, and other traders, spotting its distress, quickly drove its costs higher. Singapore jet prices flew higher to levels well north of $40, and by late 2004 they were flirting with $65. Midway through the price hike, Bourlot called Andurand.

"You saw the news," Bourlot said. "I need to buy back jet options now," he added, referring to the positions he had sold to Andurand earlier.

Andurand was irritated. Whatever Bourlot had envisioned at the outset, it now sounded to Andurand like Bourlot had essentially wanted to park his excess positions with Vitol until a better moment arose, at which point Bourlot would buy them back after having taken only limited risk himself. Andurand had no intention of selling back to Bourlot at Bourlot's direction, which he thought would have been bad timing in the markets and a sure way to leave additional profits on the table.

"I'm happy to be long," Andurand said, meaning that he continued to think the market would move even higher. In fact, he saw an extended rally coming—perhaps for another two years. He told Bourlot to find another way to add to his portfolio.

Bourlot was angry. "You're making money from having that trade," he said. "It was my idea. You should help me out."

"I'm sorry," said Andurand, "but I never bought them to sell them back. I like that position. I want to let it run."

By April of 2005, Singapore jet had practically doubled in price from where Andurand had first bought contracts on it. Andurand says he made $40 per option on the trade, for profits of some $50 million. His bosses were thrilled and his bonus reflected it.

Bourlot, however, made less money than he wanted, and told a mutual friend that he considered Andurand at least partly to blame. The two would be adversaries for years to come, right up to the point where they were raising money for their own personal hedge funds.

Vitol relocated Andurand to London after a year. He was happy to finally be at the epicenter of commodity trading. He found an apartment in Knightsbridge, not far from his office near Victoria Station, and prepared for the explosion in energy prices he had been expecting.

Andurand's job by that time was purely to speculate. He was given about $100 million to trade crude and other energy products, markets with which he was now well acquainted. Certain crude-oil futures were in "backwardation," or a situation in which the futures prices were lower than the current prices, but he thought that scenario temporary. He was spending much of his money on crude-oil calls dated multiple years into the future at significantly higher prices.

At Vitol Andurand worked with a team, but nobody really bothered him. Unlike many of his colleagues, who were focused on hedging Vitol's physical exposure as it moved crude and refined products from one location to another, he had moved beyond the more tailored deal-by-deal protective trades and was focused on the more esoteric art of predicting what other traders might do in the global commodity contract markets. Quantitative analysis that he'd learned at university helped him understand the history behind the market's moves, but knowledge of the energy industry's fundamental drivers, as well as the groupthink that helped push around prices, was crucial as well. Andurand was honing his skill for putting all those components together and coming up with a strategy for making money. And he was soon doubling his capital every year.

He also benefited from a number of built-in advantages. Not only did Vitol do business in numerous individual physical energy markets around the world, creating the data bank that helped inform Andurand and his colleagues' individual trades, it had massive scale as well. Its experiences in the petroleum markets were more than just anecdotal. Vitol was handling one of the single-biggest shares of the trading of oil in global markets—up to 10 percent of active, or "open," contracts in oil in the New York Mercantile Exchange market alone, by some estimates. Those details helped Vitol's contract traders make significant profits.

Having now mastered the art of physical hedging and gotten quite good at speculative trading, Andurand was getting bored again. It was as if all those built-in advantages made trading too easy—or perhaps, given that he wanted even more autonomy over his work to generate fast profits, not easy enough. In 2007 Andurand approached his superiors about the idea of opening his own hedge fund within Vitol. He knew it was a long shot. Domiciled in Switzerland, where the market regulation was looser and the tax rates lower, Vitol was extremely secretive. So asking it to open up its books to potential investors, just so that Andurand could make trades he was already paid handsomely to make without the glare of outside investors, was asking a pretty big favor.

Predictably, Andurand's bosses said no. They were not interested in the asset-management business, they told him. But they presented him with some parting gifts: an attractive bonus check and the assurance of a good recommendation to potential investors, should he ever need it.

Andurand resigned from Vitol in May 2007 and decided to take some time off. He wanted to have some fun. Stressful days in the oil markets had distracted him from keeping fit, normally a priority. Any time his weight crept up past 220 pounds, he knew he was overeating and it was time for a change.

Andurand had married his girlfriend from Singapore, but things hadn't worked out, and now that he was divorced, he wanted to meet some new women. So for the next four months, he made it his mission to run, weight train, go on dates, travel, and find his way back to an equilibrium from which he could start a new business.

About a month into Andurand's sabbatical, he had an unexpected caller: Dennis Crema, who had managed all the gasoline trading at Vitol. An American whose first exposure to the oil business had been working on a tanker in the Long Island Sound in his early twenties, Crema had been an impressive trader in his own right at the Swiss firm—about as successful, in fact, as Andurand had been. Crema was also older, and after years of working in the physical trading business in the U.S. and London, he had landed a job as, effectively, the head trader at Vitol, a very senior position that reported directly to the company's president and chief executive officer.

Crema proposed to join Andurand as CEO of his new hedge fund, playing the senior statesman role to Andurand's head trader. He had a long list of contacts in the investment business, he argued, and could help the fledgling fund attract new capital. He would also help Andurand figure out how to approach the markets and to interface with brokerage firms on Wall Street, which provided crucial funding and trading assistance.

"I was very flattered at the time," says Andurand. "He was a very successful trader at Vitol." So he accepted.

■

Their fund, BlueGold Capital Management, started trading in February 2008 with $120 million in capital and half a dozen employees. February was the very month when the market for mortgages tied to high-risk borrowers, known as "subprime" loans, started to flatline, signaling the beginning of the U.S. credit crisis. Those investors who had seen the drop coming were already positioned for a flurry of late payments or defaults by home-loan recipients and had bought vast quantities of insurance policies that would pay out if the loans went bad.

But commodities markets were still humming. Chinese manufacturing had by now become the engine of world consumer-goods production. In India, a massive and young population was consuming more services and products. Those two countries alone were on pace to grow their economies at an annual rate of close to 10 percent apiece, according to statistics published by the International Monetary Fund—levels that the U.S., whose economy grew by a few percentage points per year, had not seen since the early 1980s.

Crude oil would be the key to their growth. Already that winter, electricity shortages were hampering parts of the developing economies around the world. In China, the most severe winter weather in fifty years had damaged power sources throughout the country, and poor government planning in South Africa had spurred power outages that affected the entire continental region.

Amid all the demand and lack of supply, there was also an overarching fear of "Peak Oil," a 1950s theory now experiencing a renaissance, which held that the availability of global oil was soon to be maxed out, after which global supplies would be on an ever-diminishing decline. Believers in Peak Oil felt that crude oil was certain to grow more expensive.

The Peak Oil theory had some weaknesses, given the promising advancements in drilling that were being made in such hard-to-reach areas as deep ocean water in the Gulf of Mexico and the Arctic Circle. If the technology to tap those reserves could be harnessed, there would be plenty of crude oil yet. But those facts didn't prevent the market's jitters from driving crude prices up, and Andurand, who had by now been expecting price hikes for several years, also saw every indication that crude would continue on the same trajectory. Brent crude contracts, the commodity product he traded most frequently, were in the low $90s at the time. But if the demand and supply factors then present persisted, followed by a strong dose of scaremongering over Peak Oil, he thought the futures markets could go absolutely haywire, taking crude levels to $200 a barrel.

So, just weeks after BlueGold's inception, Andurand began slowly purchasing Brent contracts, betting that prices would rise dramatically to anywhere from $100 to $130. The calls were pegged to future dates as far out as two and a half years.

Andurand was already taking enormous risk, but he went a step further. In order to juice his potential returns on investment, he used complex market contracts that provided extra exposure to triple the size of his bet.

Brent crude began getting more expensive. And since Andurand's aggressive trades were winning in the short term, his assets under management were going up. By May, BlueGold was managing $500 million, an impressive rise from where it had started three months before. With the added exposure from the contracts he bought, Andurand was in fact managing a portfolio with market investments worth $1.5 billion on paper.

Suddenly BlueGold was becoming a big deal in London. Bankers who had refused to do business with the firm just a few months before were calling the office, multiple times a day. New investors were making inquiries. To the fund's junior staff, working at Blue-Gold felt like the hot new gig.

BlueGold reflected Andurand's lavish but quiet style, operating more like a library than a testosterone-fueled trading floor. On a standard day, he would only make three or four trades, building larger positions over time. In between those trades, he researched the oil markets or spoke to friends about what they were seeing and doing. Working at that slow pace, it took him several months to piece together a large position of between 10,000 and 15,000 individual contracts, in this case mostly options, or the right to buy crude at levels considerably higher in the Brent crude market.

And Brent continued moving up. By the end of May, the contract had ripped through the once-significant $100 mark and was trading above $120. BlueGold was now managing $700 million. Some of the options it had bought moved up a remarkable $27 in a total of fourteen trading sessions, the firm noted in an investor letter, shifting one of the essential oil markets from "backwardation," where future prices were predicted to be lower than the current ones, to what traders call "contango," in which future prices were expected to be higher. (The latter, which was thought to be a bastardized version of the nineteenth-century stock-trading term "continuation," meaning to keep a short-term hold on a trading account from one finalization date to the next, was exotic compared to its less imaginative opposite.)

The trade was a huge score. Around the office, though, there were no high fives or champagne popping. Andurand was waiting for things to turn.

■

By the early summer of 2008, Brent futures were trading at stratospheric prices. Meanwhile, the U.S. markets were in distress. Bear Stearns had collapsed into JPMorgan Chase's arms, Lehman Brothers was flirting with failure, and housing in the U.S. was tumbling downward. No matter how great the demand out of China, the breathless pace of commodities prices would have to slow.

BlueGold's partners told investors their optimism had cooled. After crude oil hit $135, Andurand and Crema wrote in an investor letter, the fund had sold off some of the positions it had taken when betting that crude would trade much higher in the longer term, and focused those bets more on the immediate future. BlueGold was now effectively betting that the price of crude would stay high for the next few months, but fall sharply in the coming few years.

Andurand was nervous. Every day he'd get up and pore through the overnight market reports, searching for clues. Mornings were typically slow in London's commodity markets, so he had plenty of time to bum around his Knightsbridge apartment and worry. There was a lot of noise about the broad market's movements, mushrooming crises in the banking and mortgage sectors, and stubbornly high crude futures, which had become the source of much hand-wringing in the U.S., where members of Congress were convening hearings almost weekly to address the public's outrage over ballooning costs of gas and other products.

But there was little a newspaper could tell Andurand that would ultimately change his thinking. For all his research, he traded essentially on gut instinct. It was clear to him that things had recently shifted, and that the price of crude and refined products would be depressed by the global tumult. He thought all this would bear out in the coming months; he just wasn't sure when.

The rest of the market appeared equally torn. As a result, oil prices fluctuated multiple dollars per day, in huge moves at a time. The argument for higher prices was that geopolitical issues—threats of a possible nuclear weapon in Iran, or labor strikes in Nigeria—would crimp the production of oil, leading to sticker shock for the supplies that were available. The case for lower prices was that the U.S. credit crisis was worsening, dampening orders and spending in other continents and ultimately risking oversupply of crude.

Longtime market watchers were stumped by the mixed messages, and some even argued to reporters that the oil market was broken. "This whole industry has been absolutely turned on its head," an energy analyst told the *New York Times*. Price moves that had once taken five years, the *Times* pointed out, were now taking far less time—such as the $60 upswing that had occurred over the prior twelve months. Overall, prices had been climbing for seven straight years, the *Times* added—a trend unheard of since oil drilling began in the 1850s.

On June 6, Andurand had his gallbladder removed at a North London hospital. Awakening from general anesthetic, he looked around the room hazily, focusing first on the window shades, then the shapes of a girlfriend he was then seeing and a few other friends who had come to check on him.

His first focused thought was about the markets.

"Can I have a look at the BlackBerry?" he asked. Someone handed the device over. In his dreamlike state, Andurand pressed a few buttons to check the market's prices. His eyes widened. Oil contracts were up $10 from where they had been when he had gone into surgery a few hours earlier. In fact, they were experiencing the biggest single-day increase—over $10 at their maximum point that day—they had ever seen.

It figured. Andurand was still betting on higher prices in his portfolio, though not as doggedly as he had been in early May. He wondered whether he should have reduced his risk after all, since his hunch had proved right as usual.

I should have surgery more often, he thought to himself, easing back to sleep in his hospital bed. His self-assuredness was calming. Maybe the operation had been a lucky break, he thought, providing him a few hours off at a terribly exhausting time. Blue-Gold sprinted to another set of double-digit gains for that month.

■

On July 3, crude futures in both the Brent and the West Texas Intermediate markets reached what would be their all-time high: $147 apiece. It was the Thursday before the Fourth of July holiday weekend in the U.S., and volume was somewhat light, allowing prices to throttle past traditional ceilings in the market that held firm when more parties were trading. Nonetheless, the upward price pressure, whether driven by supply threats, by continued demand in the developing world, or simply by a crowd of speculators all making the same bet, were moving prices well past the market's traditional price range.

A hundred and forty-seven dollars per barrel wasn't sustainable, Andurand knew. Unemployment was climbing in the U.S., and its gross domestic product, or GDP, the best measure of the country's overall economy, was shrinking. An actual bank failure could really topple an already shaky global financial system. The oil market had to be near a tipping point, if not already at one.

But after pulling back some of the cash he had bet in the markets, Andurand was hesitant to make another big move. "Nothing makes sense to me," he told colleagues, "so I'm going to wait."

Brent crude contracts slid off their highs, but remained elevated at $130, then below $120 as the summer dragged on. Their amped-up levels were creating new fissures in the economy. While 2008 was a bonanza for the oil companies—Exxon Mobil and Royal Dutch Shell were producing record profits—anyone who had to actually buy oil or refined oil products was struggling with the new prices. Companies like Marathon Oil, the U.S.'s fourth-largest refiner, were considering spinning off their more cost-intensive operations to preserve profits, while global conglomerates such as Ikea and DuPont were shifting to local suppliers to save on transportation costs.

Still, oil prices remained strong. Andurand's conviction was slipping. He'd gone into the summer expecting a sharp drop in oil, but the market hadn't delivered. As tenuous as things were in the financial markets, prices were resilient. He began waiting for an opportune dip in which to buy a new set of options betting that oil would go higher.

Then came September. In the course of a week, the very sorts of events that Andurand and others had feared all summer actually came to pass: a teetering Merrill Lynch was sold to Bank of America in a last-minute deal, and Goldman Sachs and Morgan Stanley rapidly converted into bank holding companies that could borrow from the government in order to assuage investors' terrors about a future bank run. The century-and-a-half-old investment bank Lehman Brothers filed for Chapter 11 bankruptcy protection. The insurer American International Group, beleaguered by bad investments in subprime mortgages that were now creating windfalls for traders to whom AIG had sold insurance policies to guard against defaults in those very same loans, had to accept a massive government bailout.

It was another roller-coaster period in the oil markets, but this time they were spinning downward. On September 15, the day that Lehman filed for bankruptcy protection, West Texas Intermediate, or WTI, oil contracts slipped below $100 for the first time in months. (Brent was already there.) But just days later, WTI experienced a record pop of more than $16 in a single day, closing once again above $120.

Andurand believed that there were two or three good trading opportunities in every year, and right now he was deep into the second one: a breathtaking crude rout. Sensing the shift in the markets, he abandoned his plans to bet again on a crude price spike and instead began betting the reverse.

"The October correction in crude has taken the market into steep contango," he and Crema wrote the following month. Blue-Gold appeared yet again to have called the inflection point in the markets. The little fund was now managing close to $1 billion, and every investor who had put money in that year had gotten returns, regardless of his or her entry point. "We believe that such an extreme contango is unsustainable," the hedge-fund managers added. "We now believe oil prices could fall lower to the $50 level."

With a variety of wagers that the crude markets would fall and a handful of more complex trades pitting WTI, Brent, and diesel against one another, and hoping to capture small profits on the price differences between the three contracts, BlueGold waited for the bigger drop in crude oil to occur.

It came. On Christmas Eve, days before BlueGold closed its books for the year, Brent sunk to less than $37, cementing Andurand's reputation as one of the most successful energy traders of all time. His fund was up 209 percent for the year.

"We made money all the way to the bottom," he says.

3

THE FIRM THAT MARC RICH BUILT

N ot far from Andurand's trading desk, a commodities giant was struggling. Ensconced in their Mayfair office tower, oil traders working for the Swiss multinational trading company Glencore International were fighting longtime business associates who were suddenly leery of trading with them.

It was the fall of 2008, the period during which Andurand made so much money as the oil market sunk toward its low point, and financial firms were all under scrutiny as the U.S. banks flailed. Nobody in the financial markets wanted to take any risk. But Glencore, an infamous trading firm known equally for its opacity and its high tolerance for risk, was now especially vulnerable. By October, the price of a standard credit default swap, or CDS, on its debt—an insurance-like policy that would pay the holder if Glencore couldn't pay its creditors—had zoomed past its already heightened levels, fueling the increasingly widespread belief that it was about to go under.

Like any trading company, Glencore borrowed heavily to finance its operations, and depended on a steady flow of credit to keep the lights on. But now Glencore's seventy-odd oil traders, who, like their counterparts at Vitol, bought and sold physical barrels everywhere from Asia to West Africa and used futures contracts to hedge their short-term exposure, were fielding concerned calls from the banks and other oil companies with which they normally did business almost daily. Glencore had always traded with the likes of Goldman Sachs, Morgan Stanley, Shell, BP, and other oil majors. But suddenly competitors were asking detailed questions about Glencore's debt levels and cash stores before they were willing to continue with buying and selling as usual.

The British driller BP, which ironically had employed Alex Beard, the trader who now ran Glencore's oil division, as a junior trader when he was fresh out of college, seemed particularly spooked. BP traders were refusing to work with Glencore under anything but the most conservative terms. Transactions had to be supported by letters of credit from banks that would pay BP if Glencore couldn't, and any bespoke commodity trades had to be finalized with a third-party registry, which would insulate BP from any issues with Glencore's creditworthiness that might arise. BP even asked at one point to be paid in advance for a delivery of ship fuel valued at $500,000—an insultingly small amount for which not to be trusted.

Glencore traders were frustrated. Hoping to improve morale, Beard arranged an emergency department call.

"We have plenty of liquidity, don't worry," he told a few dozen of his top traders, who had dialed in from Connecticut, Singapore, Switzerland, and other locations. He was referring to the amount of cash Glencore had on hand, which, in his view, was plenty. "Forget the CDS," he said, "it's a bullshit measure! It's a broken measure."

Glencore had plenty of access to credit, he assured the group:

$4 billion in bank lines, in fact. He urged them to keep calm and avoid being distracted by the inquiries from Glencore's trading partners. But it would be months, in fact, before things actually got better.

■

Glencore's oil business was one of the largest, most complex trading empires then in operation. Founded by the commodity trader Marc Rich in 1974, it had been one of the first to take advantage of the nationalization of some of the world's top oil producers by supplanting the distributors they had historically partnered with by offering to speed up the delivery of crude so that it was available almost immediately, or "on the spot." By the mid-2000s, Glencore was sourcing, loading, shipping, and delivering oil to nearly every corner of the developed world. Its logistics business rivaled FedEx's, and its financial trading desk competed with that of Goldman Sachs.

For Beard, a pale, sandy-haired Englishman who wore oxford shirts and ties jauntily and tipped his chair back for comfort during business meetings, oil became an attraction early on in life. Born outside London, he studied biochemistry at Oxford's Christ Church College and became intrigued by an entry-level program at BP during his final year of school. His first placement as a young trainee was in a Rotterdam refinery; he soon progressed to arranging long-term delivery contracts for the driller in the Middle East and Asia. The Soviet Union was dissolving, and securing crude from a newly independent Russia was big business at the time. Beard began traveling to Moscow frequently and developed an expertise in the Russian crude market, becoming a passable speaker of Russian along the way. It was an unglamorous job at times, involving long journeys to Siberia and other oil-production sites in the country's weather-bitten interior. But Beard, who was focused, competitive, and quick to anger when impatient, was willing to make the effort.

He joined Glencore in 1995. His knowledge of former Soviet states, which had made him a specialist in the region's native high-sulfur grade of crude, made him a huge asset to the oil division, where he quickly rose up the chain of command. His work life there was all-consuming. He traveled constantly and was available to clients and colleagues at any hour. During his time at the company's drab office in London, he got to know a Glencore ship operator whose job involved coordinating sea cargoes from land, and married her. Once Beard started earning more significant money, the couple bought a £7.5 million house in West London where an embassy had once stood. They had three children.

Still, Beard had limited time to relax at the house. Life at Glencore, where head partner Ivan Glasenberg insisted on having his senior team's undivided focus, was unforgiving; a news article had once described the company as "investment banking times three." If managers decided their hours were too long and began leaving early to spend more time with family, their underlings would frequently work that much harder and unseat their bosses. There was no such thing as work-life balance, a philosophy Glasenberg unapologetically embraced. But unlike other energy companies or investment banks, "there are no politics at Glencore," one employee explains. "It's totally performance-based."

Beard's tenacity enabled him to cash in on a period of unprecedented success at the company. Glencore did business in two ways: by extracting raw materials out of the ground, an undertaking handled by the firm's "industrial" arm, and by moving various commodities from one place to another, using commodity contracts to manage price risk in transit. In the latter business, Glencore's "marketing" arm, which contributed the majority of the company's revenue, Beard was exceptionally good.

In 2007, a banner year in which Glencore's top twelve executives saw their company holdings spike by $87 million apiece, Beard was rewarded for his efforts by being named head of the company's entire oil division, part of the overall energy business that was the company's second-biggest stream of revenue. It was the same year he turned forty.

Beard had high hopes for the division. He was overseeing six hundred traders, ship operators, inspectors, and other support personnel, a modest but critical fraction of the tens of thousands of staff and contract workers Glencore employed worldwide. The company had always been dominant in crude marketing, the primary activity of the business Rich founded in the 1970s, but it needed improvement in its trading of certain refined crude-oil products. Beard also craved expansion on the industrial side; with a single offshore oil block available for drilling near Equatorial Guinea, its exploration and production, or E&P, business was virtually nonexistent.

He was limited, however, by the company's finite spending power. As profitable as Glencore was, the lack of the permanent capital that could come from selling shares to the public in an IPO prevented it from investing more than a few hundred million dollars at a time on any particular mine or drill site.

Beard spent half of his first year in the job on planes traveling to Moscow, Argentina, and South Africa to visit clients and work sites while getting to know his new staff in the U.S. and Asia. He was struck by the time that human resources matters consumed. Whereas he had once managed a single trading operation, he was now buried in paperwork, interviews, and other administrative duties.

Becoming a public figurehead was also a huge transition. Beard had always prized his low profile, generally avoiding the London social scene and keeping even his charitable donations largely anonymous. (He'd soon learn what was involved in being a tabloid target, however, when British papers started publishing details of his personal life, such as his home movie cinema and his net worth and snapping photographs as he ducked into a waiting car outside his house.) One of the few things that drew Beard out was the Arsenal Football Club, whose home matches he watched from his regular seats in North London's Emirates Stadium, a behemoth celebrating the sport known in America as soccer. He also played occasional games at a London sports facility with a bunch of guys from work, five to a side.

■

The supercycle in commodities benefited Glencore tremendously. For the year 2007, the company saw record profits of $6.1 billion, as oil, metals, and other raw materials soared to astonishing price levels on their way to reaching record highs, which occurred alongside that of crude oil in July 2008.

As 2008 started off, Glencore's performance promised to be even stronger. Oil was trading higher by the day despite signs of weakness, even crisis, in the U.S. The same market denial that had benefited Andurand was helping Beard, whose ability to lock in crude supplies at cheaper rates and resell them at a premium was helped by daily price climbs of $1 or more.

Then, in the middle of the summer, prices abruptly reversed. Oil lost significant ground in late July and August, and in September it was battered by the shock waves generated by the Lehman Brothers bank failure and other close calls in the U.S.

That month, Beard traveled to Glencore's headquarters in Baar, the leafy valley town about a half-hour's drive south of Zurich, for Glencore's semiannual partner meeting. Lehman had recently filed for bankruptcy, and Brent crude was trading at about $95. The broader commodities market was off 30 percent from its high just two months earlier. Fears about a slowdown in emerging markets and slowing demand in the developed world were taking effect.

Sitting around a meeting space in the company's squat white corporate building, which was tucked between a lush hill and thickets of verdant trees, Beard was alarmed by the tone he heard. Every single division head expressed deep pessimism about prices in his respective commodity. From metals to agriculture, nothing looked good. In copper, coal, and zinc, raw materials that had prompted astonishing growth in the developing world, customers had committed to higher prices earlier in the year, when the commodities had been trading at far higher rates, than they were now willing to pay as prices sank. Painful renegotiations were occurring, raising the specter of contentious lawsuits, none of which could end well. Nobody knew how long the carnage might last, but they were all bracing for a sustained move down in the markets.

As he left the meeting, Beard called his office in London. Above and beyond the commodity contract trading they were doing to hedge their exposure to price swings in physical energy trades, he wanted his team to put on a massive speculative bet that the price of oil would fall further.

■

Glencore credit default swaps at that time had been trading at the relatively calm level of about €150,000. By contrast, the swap

51

prices attached to the major U.S. investment banks—the cost of purchasing an insurance policy that would pay its keeper if the banks defaulted and couldn't pay their debts—were growing vastly more expensive.

Around the time of the September partner meeting in Baar, Beard's team received an unusual request from Morgan Stanley, long a friendly rival in the trading of commodities and their correspondent contracts. Morgan owed Glencore $125 million for a crude shipment, a bank representative explained, but the bank at that moment was hard up for cash. Could Glencore give Morgan a little grace time, the bank wondered, as Morgan tended to crises in other parts of its business?

No problem, said Beard when the matter came to his attention. He was sympathetic to Morgan's situation.

But before long, the roles were reversed. By late October, crude prices had fallen more than 50 percent from their peak, and Glencore was battling BP and other counterparts doubting its financial health. Beard's trader call may have calmed nerves internally, but his angry swagger, while effective in creating fear and submissiveness on his own team, had done little for the marketplace at large. Swap insurance on a piece of Glencore's five-year debt was by then trading for €900,000, an enormous price.

Beard himself was in a state of astonishment. Practically every day, it seemed, he walked into his fifth-floor Berkeley Street office in London at 8:15 A.M. to find crude priced $2 to $3 cheaper than it had been just the day before. Working at BP during the first Persian Gulf War in the early 1990s, he'd seen large price moves in short periods of time, but with nowhere near this magnitude; the market of 2008 was moving with exponentially greater caprice.

Amid the drop-off, Beard went to lunch with Goran Trapp, a

tall, lean Swede who headed Morgan's commodities unit in Europe. Greeting one another at a restaurant near London's sedate Green Park, not far from Berkeley Street, they remarked on the fact that they'd never actually spent time together, despite having been in the same industry for decades. Surely they'd met at some energy-business function, they agreed, but which one, neither could say.

The conversation quickly turned to the markets. Beard, who, despite his relaxed, almost rumpled appearance, could be quite steely when annoyed, cited his frustrations with the hysteria over his company's debt load. Glencore's problem was based on false assumptions, he argued, something that Morgan had recently experienced and should understand firsthand.

"You aren't going bust, and we aren't either," he said. The whole thing, he added, seemed a bit preposterous.

Trapp, who was a calmer, more approachable trader, considered his words. "Clearly the market has some concerns," he replied. In the fog of crisis, he argued, trading partners made decisions based solely on their own long-term survival. That meant taking no chances, even with long-standing counterparts who had never given reason for concern before.

Beard sensed that something else was going on in his team's dealings with BP, which he thought was going out of its way to screw Glencore. But perhaps Trapp was right on the broader point. He reminded Trapp that Glencore had been there for Morgan during its neediest hour as a barely concealed way to extract some similar loyalty.

"We'd appreciate the favor returned," he said.

Glencore wasn't late on any particular bill at the time, but Beard wanted to know that the bank would be flexible in trading with him.

Trapp understood, and fully intended to keep trading with Glencore as usual. Still, he couldn't promise not to ask about the firm's financials. At Morgan, he said, "we do the right thing. But in order for us to maintain the position we have, we need to make sure we maintain the open line," he added, referring to the need for free-flowing communication, even if it involved sensitive financial questions about Glencore's cash and credit lines. Morgan Stanley had to be mindful of its own risk management, after all, Trapp pointed out.

Beard agreed. It was a small price to pay to take at least one item off his team's growing list of concerns.

■

Opening up their books for scrutiny, however, was something Glencore was loath to do. Insularity had been the company's operating principle for as long as anyone could remember. Glencore had always relied on Switzerland's lenient corporate laws to do business with unstable nations, even some that were considered enemies of the U.S. Many of the more notorious transactions had taken place during the Marc Rich era, which began in 1974 and ended twenty years later, but a few had occurred even after he left the company. In 2005, for instance, an independent commission report on abuses under the United Nations–sponsored oil-for-food program accused the company of paying surcharges to secure Iraqi crude oil during the Saddam Hussein regime. Glencore denied the accusations, but its long-standing use of shell corporations and complex intercompany tax and trading arrangements could make it tough to unravel a given transaction—and, ultimately, even the shadiest dealings were hard to link back to Glencore in the first place.

Glencore's willingness to do business in obscure and controversial places had also turned out to be a highly profitable business strategy. Among the European traders that handled commodities, it was one of the largest. It claimed to sell more crude than any nonintegrated oil company, its sales volume accounting for more than 3 percent of a day's global oil consumption. It was also the largest supplier of seaborne steam coal, provided at least half the zinc and copper sold on a given day, and was a major source of sugar and exporter of grain. It operated in forty different countries in every continent but Antarctica, generating $150 billion in revenue and $400 million in profit. During the 2000s, its average return on equity was 38 percent, meaning that for every dollar of shareholder capital it held, it was generating a profit of 38 cents.

Glencore's business blend was also unique. On the oil side, it competed with energy traders like Vitol, and in agriculture, Cargill and Louis Dreyfus. In mining, it faced off with Rio Tinto and BHP Billiton. About the only major commodity in which it lacked a significant presence was natural gas.

Glencore was founded by the Belgium-born trader Marc Rich, born Marcell David Reich in 1934. A Jew who had fled the Nazis with his family when he was five, Rich became an American citizen as an adolescent. After dropping out of college, he had made his name as a mercury trader at Phibro, the historic commodity trading firm, founded in 1901, that now operated a hub in New York. But Rich's real success came in the crude-oil markets during the late 1960s, when he was running Phibro's Madrid branch, from which he oversaw parts of Africa, Latin America, and the Middle East.

Oil trading at the time was dominated by the so-called Seven

Sisters: Gulf Oil and forerunners to Exxon, Mobil, Chevron, Texaco, BP, and Royal Dutch Shell. Physical barrels were often secured months or even years ahead of time and at fixed prices, making short-term gaps hard to fill. During the Six-Day War in 1967, Egypt effectively blocked Israel from importing crude, creating the first real oil embargo. In its wake, Rich was the first to embrace a novel idea: to circumvent the Seven Sisters by offering to buy oil directly from producer nations. It was the birth of what would become known as the on-the-spot, or "spot," market for oil, in which crude was secured and delivered far quicker than it had in the past, and would revolutionize the way business was done.

Shortly after the construction of a secret Iranian-Israeli pipeline in 1969, Rich began exporting oil from the Middle East all over the world. The experiment helped turn Phibro into a crucial international supplier.

Rich incorporated his own company in Zug, Switzerland—a larger lakeside city just south of neighboring Baar—after a pay dispute with Phibro. Building on the spot, or shorter-term, oil market Rich had launched at his old firm, and taking on numerous other commodities in addition, Marc Rich & Co. flourished under its name partner's aggressive, innovative style of thinking, giving him godlike status in the industry. Over time, he amassed a personal fortune estimated to be at least $1 billion, and was nicknamed "the king of oil" (which became the title of a biography published in 2010).

He also set a new, and arguably lower, industry standard by dealing extensively with rogue nations. No despot was too corrupt to do business with. Rich shipped large quantities of oil to South Africa during apartheid, brokered sugar-for-oil deals and later traded sugar with Cuba notwithstanding U.S. sanctions, and purchased oil from Iran during the American hostage crisis that stretched over 444 days from 1979 to 1981.

Rich, who eventually moved from Madrid to London and, later, to his wife Denise's native New York, comforted himself with the idea that his transactions were legal under Swiss law, and that the law was the only objective standard for business. U.S. authorities, however, were far less accepting of the way he operated. In 1983, federal prosecutors indicted him on numerous charges, including racketeering, tax evasion, and trading with the enemy during the hostage crisis. Rather than facing the charges, which he considered bogus, Rich obtained Spanish citizenship and fled his Fifth Avenue apartment for the comforting slopes of Switzerland, where, by comparison, almost anything was permissible.

Amazingly, Rich's fugitive status had little real effect on his company, which he continued operating as usual from Zug, whose charming, tree-lined shores and tasteful church spires belied the corruption of one of its richest residents. But in 1992, a large bet that one of his traders had made on zinc went uncharacteristically awry. The resultant $172 million loss damaged both the company and Rich's standing in it.

Marc Rich & Co. stabilized, but Rich himself did not. Under duress, Rich sold his 51 percent stake in the company to his partners the following year. Willy Strothotte, a German metals trader Rich had mentored and then fired amid a power struggle, returned to take on the chief executive role, and the company was renamed Glencore.

Rich retreated to a quieter life, eventually focusing more on real estate than commodities. His status as an outlaw carried with it great personal costs. His marriage crumbled, he drank heavily, and in 1996, one of his three grown daughters died of cancer in a

Seattle hospital. Her mother and sisters were by her side, but her father was only able to be there by telephone, where he listened, sobbing, in her final hours. Had he flown there, he would surely have been arrested before even making it to the hospital.

In January 2001, after an intense lobbying campaign handled partly by his former wife Denise, Rich received a presidential pardon on the last day Bill Clinton was in office. He never revisited the United States. His reputation remained stained even upon his death from a stroke, in 2013, as did those of Clinton and the lobbyists who had helped secure his pardon.

■

The commodity rout of 2008 was probably Glencore's toughest period since Rich's ill-fated zinc gamble in 1992. The company's credit default swap, or insurance-against-default, prices had retreated from their stratospheric levels, and Glencore was bringing in nearly $5 billion in net income, an amount just shy of 2007's. But its publicly traded bonds were still only barely above investment grade.

The landscape had also changed. Commodity prices were still at their lows, credit to help finance transactions was much harder to secure as banks grew more parsimonious about sharing their resources, and the troubles with BP and other companies had left the company more vulnerable to rivals.

All this was occurring at a time when Glencore's need for extra cash was most pressing. Trading vast quantities of both physical and virtual commodities was a cash-intensive endeavor. Raw materials in some markets could only be bought for hard currency, and in the derivatives markets, cash was often required as collateral on trades.

Glencore was also trying to enlarge its empire. In the years following the management buyout, the company had purchased a string of new assets around the world, deepening its commitment to commodities like coal, copper, and gold. As recently as Christmas Eve of 2008—the same day Brent hit its $37 low point—the company had spent close to $300 million to purchase a controlling interest in a distressed Congolese mining company. A couple of months later, it was forced to sell a highly profitable coal property in Colombia to Xstrata, another mining company for which it shipped certain commodities, simply to raise enough cash to maintain its one-third investment in Xstrata, which was holding a special shareholder rights offering at the time to raise some cash of its own. The distressed deal destroyed some of the goodwill between Glencore and Xstrata, which had been closely connected for years and would attempt a merger a couple of years later.

■

Ivan Glasenberg, by then Glencore's head, had taken over from Willy Strothotte in 2002. A gregarious South African, Glasenberg was a profane, fiery character whose championship race-walking skills had nearly taken him to the Olympics as a younger man. He was also a natural-born trader.

Opportunism had always been one of his strengths. In 1980, as part of a course in business finance at the University of the Witwatersrand in Johannesburg, Glasenberg had been assigned a commodities project. He was paging through some books in a Johannesburg corporate library when he heard two men doing, of all things, an international candle-wax trade around the corner. "I've got them at this price!" one of the men yelled. "What have you got?" As the second man shouted back an answer,

Glasenberg was rapt. Holy shit, he thought, the one guy sold in Brazil and the other bought in Japan. A huge international deal negotiated across three continents in a matter of seconds. He couldn't believe it.

After graduating from Wits, Glasenberg worked as an accountant. But he couldn't get the trading idea out of his mind. He went back to school, earned a master's degree in international business administration from the University of Southern California, and in 1984 he joined Marc Rich & Co. as a coal trader in his native South Africa. He married, had a daughter and a son, and began learning the nuances of the business, relocating from Africa to Australia and then to Asia, where he oversaw the region's coal operations during a time of crisis in the industry. He was a quick learner, and in 1990, he was promoted to run the company's global coal business.

There were many challenges in the commodity trade, and one was always the need for good credit. During the 1990s, as the price of coal hit a low point in parts of the Pacific region that Glasenberg oversaw, repo men were circling coal-storage facilities, where they would seize the holdings of companies that had defaulted on their debts. Sometimes they walked away with the wrong assets.

In Australia, where the industry was particularly squeezed and repossessions were a serious threat, Glasenberg ordered employees to put ropes around their coal stockpiles with Marc Rich flags to mark them off. He fretted constantly about all the bad things that could happen to his precious assets. Each time he signed off on a coal shipment, he was tortured during the weeks it took for the cargoes to arrive intact at their destined port.

In 1991 Glasenberg, his wife, and his two children moved to a town near Zurich, not far from the company's headquarters in Zug. Shortly after they relocated, Marc Rich summoned Glasenberg for lunch at his house. It was a sign that he had attracted the attention of senior management.

Rich was by then in the twilight of his career. Heavily involved with real estate investing, he had delegated much of his company's day-to-day operations to Strothotte, so even senior management had limited dealings with him. Rich was overcompensating by living hard. Over lunch at his house, Glasenberg marveled at the chance to meet the industry's king. But despite the amicable rapport the two developed, it was clear that Rich would never be a mentor.

Two years later, after Rich's zinc trade had gone bust, Glasenberg was part of the new generation that seized control, working closely with Strothotte, who took over after the management buyout. Over the decade that followed, Strothotte trained Glasenberg for a bigger job, and ultimately relinquished the CEO role to him in 2002. They functioned well together. When Glasenberg took over as chief, Strothotte stayed on as chairman.

As CEO, Glasenberg maintained a breakneck schedule. No matter what the weather, he rose at dawn for swims, cycling, or five-mile runs by the lake near Zug, keeping his body trim and prepared for long flights and all-nighters. His thinning, dark-brown hair was always neatly combed, his square glasses perched expertly on his clean-shaven face.

His attention to physical detail extended to the office, where his fixation with accounting kept him preoccupied with the company's balance sheet. Between jetting around to visit Glencore's far-flung mining, shipping, industrial processing and trading sites and conferring with his business heads over minute details of the business, Glasenberg considered how he would navigate the next decade.

From time to time he would admonish Glencore's division leaders not to dream too big about mergers and acquisitions. "Guys, you can't keep bringing big fixed assets because this company can't do it," he'd say in one-on-one meetings, referring to the costly investments they would occasionally propose. If the division heads wanted to buy billion-dollar properties, he'd tell them, only an IPO and the permanent cash it would bring with it would make a difference. "You have to go public," Glasenberg said again and again. "Think about it."

Meanwhile, Glencore was stuck with relatively small-ticket items: a few hundred million dollars here, a few hundred million there. The multibillion-dollar purchases that would make Glencore more of a global contender were simply unaffordable.

■

Amid all this, the company's shareholders were also draining its cash. Glencore had a tradition of hiring young and promoting from within; like Alex Beard, many of the company's 450 or so employee shareholders were in their forties and had been with the company for more than a decade. But when partners left, as about ten had done in 2008, they expected to cash out their equity, and the more the company's holdings grew, the more their stakes were worth.

To deal with the limited cash on hand, Glasenberg had established what he liked to describe as a financial Band-Aid: pay interest on a shareholder's equity without allowing him to actually liquidate his holdings. But that, Glasenberg knew, was only a temporary fix.

The ratings agencies, for one, were attuned to Glencore's situation. Throughout the fall of 2008, Standard & Poor's and Moody's had been asking about the stability of the company's most senior employees, given how expensive their departure payouts were certain to be, and now the questions were becoming sharper. Glencore couldn't risk a ratings downgrade that plunged it into "junk," or likely-to-default, status, making borrowing much more expensive. Commodities were hurting, and miners everywhere would soon be asking public investors for additional cash before their needs grew more dire.

During a meeting with Glasenberg and his chief financial officer late one week in December, a ratings analyst had asked what Glencore would do if faced with the resignation of one of his top twenty employees and the resultant cash the departing manager would demand. "I'm not even worrying about what if," Glasenberg told the analyst, "because it's not happening. If you are concerned, I'll have the partners sign a letter."

By the following Monday, each of Glencore's most senior officials agreed to extend their employment by at least three years.

■

During Glencore's partners meeting in the spring of 2009 in Baar, Glasenberg made a pitch for what he saw as the only solution to the firm's pressing problems, which was an IPO. He ran through the merits: a chance to raise money in the market during times of crisis; a means to take over other companies; and, not insignificantly, an opportunity to become very, very rich—but in the public eye.

Beard, who had one of the larger stakes in the company at the time, wanted to go public, never mind that it meant he was bound to lose his low profile in the London social scene. "One of the key drivers for me is increased financial firepower," he told the group, using a term Glasenberg had in the past, "to undertake larger-scale acquisitions."

Glasenberg understood. It was hard to find an attractive crude-oil drill site for less than $1 billion, and as a result, Beard hadn't even tried to present his boss with substantial takeover ideas. Realizing his goals as energy head, however, would be impossible without them.

An offering would also bring an abrupt end to decades of secrecy, however, and with it, freedom. In the more fraught parts of the world where Glencore operated, such as Zambia, the Congo, and Colombia, nongovernmental organizations would immediately home in on the company's questionable practices and dealings with corrupt politicians. Glencore would have to hire managers for investor relations and public relations—jobs that had never existed within the company. Glasenberg didn't know if his partners were prepared for the onslaught of publicity they were likely to get. Privately, he believed his own wife, a high-school teacher who worked with developmentally challenged students, might be shocked to learn his net worth, and joked that once the press reported it, he could no longer claim not to be able to afford the Louis Vuitton handbags she liked.

"Who's in favor?" he asked, looking around the table.

Everyone was.

4

THE BANKS

By 2009, the London office where Alex Beard's lunch companion, Goran Trapp, worked for Morgan Stanley was eclipsing its U.S. arm in importance. Embarrassed by the financial crisis's exposure of their weak spots, regulators were putting new pressure on Wall Street to rein in its risky behavior, and the UK, known for its hands-off attitude toward bank oversight, had become the finance industry's safe haven. Commodity markets in London were thriving, and Morgan Stanley and Goldman Sachs, now chasing profits in an environment where high-stakes, high-reward trading activity was suddenly restricted, had increased their presence there.

The focus on Europe was a turnabout for Morgan Stanley, whose commodities nerve center had for years been a converted courtyard in the wealthy suburban enclave of Purchase, New York. There, inside a brutalist-style building once used by the energy company Texaco, about seventy-five people traded both physical natural gas, crude, crops, and metals and the contracts backed by them, churning out remarkable profits. They had moved there as part of Morgan Stanley's risk-reduction policies after the terrorist attacks of September 11, 2001. By 2008, they were generating revenue of $3 billion—a substantial contributor to the bank's overall revenue of $25 billion.

Morgan Stanley wasn't alone there. Banks everywhere were relying on commodity traders to help them survive the rout in mortgage-backed securities and the resultant setbacks in other markets. At Goldman Sachs, which reported fixed-income revenues of $3.71 billion for that year and $22 billion overall, commodities contributed more than $3 billion. Even at other banks with smaller, less profitable commodities units, the trading of raw materials was a major help. Among the top ten investment banks, commodities on average made up 14 percent of their combined total fixed-income revenue. Morgan and Goldman tended to top the list, with Barclays, JPMorgan, Bank of America, and others following behind.

■

Bank commodities units made money in three ways. The first was by helping corporations involved in the physical side of the commodities business to hedge their exposure to changing commodity prices. Buyers, such as Dow Chemical or Coca-Cola, used contracts like exchange-traded futures (vows to purchase a physical commodity at a preset price at a future date), options (rights, but not requirements, to buy or sell a physical commodity at a preset price at a future date), and swaps (bilateral trading agreements that allowed parties to lock in specific future prices or in exchange for ongoing cash payments) to curb the cost of big run-ups in the price of raw materials they needed to purchase. Taken together, the various contracts were known as derivatives, because they were agreements that derived their value from a relatively simple product, like a barrel of oil, and made it more nuanced by layering on additional features, such as the right to buy or sell it later at some specific time or at some specific price. Producers, like the natural-gas driller Chesapeake Energy, faced the opposite problem: overexposure to a physical commodity whose dropping price could hurt them.

Then there were the airlines, which spent as much or more on jet fuel than they did on employee salaries and benefits. There were myriad ways to arrange a hedge, but the simplest version involved buying contracts linked to crude oil—the major commodity most closely pegged to the price of jet fuel—that gave the airline the right to buy crude in the future at a moderate price. Say, for instance, that crude-oil futures were trading at a price of $100 per barrel. Looking out on the year to come, an airline executive might believe he could handle a cost of $110 per barrel but not $120. So he'd instruct his sales trader at Morgan Stanley—a well-compensated go-between who told the actual traders what the client wanted them to do—to lock in prices of $110 per barrel twelve months into the future in an amount equal to, say, one-third of the amount of jet fuel that the airline purchased in a given year. That way, the executive got a fixed price for a portion of the commodity he would need in the coming year, protecting him against a big spike in costs. But because there was always the chance that prices would fall instead of rise, he only hedged a portion of the crude he'd actually need in order not to waste money on hedges that proved unnecessary when the commodity was cheap. It was a maddeningly difficult undertaking to time correctly, but one that was increasingly necessary, given the large swings in oil prices.

Morgan Stanley didn't make much money on the single transaction, for which it charged a modest fee (depending on the cost of the contract, pennies or even fractions of pennies for every dollar of market exposure the airline bought). But if Morgan arranged many such trades for many different clients, the fees from hedging jet fuel, copper, wheat, and other commodities quickly added up. It was a volume business, dependent on what an academic would call "economies of scale," and the revenue those fees brought in was known as the client "flow" business. It was also the least sexy of the three ways banks made money in commodities.

The second way was by owning physical assets that dealt directly with raw materials. Banks over the years had tried everything from buying refineries and coal mines to running gasoline storage silos. Goldman at one point owned both Horizon Wind Energy, an operator of wind farms, and an air-polluting power plant in Linden, New Jersey. Morgan Stanley had two assets of note: TransMontaigne Partners, which handled the shipping and storage of refined-oil products, and Heidmar Inc., a tanker-ship operator. Both provided revenue that improved Morgan Stanley's profits. But perhaps just as important, they also gave the firm in-depth knowledge of the infrastructural and regional issues in the energy business where TransMontaigne and Heidmar operated, knowledge that gave Morgan's traders an edge when it came to buying or selling crude contracts.

The third way was both complex and highly lucrative. It was house trading, otherwise known as proprietary, or "prop" trading, a bet using internal capital that often involved using commodity contracts. A prop trade sometimes sprang from a client flow trade that required taking positions that the bank wouldn't otherwise have wanted—for example, betting that natural-gas prices would fall at a time when most people expected them to go higher. Morgan probably would not make that trade of its own accord, but if Chesapeake Energy wanted the bank to do it, and no third party was willing to make the trade either, Morgan would make the negative bet in order to accommodate Chesapeake.

To avoid being stuck with a negative bet on a rising commodity, Morgan might then try to find another counterpart who would purchase its position. If it did so, it had, debatably, crossed the fine line from client flow trading into prop trading. (In the years that followed, there would be numerous arguments between banks and regulators as to what constituted a prop trade.)

Another form of prop trading was simply using Morgan Stanley's capital to take whatever positions a trader saw fit. It was speculation, much as Pierre Andurand had done at Goldman, Bank of America, and later at Vitol and BlueGold, and as Alex Beard had done when he instructed his traders in the fall of 2008 to bet on a crude-price downward spiral. The Morgan Stanley trader would be given a bit of the bank's money to start with, and then he or she would take their own view on a commodity to try to make a profit from it in the markets. Any gains that resulted were Morgan's to keep—and would usually boost the bonus of the trader who generated them. And if the trader happened to bet poorly, the loss usually belonged to the bank.

Handled well, prop trading was a big moneymaker, and the banks, unsurprisingly, barreled into it. Goldman Sachs was particularly adroit. By the early 2000s, analysts estimated that prop trading accounted for at least a quarter of Goldman's pretax income. Later, in the opening stages of the U.S. credit crisis, a small team of traders who handled mortgage indexes for clients made nearly $4 billion in trading profits by using Goldman's money to bet that the housing market would crumble.

Morgan Stanley's prop trading of mortgages had gone far less well, resulting in a $9 billion write-down and a wave of hasty departures, including that of the company's president. But the commodity side was a different story.

■

On and off the trading desk, Jennifer Fan projects seriousness. A math prodigy who graduated from New York University with a finance degree at nineteen, she started working at Morgan Stanley as a commodity trader a year later. Conscious of her youth and inexperience, she dressed understatedly: dark pants and button-down shirts or blazers, often accented by a big, fluffy scarf wrapped around her neck, even when it wasn't cold outside. She had a casual look reminiscent of Silicon Valley, even wearing things like gingham shirts and black slacks to hedge-fund conferences, as if to say that sitting in front of a computer all day in a high-stress job shouldn't require a power suit. Her main accessory, other than her piercing eyes, was her luxuriously thick, dark hair that she wore straight and down.

The daughter of studious Chinese parents who had emigrated to the U.S. to attend graduate school, Fan was more comfortable talking about quantitative theory than about her personal life, which had been subsumed by her education since heading off to a special college for gifted teenagers. After school, she had spent a year at Bank of America, where she met her future husband, an oil trader named Morgan Downey, on a trip to the company's Singapore office. Downey ran the bank's energy desk there, and at that time had recently hired Andurand, who was on the brink of his first big score in trading.

Fan was hired at Morgan Stanley in 2004, by which time both she and Downey were dating and living in New York. John

Shapiro, Morgan's head of commodities, a silver-haired micro-manager who had helped launch the business in the 1980s, was famous for his careful selection of traders who would fit the investment bank's collaborative, merit-driven culture. Shapiro gave Fan a choice of jobs: trading power supplies or working on the bank's nascent index desk. She chose the latter.

To many traders, the index desk sounded dull compared to areas like crude, where an unexpected geopolitical event could put billions at risk in a flash. Copper, the red metal that was the backbone of industrial manufacturing and such a reliable predictor of economic growth when countries bought it in large quantities that it was nicknamed "Dr. Copper," was also compelling. Even natural gas, despite the benign images it conjured of public buses and home heating, was more exciting to deal with; its contract markets were so volatile that some traders described it as the widow-maker of the commodity business.

But the trading of commodity indexes at the time was a cash cow just waiting to happen, and Morgan Stanley was playing catch-up to its rivals on Wall Street, who had spotted the opportunity many years earlier. Morgan had been particularly outflanked by Goldman, whose commodity index, the GSCI, had by the mid-2000s become a huge source of client interest. (Dow Jones, the media and index company, had paired with the insurer American International Group to create the Dow Jones–AIG index, also a popular commodity product.) So Morgan was trying to piggyback on the index fad with a more customized version of its own that took specific client needs into account. If a client called and wanted to buy the same futures contracts underlying the GSCI but with less emphasis on crude, for instance, Morgan's index trader would go into the market and buy a basket of commodity contracts that included less exposure to crude and more to other products that were poised to hit higher prices at that time. As with other client flow trades, the trader would charge a fee for doing so, and the more clients he or she serviced, the more money Morgan made overall.

The bank had been in the index business for a year or two by the time Jennifer Fan was hired in 2004, and indexing was generating about $50 million in revenue per year. Fan's job would be to help convince clients that they should embrace index trading, and then to execute the trades they wanted to make.

■

Growing up in Pittsburgh, Fan found herself in a family that was staunchly academic. Instead of watching MTV on cable like other kids in the alternative-rock heyday of the 1990s, Fan and her brother and sister did math drills at home, reviewing with their mother, a nuclear physicist, flash cards and tests designed for older students. In fifth grade, Fan and some classmates won the champion title in a math bee designed for middle-schoolers; her mother was the team's coach. Fan's older sister was even more precocious: she enrolled at Carnegie Mellon University at age thirteen (there were better schools out there, but she was too young to move away from her parents). "I am not the smart one in my family," Fan says matter-of-factly. Her sister later worked at Amazon.com devising algorithms to predict how people would shop, a complex equation that had similarities to trading. She spent her free time rock-climbing.

By the time she moved to New York for college, where she received an undergraduate degree from NYU's Stern School of Business, Fan had not yet gotten a driver's license, but as a young commodity trader in Purchase, she had to learn to drive in order to get from Tribeca, the trendy downtown Manhattan neighborhood where she lived, to Westchester County. In a rare occurrence for the star student, she failed the first driving test by sitting too long at a four-way intersection. On the next attempt, after a sympathetic driving instructor sneaked her onto the test site for a dry run, she passed.

She bought a blue BMW ragtop and began the half-hour commute from her apartment to Purchase. Before long she was ticketed for speeding along a tricky section of Manhattan's West Side Highway, where the road transitioned abruptly from a 35-mile-per-hour zone to a 50-mph zone and back again. It was a rite of passage, given that other Morgan traders had also been ticketed.

Fan was one of very few women in Morgan's commodities unit. Sitting at a five-foot desk next to her boss, a former physicist named Dan Nash, she kept busy making trades for Morgan's clients and, in short order, trading commodity contracts in her own speculative book. She arrived at 7:30 A.M. every morning, ate a cafeteria lunch at her desk, and stayed well after the close of trading to research trades. During afternoon lulls, she and Nash would amuse themselves by reading medical journals on the Internet and pointing out the ways in which the statistics didn't support the recommended treatments.

"Our corner was quiet and intellectual and everybody else was raucous," Fan says. If she took any ribbing from her coworkers, it was because she made a geek's error, as when she conflated two members of the Bernoulli family, a seventeenth- and eighteenth-century mathematical dynasty in Switzerland that produced important theories on probability and fluid dynamics. (It was an uncle and his nephew who generated those respective ideas, not the same individual, as she had initially thought.)

The index group was a relatively bare-bones operation. It handled its entire collection of trades with a spreadsheet that Nash, who disliked the cut-and-paste bank models that other people used, had built himself. The work was labor-intensive. Replicating commodity indexes was a piecemeal process that required signing flurries of private trading contracts with clients. And Morgan was trying to compete with the more entrenched players by offering lower fees.

It worked, helped in no small part by the broader market trends at play. Commodity indexes were soaring in popularity as clients embraced the supercycle—that is, the notion that economies were in the middle of a robust, twice-a-century upswing in prices—and the idea that they could mitigate their vulnerability to price inflation by owning raw materials. Morgan benefited from that added volume. Nash added another salesman and a couple of additional traders to the team, and let Fan start trading "relative value" positions, or sets of commodity contracts where she saw potential profits from pitting the different components against one another, for the company's benefit. She had to ask Nash for permission to make the trades, and, like Jean Bourlot at Vitol with his Singapore jet-fuel gambit, she was subjected to strict risk limits.

■

Late in the spring of 2005, Fan made a small bet in the U.S. gasoline market. There was plenty of gas in storage at the time, and futures contracts linked to September and October looked relatively cheap. But Fan had a theory that summer "spec" gasoline—a specified blend designed not to evaporate easily in hot conditions—might go into short supply over the summer, raising its price as the season progressed. So she bought September gas futures and concurrently bet on a price fall by their October counterparts, hoping to benefit from an eventual price discrepancy between the final contract linked to summer and the first one of the winter season, at which point summer-blend gasoline would go out of favor. Her goal was to make about two cents a gallon, or total profits of a little over $250,000.

Months later, when Hurricane Katrina made landfall near New Orleans, she was the only trader on Morgan's index desk who was actually in the office. It was early on Monday, August 29, and many of the energy traders had been in Purchase all weekend to be ready for a potential price spike in commodity contracts that they thought might result from hurricane damage to refineries or drill sites around the Gulf of Mexico. Nash, however, was on a long-planned family vacation and had left Fan on her own.

Initially, commodity prices fell, as the immediate damage from the storm appeared less severe than the market had feared. But things soon turned catastrophic. The death toll eventually topped 1,800. Levees around New Orleans failed, 80 percent of the city flooded, and big chunks of the roof of the Louisiana Superdome, where thousands of refugees had gone for temporary shelter, were ripped away. Meanwhile, the Gulf region's energy infrastructure, which accounted for a quarter of the country's crude-oil production, was badly damaged. Fan heard that one refinery control room had an alligator in it. Gas shortages seemed inevitable, and the pipelines that fed oil tankers on coastal shores were surely compromised too.

Fan was distraught. The human impact was horrific, the market impact uncertain. Most of her clients were betting on a rise in commodity contract prices somehow, so as the market surged as bad news raised fears of crimped supplies, they would probably make money. But Morgan, which had taken the other side of many of those trades, wasn't in the same position. One of the few bets that actually stood to be profitable in the bank's prop books during the storm's aftermath was Fan's gasoline wager.

On August 30, gas contracts rose 20 percent as pump prices soared to $3 or even $3.50 per gallon across the country. On August 31, they rose another 6 percent, as fuel lines formed in many states. To address the shortages, President George W. Bush vowed to tap the nation's Strategic Petroleum Reserve, a stockpile of hundreds of millions of barrels of crude that the U.S. government drew upon in times of emergency.

Amid the drastic turn of events, Fan's side hunch on a summer gas shortage turned into a 30-cent-per-gallon gain. The trade generated about $3 million.

■

Despite the performance of its occupants, the commodities building in Purchase remained a cultural backwater at Morgan. There was relatively little contact between the bankers and other traders in New York, where the firm was situated in a flashy tower near Times Square.

Morgan chief executive John Mack, a veteran who had left the firm after a bruising boardroom battle only to be reinstated as chairman and CEO in 2005, was one of the only senior executives to visit the Purchase building regularly. Even then, it was only to use the gym on his way from home in nearby Rye to midtown Manhattan. Senior-level sightings were so rare that when Boris Shrayer, one of the top salespeople in the commodities division, was named managing director, he joked to Mack, whom he had seen frequently in the locker room, that he didn't recognize him with his clothes on.

Mack, a Duke-educated former bond trader with Lebanese roots, could handle a blue joke or two from a subordinate. But when it came to the commodities unit's general attitude, he was less amused. During one particular dinner with some of the commodities traders in Westchester, Mack was astonished by the group's arrogance. Sure, they were generating billions in annual revenue, grabbing business from their competitors, buying physical assets, and trading lots of volume. But their demands for huge bonuses suggested that they thought the bank itself had nothing to do with their success, as if the Purchase trading floor was an island with no need for Morgan Stanley's considerable resources. Mack left the dinner with a sour feeling. At some point, he thought, I've got to crush these people.

The key, as it turned out, would be for the commodities unit to not crush the bank first. In 2008 John Shapiro, Morgan's head of commodities, retired. In the first half of that year, oil was peaking and the division seemed well on its way to a standout year in revenue terms. (And, to be sure, it was.) But when the market reversed that fall, a seemingly innocent crude-oil trade suddenly threatened to leave Morgan with billions of dollars in losses, and Shapiro, the godfather of the division—whose impeccable memory for detail was a source of both irritation to subordinates and, on the upside, prudent risk management—was no longer there to prevent it from happening.

The trade in question, a hedge meant to manage jet-fuel price risk for Emirates Airline, was the brainchild of Jean Bourlot, the irritable Frenchman who had fought with Andurand over the Singapore jet-fuel trade. Emirates was the official flyer of the United Arab Emirates, the tiny constellation of states east of Saudi Arabia. A government-sponsored company that had grown quickly from its inception in the mid-1980s, it had a unique set of needs when it came to jet fuel. Emirates was a transportation hub for international flyers traveling to and from Dubai, the UAE's financial capital, from thousands of miles away. To service those routes, Emirates operated some of the world's biggest aircraft, including the two-deck, 525-seat Airbus A380. The airline had spent $3.2 billion on an order for a dozen of the 777-300ER, a sleek new Boeing aircraft, as well.

By 2004, the carrier's annual fuel bill was nearing $1 billion, overtaking personnel as its number-one cost. And unlike some of the more conservative U.S. airlines, Emirates was willing to hedge its jet risks creatively, making it a perfect target for innovative bank commodities traders.

Bourlot, the Morgan commodity trader still fuming over the China Aviation Oil Corporation trade on which he believed Andurand had stiffed him, was then a rising star at the company's London energy-options trading desk. The same year his China Aviation trade exploded, Bourlot helped arrange a hedge for Emirates that seemed guaranteed to make it money in the crude market under anything but a wildly volatile price scenario. The only problem was that was exactly the scenario Emirates encountered.

Because the jet-fuel derivative market was relatively small, making it tough at times to get in and out of trades, airline fuel hedges typically employed a basket of contracts tied to various liquid energy commodities—usually crude, but also other contracts that were related to it, like heating oil and diesel. Bourlot's trade involved using various options to set the expectation that crude oil would trade within a certain price band at a certain dollar amount above and below where Emirates management expected crude prices to actually be. If prices stayed in the range—which, statistically speaking, they almost certainly would—Emirates would achieve significant cost savings on crude.

But the trade also had some other features. Emirates had layered an additional batch of commodity contracts to widen that original range. So, instead of only being price-protected in a price range that was $30 wide, a second set of options contracts locked in oil prices at a range about $50 wide (the exact prices would change every year based on the market price of crude oil, but the size of the price range remained about the same). Emirates sold put options, which represented the right to sell oil, and calls, the right to buy it, to Morgan Stanley, which in turn sold other instruments back to Emirates.

It was a relatively simple concept with a complex execution, and it had a Seussian name to describe it: a "cap-swap double-down extendable." There were layers upon layers of different trades between the parties, and no one bothered to track the amount of money one party had paid to the other overall. For Morgan Stanley, however, the "extendable" part was key. If the trade went well for the client—and it did for a number of years—it was simply rolled into the new year and reinstated at new price targets.

"For years and years, they were happy, and the firm was happy," says a onetime Morgan official who was involved with the trade. Oil prices rose within the ranges expected, and Emirates effectively locked in cheaper fuel prices at just the right time. The carrier had recently initiated nonstop flights from Dubai to New York, and was planning to add a route from Dubai to San Francisco as well. The airline's executives, led by Sheikh Ahmed bin Saeed Al Maktoum, whose nephew was the ruler of Dubai, were happy to remove some of the uncertainty from their biggest liability. Over time, the program saved the carrier at least a billion dollars on fuel; for the fiscal year that ended in March 2008, Emirates reached a record profit of $1.4 billion.

Then things changed. In early May, West Texas Intermediate crude contracts—the standard oil contract in the U.S. at the time and the one Morgan had used to structure the Emirates hedge—soared past the $120 upper limit Emirates had imposed. That meant not only that Emirates was paying sky-high prices for jet fuel as cash prices moved higher, but that it was no longer protected by the hedges it had paid to create.

Oil's $147 peak in July 2008 was an expensive miscalculation for Emirates, but its reverse was far worse. In five short months, West Texas contract prices collapsed from their height of nearly $150 to less than $70 and kept going. The floor of the Emirates trading range had now been pierced, and although the cost of West Texas crude was by now impossibly low—ranging in the $50s by November—the cost of the "swap" portion of the trade the airline had arranged with Morgan Stanley, which was repriced every day based on the latest market movements, was exploding.

At that point, Morgan made a massive "margin call," or demand for additional cash as a down payment on the ongoing swap trade, to Emirates of more than $4 billion. The put options, or rights to sell crude, that the carrier had sold to Morgan were by now well below their "strike," or target price. While the details of the paper transaction were confusing, the economic impact of it could be understood simply: if Morgan Stanley had wanted to collect on the puts, Emirates could, effectively, have had to buy crude oil from Morgan for $70 per barrel and receive as little as $50 per barrel in return. Although Morgan had not yet invoked its right to sell the oil to Emirates at those inflated prices, it wanted reassurance that the money Emirates would owe it if it chose to use them would be there. So, late in 2008, it issued the margin call, a demand for additional cash from the airline.

Emirates executives scrambled. They didn't have billions of dollars in cash handy, so they had to source it from elsewhere. Letters of credit from various banks were issued, and at one point, Emirates put about $2 billion in cash in its margin account. But the full amount, of more than $4 billion, was not forthcoming, and West Texas prices were going even lower.

Some Morgan Stanley executives, who had reduced the overall margin demand thanks to their long-standing ties to Emirates, grew alarmed. True, the Emirates debt was unlikely to become an issue unless the airline suddenly went bankrupt. But they couldn't rule out that possibility. The U.S. banking community had barely recovered from the financial crisis, even after a nearly $700 billion taxpayer bailout the October before, and cash was critical. The Federal Reserve's office was asking questions, and so were Morgan Stanley's board members.

"The psychology in those days was, if Lehman could fail, anything could happen," says the Morgan official who was involved at the time.

■

Early in 2009, with West Texas contracts trading in the $40 range, John Mack and two lieutenants flew to Dubai to meet with Emirates management. They had been invited to see the city-state's ruler, Sheikh Mohammed bin Rashid Al Maktoum, in his desert lodge, about 45 minutes' drive from Dubai, for evening tea.

Using his limited Arabic, Mack greeted Sheikh Mohammed bin Rashid, nicknamed "Sheik Mo," and his uncle, Sheikh Ahmed bin Saeed Al Maktoum, the Emirates chairman. Mack was warmly received. In addition to their business dealings with Morgan Stanley, Sheik Mo and three of his sons had visited with the bank's board during a scheduled gathering in Dubai in 2006 (designed, no doubt, to curry favor for the booming and increasingly indebted metropolis). They liked the firm, it seemed, and were impressed with its embattled chief executive, who, despite his modest grasp of Arabic, had Middle Eastern roots himself and took the time to call on them regularly.

The group settled into their seats, and coffee and tea were served. "Tell us what's going on in the world and on Wall Street," the ruler asked Mack. "When is all this going to end?"

Mack and Sheik Mo commiserated over their respective dilemmas. Mack had narrowly avoided a bank failure in September, and Dubai, which had become an international hub for real estate, finance, and tourism under Sheik Mo's watch, was being criticized for overbuilding and amassing huge debts. Perhaps more embarrassingly, the arrest of two drunken British travelers for having sex on a local beach had brought months of headline damage to Dubai, where people took offense at such vulgar public activities.

The sheikh seemed incredulous about the sex scandal. "If you, in the U.S., find two people on the beach who are not married having sex, and the policeman tries to tell you you cannot do this and the woman gets up and slaps the policeman, would you arrest them?" he asked.

"Of course," said Mack sympathetically. It was a no-win situation, he added.

Mack soon turned the topic to the financial struggles in Dubai. "How are you getting through this?" he asked gently.

"We're suffering the same issues as everybody else and we're going to walk through them," the ruler replied. "We are one country, we are one state, and if we need to financially assist institutions, we will do that. Nobody will ever lose a dollar in Dubai."

It wasn't a clear promise of money in the bank, but it was as strong a reassurance as Morgan Stanley was going to get that Emirates was good for its money.

■

Morgan reported profits for that year of just $1 billion. Commodities results, the company noted, were affected by a lack of client business and a weak economic environment. Emirates Airline, whose fiscal year comprised the worst possible period for the contracts it had bet with—the latter half of 2008 and the first half of 2009—reported fuel-hedging losses of $428 million. Its fuel hedges had met with "challenges," the carrier noted, and had protected it only in a certain price range.

Jennifer Fan sensed internal change coming that winter. She was friendly with Jean Bourlot, who had moved on from trading jet fuel to develop a new agricultural-commodity trading desk, and who had heard rumblings of the Emirates problem. Moreover, since the credit crisis, Morgan was being more frugal in deploying its cash for house trading, and it was having some difficulties in getting credit from market counterparts, making it tougher to trade.

Fan, who had married Morgan Downey the year before and was still living in Tribeca, had never been good at artifice. She said what she thought most of the time, and what she didn't relay verbally was usually made clear by her body language. She wasn't above rolling her eyes during a boring speech at a public meeting, and her terse e-mails made it clear when she thought she was fielding a stupid question. Long silences in conversation with her weren't unusual, nor were boasts about her trading prowess in the company of rivals.

By early 2009 at Morgan Stanley, she was mostly frustrated with her annual bonus, which had been in the low millions despite her trading profits for the year of $35 million. Standard pay for a hedge-fund trader was 10 to 15 percent of the P&L, or profit they made in a year, so she figured she was entitled to at least $4 million, if not substantially more. Morgan Stanley had never paid its young commodity traders terribly well, and Fan was getting the usual treatment.

One day that May, she walked into the Purchase office and gave notice of her resignation. She'd been offered her own portfolio to manage at a newly formed commodity hedge fund in Stamford, Connecticut, and at twenty-five, she planned to take it.

5

THE REGULATORS

Early in 2009, Carl Levin, the powerful Democratic senator from Michigan, met with Gary Gensler, the former investment banker who had been named to run the Commodity Futures Trading Commission. Established in 1974, the CFTC was a somewhat overlooked sibling agency to the Securities and Exchange Commission. Its responsibility was to regulate the nation's swelling commodity and futures contract markets, but it barely did.

Commodity trading oversight, despite being an unloved agenda item in Washington that was handicapped by a modest budget from Congress and protective laws set during the Clinton era that walled off big sections of the markets from regulation, was a huge concern to Senator Levin. Gyrations in oil and gas prices were hurting consumers in Michigan, the home of the big three automakers, and beyond, and the demise of the energy trader Enron in 2001 had exposed manipulative activity in the natural-gas and power markets. About to serve his last term before retirement at the time of Barack Obama's election in the fall of 2008, the smiling, portly senator, who had no problem interrogating the titans of Wall Street with hours of embarrassing questions, was determined to address runaway commodity trading.

During the 2000s, the septuagenarian senator's Permanent Subcommittee on Investigations—a panel of a dozen or so publicly funded detectives who used cajoling and, occasionally, subpoenas to gather information then used in televised public hearings and excoriating reports the size of coffee-table books—conducted five different inquiries into commodity markets. Its seminal report, issued in 2006 as the commodities bubble was building, found that speculative trading was affecting commodity prices greatly, perhaps padding the price of oil by as much as $20 for every $70 barrel of crude.

Levin knew that a Goldman alumnus like Gensler would face a tough confirmation process before he could start the job, and that demands for tighter oversight of speculators after a period of witheringly high energy prices would inevitably arise. He thought it might be his moment to steer the CFTC toward neutering some of the commodity traders whose behavior he considered most abusive.

Levin, two of his senior staff members, and Gensler met in mid-January 2009. Sitting on a couch in his Senate office at a right angle to the CFTC designee, Levin got immediately to the point. "Does speculation affect prices?" he asked.

"Yes," said Gensler.

There was a long silence. The answer had come with astonishing ease; this was not the sort of frankness previous CFTC chairs and commissioners had given. Levin and his aides, staff director Elise Bean and a lawyer named Dan Berkovitz, both of whom had been deeply involved in the subcommittee's commodity research, looked shocked.

Gensler, whose confidence was not easy to dent, glanced around the room. "Why is my answer having this effect?" he finally asked.

"It's not what we've heard before from other people at the CFTC," Levin answered. He repeated the question: "Does speculation affect prices?"

Gensler repeated his answer. "It's what I feel," he said. "We had an asset bubble in housing, and we also had an asset bubble in physical commodities," he added. He spoke about how in the mid-2000s, commodity contracts had become a product for the masses, not just the professionals, drawing in large volumes of investments betting on a rise in prices that, in fact, pushed prices higher. "We saw that bubble burst in 2008," he said, referring to the steep crash that had sliced crude-oil prices from nearly $150 per contract to a $40-per-contract level, where the market was still trading that January.

To Levin and his team, Gensler's answer provided some hope. Here was a potential CFTC chairman who actually agreed with some of the subcommittee's conclusions—and might even construct policy to combat the more harmful behavior in the market.

Levin said he would follow up with a list of written queries that he wanted Gensler to answer before his confirmation hearing.

"I look forward to reading them," Gensler replied. Levin, who was accustomed to battling unenergetic market regulators, seemed to find that humorous.

■

Speculators had had a bad reputation in the commodity markets long before traders like Andurand, Glasenberg, or Fan came onto the scene. In fact, it was concern that speculators were manipulating raw-material prices that had led to the founding of the Commodity Futures Trading Commission a quarter-century before.

Congress established the CFTC the same year Marc Rich & Co. opened for business in Zug. Commodity contract trading around the world had grown dramatically, and so had big fluctuations in commodity contract prices. The lines were blurring between the so-called hedgers—farmers, corporations, and ranchers who traded futures to help manage the risks associated with their physical positions—and speculators, who made bets on the future of prices without the underlying physical positions. Back then, market watchers made a sharp distinction between the two.

By the terms of the Commodity Futures Trading Commission Act of 1974, the CFTC was meant to oversee the trading of all commodity contract products, which by the 1970s tracked a large array of physical commodities, from silver to Maine potatoes. The agency would crack down on any violations of trading laws, including manipulation. It would have enforcement capabilities and emergency powers allowing it to step in and halt trading during especially trying market circumstances.

In 1975, it opened for business in the basement offices of the U.S. Department of Agriculture. The nascent CFTC had desks, typewriters, and a small staff with little or no direction. William Bagley, the chairman, had no background in the commodities industry at all, but he had recently lost the California state controller's race and was an acquaintance of President Gerald Ford. "You can be the Joe Kennedy of the CFTC," joked the presidential staffer who offered Bagley the job, referring to the Kennedy patriarch who had been the Securities and Exchange Commission's first chair.

Building a culture of openness and tough regulation proved arduous for Bagley. In short succession, his CFTC faced a soybean-market manipulation by the Hunt brothers, a wealthy family of

Dallas commodity traders who tried to corner the market for soybeans by buying an enormous number of physical bushels in hopes they could drive prices higher. It also faced a group of con men that were selling phony contracts in the London commodity markets to unwitting Americans. By then situated in its own offices on Twenty-First and K Street, the CFTC jumped to stop the London swindles, which had been perpetrated from the U.S., but found it had essentially few tools at its disposal. "We had no body of law," Bagley says, "no precedents."

New as it was, the CFTC was already crippled by a bureaucratic Washington mentality—as Bagley discovered when he realized how many CFTC documents were stamped "confidential" in red ink. Since there were no established rules around the secrecy of documents, Bagley considered the stamps unnecessary, and he sent an employee around the office to collect them all so he could toss them into the Potomac River. Bagley had hoped the photographer he'd invited along for the purge would promote it as a needed push for transparency. Instead, Bagley was chastised for polluting local waterways.

By the 1980s and early 1990s, a new breed of trader was trickling into the commodity contract markets, where products tied to West Texas Intermediate and Brent crude oil were taking off. Refineries and other energy buyers were experimenting with oil contracts as a way to hedge their risk of rising prices, and independent money managers were betting on commodities.

The CFTC had strengthened during its first three decades, but it was still considered very cozy with the commodities industry. CFTC commissioners, the body of five appointees with ultimate authority over the agency's actions, spanned a mix of backgrounds and agendas—often with connections to physical commodities.

Farmers and industry lawyers were common, as were politically advantaged figures with no background in commodities at all, such as the wife of a prominent Washington arms negotiator who served during the 1990s. At one point, the group even included a veterinarian. Yet the Commission's presence in the President's Working Group on Financial Markets—a board, sometimes referred to informally as the Plunge Protection Team, established by President Reagan after the market crash of 1987 to invite discussion between representatives from the Federal Reserve, the Treasury, the SEC, and the CFTC—gave it access to the White House. "It was a quirky place," said a lawyer who worked there in the 1990s, recalling a female commissioner once wearing a spaghetti-strapped evening dress to a Working Group meeting and a narcoleptic commissioner who nodded off at some of the worst possible times.

Perhaps unsurprisingly, the CFTC was not prepared for the public backlash it faced in the late 2000s as the prices of major commodities swung higher. By June 2008, the price of West Texas crude contracts had soared into the $130 range, and gas prices were reaching $4 per gallon in some parts of the country.

Voters were outraged. During that summer, Congress held dozens of hearings on energy-related issues. Notwithstanding the Levin subcommittee report from 2006, there was scarce hard evidence to show who, exactly, was responsible for the astonishingly high prices. But in the few years before 2008, speculators as a percentage of the market had rocketed higher as more passive investors piled into commodity indexes on a large scale. Commodity prices surged accordingly, with the empirical data arguing strongly that speculators could be partly responsible. Many motorists and corporate fuel buyers thought so, and were demanding that the government somehow put a stop to their influence.

Inside the CFTC, the general assumption was that the basic realities of finite supply and increased demand were the reasons for triple-digit-per-barrel oil. It was essentially the same "Peak Oil" theory that Andurand had spotted in the contract markets, that crude oil deposits around the world were soon to run out, driving prices for what still existed to nosebleed levels.

That attitude struck CFTC commissioner Bart Chilton, who had been sworn in in 2007, as far too blasé. Chilton, a Indiana-born Democrat who sported a long, blond mane reminiscent of a hair-band rocker, had never traded commodities himself. But he had worked for a family farm union and spent time at cattle auctions as an advisor to Tom Daschle, the onetime Senate majority leader from South Dakota, where, after hearing a series of public bids, the price of a head of cattle was settled by a couple of guys whispering to each other at auction. Even on that tiny scale, the fact that a private oligopoly could decide cattle prices had always bugged Chilton, a die-hard liberal who loved to wax outraged about the travails of plain folks while clad in his signature cowboy boots. Now he believed a cabal of traders were pushing around commodity prices in the oil and agriculture markets to benefit their own bank balances.

During a meeting with one of the agency's senior analysts in 2008, Chilton brought up the cattle-auction anecdote as a possible explanation for rising oil.

"It's nothing like that," the analyst told him. "You don't understand it." For every buyer there was a seller, he added, and speculators simply couldn't move prices around willy-nilly.

Chilton was miffed, but gave the staffer the benefit of the doubt. Bombastic as he could be at times, Chilton knew his limitations. After all, he lacked the education to back his claim about speculators and commodity prices; whereas the analyst in his office had been studying the markets for thirty years. Still, Chilton couldn't help thinking there was something strange about what was happening to oil.

"The staff was writing me off," he remembers, "trying to tell me to go in a corner and hush up, and 'you don't understand it, Bart,' and oil prices started going higher and higher, and I kept saying to the staff, 'Really? Really?'" The only encouragement he got came from his own staff lawyer. "Just keep asking the question," she said.

Chilton was not without support on Capitol Hill, where a number of legislators had been promoting bills to curb speculation in the energy markets. Late that July, not long after oil reached its zenith of $147 a barrel, the Senate passed a motion to proceed with a vote on an antispeculation bill that Senate Majority Leader Harry Reid of Nevada had been promoting.

Chilton was pleased. But on July 22, while grabbing a bite at the M Street Grill near the CFTC, he read on his BlackBerry that the agency had issued a press release on its oil-price task force's preliminary findings. "Fundamental supply and demand factors provide the best explanation for the recent crude oil price increases," the statement read.

Chilton nearly choked on his Cobb salad. This was politically motivated, he was sure. The CFTC's task force, convened in June 2008 under pressure from Congress, had only been meeting for a few weeks and had barely any data to go on. Among other things, the CFTC had issued a special request to certain market participants to share their "swap" or bilateral commodity trading contracts as part of the study, and only a handful of parties had even responded.

Chilton, who was the sort of appointee never to avoid a news camera, rushed back to his office and began calling reporters. The task-force findings were preliminary, he insisted, and it was too soon to render judgment. Just because speculators weren't the only driving force behind oil prices didn't mean they should be discounted entirely, he insisted.

He also confronted the CFTC's chairman, Walter Lukken, as to why he had issued the release with such a thin basis. But he never got a satisfying answer, and it was too late to change the story line. Three days later, Reid's bill was killed in the Senate.

■

The idea that Gary Gensler might be too tight with Wall Street was understandable. Before coming to Washington, he had spent two decades at Goldman, where he worked with media companies on mergers and acquisitions. In 1990, he advised the National Football League on the sale of its broadcast rights to television networks over the coming four years. (One of Gensler's tactics, which involved withholding the rights to broadcast the 1994 Super Bowl, helped net the league a record $3.6 billion package.)

He had also worked overseas, relocating in 1993 to Tokyo, where he ran the Asian branch of Goldman's sprawling fixed-income, or bond, division. The job put him in close proximity to a major financial scandal: a series of futures contract trades at the Singapore office of the UK-based Barings Bank on the direction of the Japanese stock market and certain interest rates that ultimately brought Barings down. For Gensler, who knew little about such contract markets before living in Tokyo, it was an education in the perils of trading complex products across borders during times of market stress.

As a Goldman executive, he handled the crisis self-interestedly, telling the Goldman staff not to wire any money, property, or security of any value to Barings. "Let the lawyers figure it out later," he said. He had to protect the firm's soundness before anything else.

In 1997, Gensler, his wife Francesca, and their three daughters moved from New York to Chevy Chase, Maryland, for a new job he'd taken in the Treasury Department. A strong believer in the importance of government service, Francesca, whose father had been at Pearl Harbor, had encouraged Gensler to leave the private sector and had helped him compose a letter to Robert Rubin, the fellow Goldman alum who was then treasury secretary, inquiring about a post. Gensler had already made a lot of money at Goldman, and a job at Treasury seemed worth uprooting their lives for.

It was an era of light regulation in Washington, and it was the dot-com boom: Internet companies like Netscape, Yahoo, and Amazon were hitting the public markets with wild success, and small investors were shifting in mass numbers into stocks.

Under the guidance of the conservative Fed chairman Alan Greenspan and, later, Rubin's successor at Treasury, Lawrence Summers, officials were beating back attempts to curb trading in off-exchange commodities and other risky contracts—including a notable push by Brooksley Born, the female lawyer who was chair of the CFTC. In 2000, President Clinton signed the Commodity Futures Modernization Act, a piece of legislation supported by Summers, Gensler, and other Treasury staffers that preserved almost complete autonomy for banks and speculators in the trading of private contracts known as "over-the-counter derivatives," positions betting on the price movements of stocks, bonds, or commodities in some way. The idea was to let markets run their course, presuming that broad growth would follow, and it did—right into the housing boom of the next decade.

"Knowing what we know now about how derivatives evolved, I think we should have done more at that time," says Gensler. "But, back in that context on derivatives, they weren't regulated in Europe, Asia, North America, or Latin America, and there had been a worldwide consensus on that."

By the time Gensler was designated to run the CFTC in December 2008, the environment had changed dramatically. Upheaval in the banking system and a series of government bailouts had fueled calls for tighter market oversight, and Gensler would have to agree to tighten the policing of speculators to overcome his record in the Treasury. Even after the defeat of his July 2008 speculation bill, lawmakers like Harry Reid and Congressman Bart Stupak (D-Mich.) were still angling for curbs on the size of commodity futures wagers, otherwise known as "position limits."

During rehearsals for Gensler's confirmation hearings—also known as "murder boards" in Washington since the intention was to help the nominee handle hostile questions that could scuttle his or her chances of being confirmed for a job—he spent a good deal of time justifying his historic stances on regulation. His coaches, including a staffer for a key Democrat on the Agriculture Committee and a hedge-fund official from New York, interrogated him on his years in the Clinton Treasury. Bart Chilton pitched in, as did Dan Berkovitz, the subcommittee lawyer on Carl Levin's staff who attended Gensler's first meeting with the Michigan senator.

During the actual hearing, Gensler was asked more than once about his surprising theory that speculation did indeed affect commodity prices. One senator on the Agriculture Committee repeated Gensler's own testimony as a younger Treasury official arguing that imposing regulation would be a "burden" to the market's functioning. Senator Kent Conrad pointed out that Gensler bore "responsibility" to fix the harms that led to the financial crisis, because "you gave us bum advice" in the run-up to the housing collapse.

"What would you say to assure us that you would be part of the solution?" Conrad asked.

Gensler was humble. "We should have fought harder" to harmonize the oversight of all commodities and not just a few, he replied. He and his colleagues in the Treasury and Fed hadn't realized the looming threat from "swap," or hand-tailored products settled by private contract, he added, which in the late 1990s were just "dots on the landscape," not the enormous market that derivatives later became. He mentioned *The Great Mutual Fund Trap*, a book he had coauthored, about shoddy performance and excessive fees in the mutual fund industry in 2002—probably the first public manifestation of his own apparent change of heart on financial regulation. The book itself was ironic, given that Gensler's twin brother, a libertarian thinker named Robert, was a celebrated mutual-fund manager at the investment firm T. Rowe Price in their hometown of Baltimore.

■

Late in May 2009, Gensler was sworn in as chairman of the CFTC. In his acceptance speech, he promised to work "vigorously" to protect citizens from "fraud, manipulation, and excessive speculation."

He would have limited resources with which to do so. Reduced funding had taken the CFTC to a five-hundred-person staff, the same size it had been back in William Bagley's day in the late 1970s. The agency desperately needed additional lawyers to enforce its existing laws, as well as to develop new ones. A request to add nearly two hundred people to the staff was pending.

For Gensler, it was also a time of personal transition. After a long fight with cancer, his wife Francesca had died in 2006, leaving him to raise their three children on his own. During her final weeks at The Johns Hopkins Hospital in Baltimore, bedridden and wearing an oxygen mask, she had exhorted her family not to think of her passing as unfair.

"This is just part of life," she had said as Gensler tried to comfort the girls, "but life's been fair to us."

Gensler repeated the mantra often in his years at the CFTC. He was "blessed" with two decades of marriage to his late wife, and also blessed to serve the government, he'd say. It gave his professional persona, which could turn caustic over seemingly small issues, a sense of mission.

Gensler didn't work for two years after his wife's death, wanting to focus on his daughters instead. But once on the job at the CFTC, he wasted no time with opening pleasantries. During his first financial-services industry speech, to the Managed Funds Association in June 2009, he recommended that the "entire" derivatives industry—at least those parts of it that traded privately rather than on a public exchange, be subjected to robust regulation. That meant that every type of swap, or two-party trading contract, from interest-rate to commodity, would be under his purview. He added that he would be scrutinizing the hedge-fund industry, and deferred to a wheat-market study that had been conducted by Senator Levin's investigative subcommittee, a particular enemy of Wall Street interests, as a source for further discussion.

Traders were shocked. Nearly every government official paid lip service to protecting the public good, but no one had launched their new regulatory regime like Gensler. Short, slim, and brainy, the CFTC chairman was not physically intimidating; during the course of a long meeting, he might even kick off his shoes and prop his feet up on a coffee table to create a more casual atmosphere. He spoke of using the D.C. Metro service and the Baltimore commuter rail, mentioned often that his girls had no nanny, and held lunch meetings at a nondescript Chinese restaurant near his Twenty-First Street office (which was huge and had a view). But when the former Goldman banker took the podium at a large securities conference and told Wall Street that he was essentially coming for it, that was something.

■

The debate over speculation continued to roil. Late that summer, a pair of Rice University academics, Kenneth Medlock and Amy Myers Jaffe, published a paper arguing that speculators might be influencing prices. They used CFTC market data to illustrate their point. Noting that the proportion of speculators in the market had spiked to nearly 60 percent in July 2008, as oil reached its peak price, they argued that the former condition may have caused the latter.

Some market analysts immediately panned the study. "Ken Medlock and Amy Jaffee [*sic*] play the drunk looking for a wallet under the lamppost" in their study, argued University of Houston professor Craig Pirrong, an expert in commodity trading who was skeptical of the idea that speculators were responsible for raising oil prices and thought the data proved little. Hobbled by faulty logic and grand, baseless assertions, Pirrong added, the Rice study "is about as weak as it gets."

That summer, the CFTC held three rounds of hearings on position limits, the takeaway of which was that no one could agree on almost anything. Energy users like the American Trucking Association demanded that the agency place curbs on positions that, they felt, led to spikes in the price of futures that they used to hedge the cost of diesel. Wall Street traders such as JPMorgan argued that large-trader reporting was fair, whereas position limits on client flow trades were not. The head of the Chicago Mercantile Exchange claimed that it should be the one to monitor speculative activity by curbing large positions; whereas its arch-rival, the IntercontinentalExchange in Atlanta, argued that such supervision should be done by the CFTC.

Gensler's own mind was already made up. "I came away with the feeling that it was not so much a question of whether we were going to do a proposal on position limits, it was just a question of the details," he says.

On January 26, 2010, less than a year after the new chairman had taken office, the CFTC published its proposed energy position limits in the *Federal Register*, the government's daily publication of official notices and new rules to the public. Noting the wild prices of 2007 and 2008, the rule filing stated that "large concentrated positions in the energy futures and options markets can potentially facilitate abrupt price movements and price distortions." To limit that risk, the CFTC planned to contain the size of the position that any one party could hold in major energy commodities like crude and natural gas. Exceptions would be made primarily for traditional hedgers, such as airlines, or for swap dealers using large positions as risk-management tools.

Almost immediately, industry members torpedoed the proposal along much the same lines that they had argued during the summer hearings. Nearly 15,000 comment letters poured in—an all-time record for the agency. Gensler was unmoved. Asked during a lunch at the upscale Waldorf Astoria hotel in New York with representatives from Goldman Sachs, Credit Suisse, and other banks what the biggest hurdle to improving the derivatives world was, he pointed to his hosts and said: "The people in this room."

Even among the CFTC's commissioners, the position limits were controversial. Chilton was pleased, but three of his counterparts had significant doubts. Imposing specific limits on one universe of commodities contracts that didn't exist in others would be too confusing, argued one, and stiffer oversight in the U.S. risked sending traders fleeing to more hands-off regulators in Europe and elsewhere. Another argued that although he was in favor of publishing the proposal, it was only because he wanted to see the industry's comments, not necessarily because he agreed with what was in it.

Congress and the White House soon came to Chilton and Gensler's aid. For several years, Representative Bart Stupak of Michigan had been pushing a bill to rein in speculation that he called the Prevent Unfair Manipulation of Prices Act, a proposal better known by its cheesy acronym: the PUMP Act. Among other things, Stupak's bill called for the extension of position limits in energy products across all derivative markets. Backed by the Teamsters Union, an airline trade group, and numerous corporations, it would enable the CFTC to "prevent market manipulation and help eliminate the unreasonable inflation of energy prices caused by excessive speculation," Stupak argued in congressional testimony, helping American consumers to avoid runaway costs. President Obama and Treasury Secretary Timothy Geithner also appeared to be in favor of position limits.

Those views were crystallized in a key section of the Dodd-Frank Act, a legislative behemoth passed in 2010 that was years in the making. Embracing many prior congressional attempts to curb derivatives trading, Dodd-Frank articulated new protections for consumers who used credit cards and basic banking services, set up new authorities to monitor the financial system, and forced major financial institutions to create contingency plans to protect the broader system from their own demise.

House and Senate leaders spent much of the spring and early summer of 2010 finalizing the bill, which ultimately filled 848 pages. Dodd-Frank mooted the position-limits proposal that had been published that January (which, ironically, was too narrow to meet Dodd-Frank's requirements). But it reinvigorated the cause by curbing large trades in contracts connected to twenty-eight major commodities rather than just a handful, including gold, copper, natural gas, sugar, and crude. It also called for the central "clearing" of most swaps (a move that, as with BP's late 2008 transactions with Glencore, insulated market participants from the credit problems of their trading counterparts) and gave the CFTC more oversight of contracts traded on foreign exchanges.

Gensler, who had been in the room throughout the all-night congressional session at which Dodd-Frank was finalized, was delighted. He was a huge proponent of Title VII, the portion of the act dedicated to contract trading and commodities, which promised to empower the CFTC substantially. Along with Dan Berkovitz, the Levin committee lawyer he had hired as the Commission's general counsel, he collaborated with lawmakers like Arkansas Democratic senator Blanche Lincoln to fashion the final language. Being on the Hill frequently enabled Gensler to tinker with the act's details up until the last minute—including huddling at

5 A.M. with a New England senator to broaden an important swap-reporting requirement.

Days before President Obama signed Dodd-Frank into law on July 21, word of a new commodity-market disruption hit the press. Anthony Ward, a London hedge-fund trader who had gotten his start at Phibro, the same company that trained Marc Rich, had amassed a huge physical position in cocoa that amounted to nearly every bean in the London cocoa exchange network that he could physically get his hands on. The price of physical cocoa beans, tropical products that were used to make chocolate, had shot to their highest price since 1977.

The stratospheric prices of physical cocoa sparked fury in Britain, where, as in the U.S., many people were still reeling from the financial recession. The thought of some mysterious, deep-pocketed hedge-fund manager driving up the price of everyday goods like Hob Nobs cookies and fine chocolates at a time when so many people were suffering seemed grossly unfair. The London tabloids dubbed Ward "Chocfinger," a play on the notorious James Bond antagonist Goldfinger, and published pictures of him looking dark-tanned and hokey in a tieless suit. On Facebook, someone created a Chocfinger graphic by superimposing Ward's face on a pig's body, headed for the trough. A television camera camped for a day outside Ward's stately London office on Curzon Street, part of the same moneyed enclave where Glencore's traders worked.

Fellow commodity traders were almost as incensed. The German Cocoa Trade Association reportedly dispatched an angry missive to the London International Financial Futures Exchange where cocoa is traded, charging that Ward's company, Armajaro Holdings Ltd., had engaged in manipulation. Behind the scenes,

Armajaro fought back, arguing that they had been set up for a media drubbing by market opponents betting that cocoa prices would fall, and that their trades were entirely legitimate. Ultimately, after a brief spike, the price of cocoa fell dramatically and Ward had to unload his physical position in a hurry. No public regulatory sanctions were ever brought.

■

In the months after Dodd-Frank's passage, CFTC teams began crafting the rules that would actually execute the act's directives in the markets. Thirty-four rules were prepared by December, a remarkable accomplishment for an agency that had been far less prolific in the past, but commodity position limits weren't among them.

Because the commissioners were still at odds over the limits, Gensler proposed to Congress a phased implementation. To strengthen market oversight in the meantime, Chilton, who was irked about the delay, proposed implementing "position points," threshold position levels for commodity contract traders that would trigger the CFTC's notice and, potentially, a directive to the traders who attracted notice to downsize their positions.

On December 16, the Commission held its eighth public meeting to discuss its progress on Dodd-Frank. After listening to the back-and-forth between the staff and his colleagues about the problems with checking large commodity contract positions, Chilton, who was pressing the position-points idea, lost his temper. He cut off Berkovitz midsentence during an answer to one of his own questions, and implied that Steve Sherrod, the CFTC's head of market oversight, was being lazy in balking at Chilton's request to flag the Commission on large commodity contract trades.

"This isn't just some little thing you may or may not do if you get around to it," Chilton told Sherrod, as reporters and staffers watched. "This is a proactive responsibility on your division . . . to come to us and make sure we know what's happening. We're the people that have these things on our wall."

Gensler tried to smooth things over. "I have such respect for the staff," he said, pointing out their long hours and willingness to solve problems. "They're just pros."

"Remember Reagan?" asked Chilton. "Trust but verify."

Gensler told Chilton that as part of its weekly market surveillance, the staff would report to the Commission on parties with especially large positions—even though the parameters for doing so were still fuzzy. "I think that's what I asked them to do forty-five minutes ago," he said.

"Okay, good. I'm done for now," said Chilton.

Gensler, apparently sensing the resentment around the room, called for a ten-minute break. When the meeting reconvened, Chilton was mysteriously absent.

After an excruciating pause, during which Gensler went looking for Chilton, the long-haired commissioner finally returned to the room. Gensler was arguing for an adjournment.

"This one might just need a little more time to ripen," Gensler said with a characteristic half-smile.

6

THE HEDGER

Jon Ruggles was working in his Houston office one morning early in 2011 when a headhunter called with something intriguing. Delta Air Lines was searching for a vice president of fuel, the recruiter said, and the person they hired would rebuild the carrier's commodity contract trading, or hedging, from scratch. Delta wanted to do everything differently, he explained; it was a serious opportunity, or he wouldn't have bothered to call.

Ruggles, whose floppy hair and innocent face gave him a boy-next-door quality even at thirty-seven, was content at Bank of America's Merrill Lynch brokerage—or, at least, as content as someone who moved jobs every few years could be. Merrill, which had been purchased by the larger bank at the nadir of the financial crisis in September 2008, lacked the pedigree of Goldman Sachs or Morgan Stanley. But as a subsidiary of a massive commercial bank with close to a trillion dollars in deposits, it did have something they didn't: a huge stash of cash to lend to clients. Plus, Bank of America Merrill's commodities division, which Ruggles was trying to help expand, was a fun place to work; it was run by an affable former investment banker, employed a number of smart traders, and seemed to be gaining momentum in the years after the emergency acquisition. Despite occasionally being mocked for his designer jeans and know-it-all attitude, Ruggles felt comfortable at the place.

That hadn't been the case everywhere. Ruggles's résumé was filled with two- and three-year stints. Over the nearly fifteen years since leaving a post in the army, he'd worked in practically every part of the energy-trading business, from drillers to traders and consultants. He'd lived temporarily or more permanently in Houston, London, New York, Los Angeles, and Moscow. But the airline industry, which was notorious for bad trading decisions and a stodgy culture, was one area where he'd never thought to work. Airlines had a reputation for being comically bereft of any trading savvy, as exemplified by disastrous bets like the one that had led to Emirates Airline's multibillion-dollar margin call during the crude-oil rout of 2008 and 2009. US Airways Group, also seemingly incapable of navigating the energy markets, had recently given up on hedging the price of fuel through commodity contracts altogether. Others were still tinkering with their programs after experiencing setbacks. Only one, Southwest Airlines, was known for betting correctly over the years, and even its track record had been mixed.

Still, there had to be room for improvement. Airlines were the world's biggest consumers of fuel after the U.S. government, and after a wave of bankruptcy filings in the mid-2000s, the need to better manage their costs was paramount. Ruggles had never heard of an airline giving to a fuel-hedging team the autonomy that the headhunter was describing, but it made Delta sound serious. So he took a meeting about the job.

Once he passed the first few rounds of interviews, Ruggles flew to Atlanta to meet Delta's president, Edward Bastian, and its chief executive, Richard Anderson. The executives were frank about their problems. Delta had been unsuccessful in hedging jet fuel, they explained, and had been burdened with the cost of purchasing hundreds of millions of dollars in commodity contracts that hadn't bet accurate future market prices, making them useless as a way to curb jet-fuel costs. Delta had bought oil contracts when prices were racing higher and then sold them when prices were lower—the exact opposite of what a good investor would do. Its fuel-hedging loss for 2009 alone had been an astonishing $1.4 billion, a bill that put the company into the red for the year. Since then, Delta had slowed the hemorrhaging of money, the executives said, but there was much more still to accomplish if they were to make their hedging efforts truly worthwhile.

In the meeting, Ruggles kept his characteristic bluntness, which often got him into trouble at work, in check. In his mind, he was horrified. Some of these trades were just galactically stupid, he thought. Even as the three men spoke, Delta held a collection of crude-oil contracts, the products most often used to smooth out swings in the price of jet fuel, that were costing hundreds of millions of dollars to keep active. The contracts had been costly to purchase and wouldn't pay profits unless crude prices rose substantially from the $100 level where West Texas oil contracts then were. Keeping all that in mind, Ruggles told the executives that their concerns were warranted.

Delta, which was spending $9 billion a year at that point on fuel, was not alone. Jet fuel was now the single biggest expense for many carriers, and they could only pass on a limited amount of the pain to cash-strapped flyers, who would abandon them altogether if prices grew too dear. Jet-fuel fees were "out of control," the chief of Virgin America Airlines had recently told a reporter, calling the rising expenditure "a silent killer." It almost made labor talks with pilot and flight attendants, once the industry's biggest headache, seem easy by comparison.

Anderson, who was relatively new to the airline, was considering making fare hikes. But in addition to bolstering Delta's use of commodity contracts to "hedge," or iron out the impact, of fuel costs, he had also contemplated a more radical move: the purchase of a physical oil asset, such as a driller or a refinery, that would win Delta greater control over the fuel that it bought.

He and Bastian broached that subject with Ruggles.

"You can't buy an upstream operation," Ruggles replied, using the industry's term for a production site that actually drilled oil. He thought such an endeavor would be too cumbersome for Delta to manage, given that it had no experience in the exploration and production of oil.

A refinery purchase, however, had potential. Having helped manage refineries—crude-oil processing plants that turned the raw commodity into more usable products—and, as a consultant, advised clients on running and purchasing them, Ruggles knew a fair bit about the business. Two and a half years after the financial crisis, refiners on the East Coast had reduced capacity as a result of slowing demands for their products, meaning that there were plenty of processing plants that might be for sale. Given that, Ruggles told the Delta executives, the airline might be able to buy one more cheaply.

Anderson and Bastian seemed to like what they were hearing. Ruggles was offered a job on the spot, with a $1 million signing bonus and a salary of $300,000. If he were willing to start work immediately, the executives told him, they'd provide temporary housing in Atlanta and a clothing allowance so he didn't even have to fly back to Houston to get his things.

Ruggles demurred on the more immediate offer, thinking he should end things properly with Bank of America, to which he would have to give fair notice. He agreed to start in early April.

■

Delta had been through a rough few years. Clobbered by competition from low-fare rivals and beleaguered by jet-fuel costs in the aftermath of Hurricane Katrina, the carrier had filed for Chapter 11 bankruptcy in September 2005, the very same month in which Jennifer Fan made her $3 million gasoline trade. A year and a half later, Delta reemerged, having cut six thousand jobs, restructured its fleet, and added more profitable international routes. But its ability to borrow money from banks was tarnished, it had lost its spot in the venerable S&P 500 index of blue-chip companies, and its shares were trading on a dodgy stock market called the "pink sheets," whose companies didn't meet Securities and Exchange Commission requirements, for just 13 cents apiece.

Anderson, a Delta board member, was named CEO in September 2007. Although he was in the health-care business at the time of his hiring, he had run Northwest Airlines years before, and he had been a key advisor to Delta through the final stages of its restructuring.

A Texas native and a former assistant district attorney in Houston, Anderson was understated and folksy. Tall, bespectacled, and speaking in a charming southern drawl, he was known for volunteering to build homes for the poor and dealing personally at times with consumer complaints. He often reminisced about growing up in Galveston, his hometown, and drove a pair of

Toyotas rather than using a chauffeured car. At Delta, he adopted a desk that had belonged to Delta's founder, Collett Everman "C.E." Woolman, who had fashioned a crop-dusting company into a passenger airline in the late 1920s; Anderson told a reporter he hoped the entrepreneur's good vibes would "rub off" on him as the new chief executive.

By the end of 2007, after Anderson's first few months in office, Delta had returned to profitability, establishing a $158 million employee profit-sharing pool for the first time since filing for bankruptcy protection. Passenger revenue increased, a valuable agreement with Air France that provided Delta with a greater foothold in the European markets was struck, and the airline ranked at the top of the industry for on-time arrivals. In April 2008, plans to merge with Northwest in a deal that would create the nation's largest airline were announced.

Anderson was off to a bold start at Delta, but fuel prices remained an albatross. Unbeknownst to it at the time, the airline was headed into the most expensive period for oil in world history, and the carrier's modest contract-hedging effort was not sophisticated enough for what was to come. Expecting additional price hikes, Delta increased its hedges to half its expected consumption for the coming months, reduced or eliminated unprofitable flying routes for the rest of 2008, and tried to preserve as much cash as possible. Still, with the expense of the Northwest merger and the climbing cost of fuel and attempts to mitigate it, Delta ended the year at a financial loss yet again.

Then came 2009 and the airline's embarrassing $1.4 billion loss from ill-conceived commodity contract wagers. Delta had bought contracts meant to smooth out its 2009 costs as far back as 2008—in other words, during the bubble period in which prices were expected to continue rising. But instead, those peak prices from July 2008 had reversed, dropping the U.S. oil contract price based on the future price of West Texas crude from nearly $150 to about $34 during the winter of 2008 and 2009, turning what Delta had thought would be insurance policies to help it survive inflated jet-fuel prices into expensive liabilities. The airline's bad timing had been such that at the end of 2008, unexpectedly low crude prices had resulted in margin calls, or demands for additional cash from its banks, of $1.2 billion, the sum required simply to keep the poorly functioning hedges intact. It was much the same scenario that Emirates Airline had faced during that period, when Morgan Stanley's ingenious plan for curbing the Middle Eastern carrier's exposure to runaway fuel expenses led instead to a crushing margin call of more than $4 billion, prompting John Mack's emergency visit to Dubai.

Compared to 2009, the year 2010 was far better for Delta. But it still involved a slight loss from its attempted hedges of $89 million. Oil prices, now at about $90 in the West Texas Intermediate contract market and far closer to where their fundamental drivers of world supply and demand would have dictated, were still proving awfully hard to predict. Still, a successful hedging program would have saved Delta money rather than costing it an eight-figure sum, no matter what the market prices chose to do.

And oil in 2011 was hit with a fresh wave of political events that again drove prices higher. The problems started with agricultural commodities like wheat and corn, whose prices had shot high in the latter half of 2010 as a result of extreme weather in important grain-producing countries like Russia, China, and Australia that crimped the supply of crops. By early 2011, world food prices were hitting a new record high each month, according to the Food and

Agriculture Organization in Rome, surging past their mid-2008 levels and making food far less affordable. Parts of the Middle East were hit particularly hard by grain costs and other economic troubles. In December 2010, a twenty-six-year-old Tunisian fruit and vegetable vendor, devastated by poverty and political corruption, set himself on fire outside the headquarters of his provincial town two hundred miles south of Tunis, the country's capital. Fellow workers in his town took to the streets in protest, using cell phones to film their activities. Their videos were fed onto Facebook, Twitter, and other social media, and the demonstrations story soon went viral.

In January, the movement, which came to be known as the Arab Spring, gathered steam. Demonstrators fed up with autocracy and economic malaise gathered in town squares in Algeria, Jordan, and Egypt. Within weeks, tens of thousands of protesters filled Tahrir Square in downtown Cairo, demanding the resignation of Hosni Mubarak, the Egyptian dictator who had ruled for thirty years. Their ranks soon swelled to hundreds of thousands, and violence broke out. Hundreds were arrested, and hundreds eventually died, as Mubarak's security forces sought to quell the protests with brutal tactics.

In the aftermath of the Arab Spring, some have argued that food prices were a particular stressor. In Egypt, where bread constitutes one-third of an average diet and food costs amount to more than one-third of the average household's income, rising wheat prices had an enormous impact, argued Troy Sternberg, a research fellow at Oxford's School of Geography, in an academic study.

The political unrest was soon affecting the oil markets. By February 2011, rebels challenging the Libyan dictator Muammar el-Qaddafi were moving in on its capital city. Soon the country, which produced about 1.6 million barrels of crude per day, was operating at only a fraction of its capacity. Some hedge-fund traders, convinced that the threats to supply would be long lasting, were predicting $200 oil in the contract markets.

By the time Ruggles arrived at Delta in April 2011, Brent crude, the European oil contract he and an increasing number of U.S. traders followed most closely, was trading at more than $120. But the contracts Delta had bought to hedge jet-fuel costs during the period had bet prices of $110, and had cost about $8 apiece. Ruggles thought that was an exorbitant price to pay for a simple crude contract, one that practically wiped out the $10 Delta stood to make by having locked in lower crude prices. Recognizing the mistake, Paul Jacobson, Delta's treasurer and the usual point man on hedging decisions, worked with Ruggles to sell the existing contracts.

Delta's commodity contract purchasing had until then been basically ad hoc. Decisions were made by a small group of executives—usually including Jacobson, Anderson, and Bastian—who would set the company's plan. Once they decided how to bet in the markets, they, like Andurand at BlueGold, would then turn to underlings to actually buy the proper contracts and watch their performance day to day. Ben Bergum, a graduate of Montana State University's accounting program who now handled many of the details, had just been hired. He worked with other employees in Delta's supply-chain management area who tallied the amount of fuel the airline needed and what its price exposure might be as a result. The group sat in the flight-operations center of the Delta campus, isolated from Jacobson and other finance employees, and Bergum himself worked in a cubicle that was crushed against a thick column, next to a printer, envelopes, and other office supplies.

Once on the job, Ruggles stopped the self-editing he had labored over in the interview with Anderson and Bastian. Spotting textbooks on topics like advanced corporate finance and hedge ratios in Bergum's area, he lambasted the airline's simple-minded approach to commodity contract trading.

"I don't care about anything you've done before," he said, tossing the books into the trash. "We're going to do this my way." His view was straightforward: since Delta always needed jet fuel, it was by definition short the commodity, and should have a sophisticated hedging book, or investment portfolio, dedicated to preserving the most attractive possible prices. The book would use all available techniques to do so, just as that of a hedge fund or a bank like Goldman Sachs would.

But Delta's conservative hedging policy, which forbade the use of complex commodity contracts, restricted the possibilities. In general, Ruggles was limited at the time to using options, the right to buy or sell crude at predetermined future prices, and other commonly traded products. But he could put together more sophisticated positions if he did it in a piecemeal fashion, buying single components of the overall bet to build the broader wagers over time.

Using the more incremental approach, then, Ruggles revamped Delta's market bets with a series of options trades tied to a spectrum of different crude prices. The resultant position was similar to the nerve-racking "cap-swap double-down extendable" that Emirates had used in the mid-2000s. With Brent crude contracts trading at $110 in the middle of May, Ruggles effectively forecast that prices would stay somewhere between $95 and $122 in the months to come. Depending on where, exactly, crude contracts went, Delta would either come out slightly ahead or make a lot of money; barring an unpredictable calamity, it wasn't expected to lose money.

The strategy worked well. Crude stayed in the desired place for the next several months, and Delta's cost of hedging fell substantially.

Satisfied, Ruggles turned his attention to the physical and technical operations of Delta's fuel-hedging business. He hired a few more traders and moved the entire group over to the finance floor, where they could be closer to their overlord, Jacobson. He also put up Bloomberg market-data terminals, which were ubiquitous on Wall Street trading floors, and set up exchange accounts for Delta on both the Chicago Mercantile Exchange and the IntercontinentalExchange. He arranged for Delta to trade directly with places like Cargill and Koch Industries, rather than contacting them through middlemen. When two-foot-deep desks designed for flight reservation takers arrived in his team's new workspace, Ruggles sent them back, insisting that the group work off a traditional trading desk, which would allow them to work together better.

■

It was a Wall Street trading floor that had lured him into trading in the first place. In the mid-1990s, Ruggles was fresh out of a back-office posting in the army when he was offered a chance to help Citibank transition its trading systems from Unix, the software he had used as an information-technology specialist in the military, to Microsoft Windows. Eager for the shot, he traded in his 1986 Toyota Celica, which had nearly 200,000 miles on it, for a little bit of cash and a ride to New York.

Like Pierre Andurand, Ruggles had grown up with a liberal-minded father who was suspicious of financiers. The indoctrination was worse for Ruggles, though: his father was a professor of finance in Ohio and had actually researched the system as part of his living.

In 1987, his father took him to see the movie *Wall Street*, the portrait of corporate greed starring Charlie Sheen as an ambitious young stock trader and Michael Douglas as Gordon Gekko, his sleazy, amoral business mentor. "We left the movie and we had very, very different views," Ruggles remembers. "I had a hard time understanding that Gekko was the bad guy. I'm thinking, 'This is what I want to do when I grow up.'"

After graduating from what he joked was "the 200th best high school in Ohio" in the depressed steel town of Youngstown, Ruggles attended the University of Michigan, where he remembers maintaining a 4.0 for a while. He was sharp, but lacked focus, skipping classes until the last week before the exam. Prior to that, he'd bum around campus attending other things he found interesting—business school lectures, for example. Then he'd show up to the class in which he was actually enrolled and, hoping to bone up on the topic quickly, ask fifteen questions during a lecture. Classmates found him infuriating. "I didn't have a lot of friends," he says. He eventually transferred to the University of Texas, where the tuition was less than half of what it was in Michigan, and got a part-time job. Over the next year and a half, he lived on the cheap, worked as an assistant manager at an ice rink, and did other retail jobs to make ends meet. He never quite managed to make it work, though, so with one unpaid tuition bill standing in the way of getting his degree, he joined the army, where he finally earned enough to pay UT.

Arriving on Citi's bond and commodities trading floor in 1997, Ruggles was immediately smitten. He loved the high-octane ambiance and the camaraderie. Plus, he witnessed some major market meltdowns right up close. He was there for the Russian currency crisis of August 1998 and the Long-Term Capital Management hedge-fund bailout a month later, periods when the traders sprang into action and hundreds of millions, even billions, were lost in a single day. It seemed to Ruggles that the market was a living organism in itself, with moments of complacency, fear, and sadness, just like people had. When crisis was stirring, "you could almost sniff it out," he says of those wild days on the floor at Citi. "It starts out as a normal morning and all of a sudden people are yelling and screaming."

Ruggles was paid to tweak technology systems, but he began paying attention to the mathematical trading models instead. He also got to know some of the traders whose computers he fixed. One of his mentors was David Becker, a rising commodities trader. Sitting next to Becker for several weeks, he learned about the nature of the job and how to interpret what was happening in the market. At that point, Ruggles had "job envy," he says. "I liked what I was doing, but I would much rather be doing what he was doing."

Ruggles applied to business school at the University of Texas and won a spot in a program funded by Enron for aspiring energy traders. The summer before school started, he went to Venezuela to study Spanish and visit some of the country's oil rigs. A second language would help his career, he reasoned, and Arabic seemed too difficult to learn.

During his summer in business school, Ruggles got an internship at a major oil company in Houston. It was 2000, and he was young and single. One night, a couple of friends took him to an after-hours Latin club housed in an abandoned apartment complex. Inside, with the music booming, he was introduced to a pretty young accountant named Ivonne Gonzalez and they started talking. Ruggles was impressed with Gonzalez's drive and business savvy. She worked a junior position at Ernst & Young, but had plans to go much farther in the corporate world.

Ruggles wanted to go out with Gonzalez, but one of his friends asked her first. Gonzalez went on a couple of dates with Ruggles's friend, and Ruggles saw her again during a group outing about a week later. During the walk home, he pulled her aside. "We should go out," he said. "Sure," she replied.

The next night they went to a movie and a Tex-Mex restaurant. Over dinner, Ruggles pitched Gonzalez on why she should date him and not his friend.

"That guy you're going out with, he's not a good guy," Ruggles began.

"I know that," she said. She was barely out of school and not looking for anything serious. "Why does it matter?" she asked.

"You should be dating me," Ruggles pressed. "I'm an honest guy, a good guy, and I know what I'm going to be doing in my life." He laid out a prospectus that included working at an oil major, making lots of money, and traveling the world together.

She was convinced. After a few years of dating, they married in 2003 at a Baptist church in Houston. Fittingly, the reception was held at the Petroleum Club.

■

The next year, Ruggles was hired by Trafigura, the secretive Dutch trading firm founded by, among others, a pair of Glencore alumni. "Trafi," as the firm was known, was one of a handful of European commodity trading firms that did the same type of work as Glencore but on a smaller scale: moving physical quantities of oil and metals from one place to another, operating or processing the commodities it shipped, and hedging its exposure to changing prices through commodity contracts.

At Trafi, Ruggles worked in London, trading crude and other products on a speculative basis. His boss, a more experienced trader named David Mooney, had introduced Jennifer Fan to her future husband, Morgan Downey, when Downey worked for him at Bank of America. From Mooney, Ruggles learned the importance of betting smartly on energy prices not only when markets were volatile, but also when they were serene; that way, there was always a strategy for making money. He also realized he was better at finding trading inefficiencies between one commodity contract market and another—such as when heating oil was trading at an inexplicably cheaper level than natural gas—than he was at betting purely on the future direction of a single market, such as crude. In the first realm, Ruggles had real talent.

Outside of work, he began trading crude in a personal account, registered under his wife's name. Since Ivonne, who had changed her surname to Ruggles, handled all their finances anyway, it seemed a natural step.

Trafi also exposed Ruggles to the energy-trading business's seamier side. In 2005, he was in Houston helping to set up a new company office when government investigators arrived out of the blue, seizing computers and documents. "They came in, had a subpoena and just took everything," he recalls. "I think it was related to either oil-for-food," he says, referring to the U.N. program that Glencore and other traders were accused of abusing, "or the Ivory Coast government collapsing . . . or some other thing," Trafi faced.

He thinks the authorities came from Interpol, but still isn't sure. "In a trading house," he says, "what you don't know, you should not ask about."

Friends whom Ruggles told of the unnerving experience said to shrug it off. "The oil business is very litigious," he says. Associates warned him that things like the Houston raid would happen, and that he had to protect himself by following the rules and having a good lawyer on hand. But the threat of investigations and court shouldn't dissuade him from keeping on in the business, they insisted.

Ruggles spent the next six years hopscotching around the world, eventually landing at Bank of America. He had made good money by getting better jobs every few years, and also profited from some of the trading in his personal account. His intellect and creativity were respected, even if his attitude sometimes rankled. All in all though, Ruggles was restless. He was ready for the next challenge.

■

With the fuel book well in hand by mid-2011, Delta management returned to the refinery-purchase idea. Ruggles and others had been pondering the options that year, and had hired a refinery operator as a consultant on the project. Having done a good amount of research, the list of prospects had been narrowed down to two.

Late that summer, Ruggles, Jacobson, and others went to Richard Anderson's office for a meeting to discuss the possibilities: a 185,000-barrel-per-day refining facility in Trainer, Pennsylvania, not far from Philadelphia, or a 250,000-barrel-per-day plant near New Orleans.

Anderson eyed the two huge printouts that were spread across his conference table. They contained detailed satellite images of the two facilities, both of which were owned by ConocoPhillips. "How much is this one?" he asked, pointing to the Trainer plant. About $100 million to $120 million, he was told. The other, the group believed, would command a far higher price—as much as $800 million.

The Trainer facility, while far cheaper, was nonetheless part of a struggling refinery belt in the mid-Atlantic region, where numerous facilities were being idled because of waning demand for gas. Among other things, Trainer needed a complete physical overhaul, known in refining as a "turnaround," if it were to be in full compliance with environmental and other federal regulations. That meant the ultimate price could be twice what Delta was paying for the facility itself. Still, Ruggles, who had dealt since business school with refineries as either an operator or a consultant to clients who bought and ran them, felt that Trainer was a good value. The turnaround costs would be considerable, he felt, but Conoco had kept the plant in pretty good shape, and if Delta could keep the repair process to a tight enough schedule, it could limit the delays and expenses involved.

Anderson agreed. He told the executives to pull together a due-diligence team to take a closer look.

■

Thanks in part to its new hedge book, Delta was in much better financial shape by September. Still, unexpected setbacks, such as the Fukushima Daiichi nuclear meltdown in Japan in March and a winter storm that had forced Delta's Atlanta hub to cancel a wave of flights, meant that the airline was now projected to be $100 million short of funding its employee profit-sharing pool.

In a meeting with a half-dozen of their senior division heads, Anderson and Bastian asked what could be done. Budget trims were possible in the supply-chain area, they were told, and perhaps some of the airline's borrowing agreements could be rejiggered to free up cash. But even with those tweaks to the financial picture, they still had a big gap before the bonus pool was ready.

Bastian turned to Ruggles. "Fuel," he said. "Anything we can do?"

"We could probably trade a bit and make some money," Ruggles replied. Bastian appeared open to the idea. If the fuel group could generate $40 to $50 million, he said, it would help matters greatly.

Ruggles sensed an opportunity in heating oil. Often used as a hedge for airlines and other energy traders because it was correlated to crude and jet fuel, heating oil had been volatile that fall, and its trajectory might continue to be ragged. But Ruggles thought it would stay in a certain range until the end of the year, and figured that if he was right, he could make some money.

With heating oil then trading at about $2.80 per gallon in the contract markets, Ruggles made a complicated wager consisting of multiple parts, including the right to buy heating oil at particular prices and the right to sell it at others. Overall, though, his position targeted a basic price range in the coming months of between $2.50 and $2.90.

A couple of days later, Ruggles got a call from Trey Griggs, a senior salesman at Goldman Sachs, which was one of Delta's primary brokerage firms. "What the hell are you doing?" Griggs asked. He demanded to know why the airline, whose primary need was to buy jet fuel, would possibly want to reserve the right to sell a commodity like heating oil, which seemed like a trade pretty far afield from its core needs.

Ruggles explained that he had a plan that had been approved by Delta management, but Griggs's call, he knew, was a serious one. As a broker to the airline, Goldman had a responsibility to protect Delta's financial interests, and a purely speculative trade like Ruggles's might have seemed inappropriate. "The last thing you want to do is have the company blow up with wrong-way risk," says a Goldman employee who was briefed on the Delta discussions.

Delta arranged a conference call with Griggs to explain their rationale for the trades. Managers vouched for Ruggles, who was by then on his way to making $100 million on the heating-oil gambit, helping to push the airline's profit-sharing pool into the black. All in all, Delta's hedge book generated $420 million in gains for the year, capping what could only be considered a remarkable turnaround from where it had been less than a year before.

But even though he escaped that particular attack, Ruggles was in other ways off to a very bad start. "From day one," says the Goldman employee, "everybody in the industry thought he was a lunatic."

7

THE WILDERNESS YEAR

Two and a half years after his record performance, Pierre Andurand was still doing incredibly well. His returns in 2009 and 2010 had been strong, if not superlative, and BlueGold had established itself as a major player in London's commodity-trading business. The fund, which now occupied a gracious office in the city's pricey Sloane Square neighborhood, an area famous for a particular brand of British gentry known as the "Sloane Rangers," was a fixture in the international financial press and managed billions of dollars in client money.

Since its inception, the firm had returned more than five times its invested cash, or capital—all during a period in which the Goldman Sachs Commodity Index and the S&P had fallen hard. Noting the wild range of prices in the oil markets, "we are pleased with how we have navigated all of these energy markets—bullish, bearish, and last year's trendless range bound market," Andurand and Crema wrote in their January 2011 investor letter. In other words, even when there was no apparent direction in the markets, BlueGold made money, sacks of it.

That winter Andurand, who was by now an internationally

known hedge-fund manager living on Walton Place, a lush but quiet side street of West London near the department store Harrods, had also fallen madly in love. A friend had introduced him to a former model named Evgenia Slyusarenko at KX, the gym where he worked out most mornings in West London, and he had proposed to her after a brief courtship while lying in one day in bed.

Born in Vladivostok, on Russia's easternmost tip, Slyusarenko, or "Genia" for short, had come to Paris as a teenager with no knowledge of French and little English. A soft-spoken, willowy brunette, she was taken in briefly by the Karin agency, which trained her to walk the international runway for brands like Chanel and Dior. But Slyusarenko resisted the physical toll of modeling, including the constant pressure to lose weight and to work exhausting hours. By the age of twenty-three, she had earned a degree from Vladivostok State University and relocated to Moscow. There she took up with the financier Nathaniel Philip "Nat" Rothschild, a British commodities investor and a member of a well-known European banking family, and eventually moved to London with him, where she switched careers and became an interior designer.

It was after her breakup with Rothschild that she met Andurand. Now Slyusarenko was newly pregnant and planning an August wedding with him near St. Petersburg. Furniture was to be flown in to the Catherine Palace, which the couple felt was lacking in elegant partyware, and Slyusarenko's dress was being custom-made for €60,000 in Paris.

Andurand was still optimistic about prices in the crude contract market. He knew that the Arab Spring was creating a volatile period, but he felt that oil was still significantly cheaper than its natural levels and expected a rise over the next year or two.

During the first few months of 2011, he had purchased both Brent and West Texas oil contracts. Some were tied to prices in the near future, and others were tied to prices as far out on the "curve," or calendar, as 2013. By buying both sets, Andurand spread his position over a longer period of time.

BlueGold was by that point managing about $2.4 billion in cash, mostly from outside investors. But, as usual, Andurand liked to think bigger, and he had used complex trades to triple his market exposure, leaving the fund with wagers on a rise in crude prices that amounted to about $8 billion.

London markets were quiet most mornings, so Andurand kept to a leisurely work schedule. He would usually sleep until 8:30 A.M. or so, check the e-mails that had come in overnight for any oil-moving news, then have a bite to eat. Perhaps because of his pending nuptials, he was keeping healthy at the time, relying on foods like toast with goat cheese or salmon or fruit and yogurt for breakfast to stay trim. Each morning he would look at the Bloomberg computer terminal in his home office, read some relevant stories, and, if nothing earthshaking was going on, he'd head the few blocks to KX for a hard-core workout. After that, he would shower and throw on his usual casual ensemble of jeans and a button-down shirt, getting to the office at Sloane Square by about 11:30 or noon.

Crude had been trading in a range for some time now, and it was at a lower level than Andurand wanted. He had been astonished by the market's fall in the aftermath of Osama bin Laden's death, and was growing annoyed by the stagnancy of his positions. Come on, Andurand would think, looking at Brent contracts that were then stuck in the mid-$120s. When were they going to budge?

Good things rarely happened when Andurand got impatient; he knew that much. A methodical trader, he normally laid the groundwork to support his market thesis and waited calmly for it to become profitable, even if the process took weeks or months. But this time around, he was becoming antsy. He couldn't help it.

Placing a big market wager was tedious work, involving the buying and selling of relatively small bundles of commodity contracts at a time followed by long waits to see how the trades fared. If BlueGold's positions didn't affect prices unfavorably, it could keep adding new contracts until the bets reached their desired size. But if prices moved against the firm, it would pull back, waiting hours, days, even months for a better moment to increase the stakes. It was the same painstaking book-building that Ruggles underwent. Little by little, BlueGold would build its positions, monitoring them constantly as contracts matured and market prices changed, assessing whether that left the firm's portfolio up or down as a result.

In 2008 Andurand had done all the trading work himself. But after BlueGold's first flush year, he and Crema had hired a pair of so-called execution traders to do the work for them. Neel Patel, the more senior of the two, was Andurand's proxy when he was out. Early in the morning, Patel commuted in from his country house to check the markets and send his boss updates, and he'd continue doing so throughout the day, putting BlueGold's market holdings in the context of the commodities market as a whole and warning Andurand when certain positions became a risk.

On May 5, the calamitous day in which BlueGold nearly lost a bundle on Andurand's overoptimistic crude bet, it was Patel and his colleague Sam Simkin who first noticed the spiral. Andurand had spent the first hour or so of the disaster meeting with the author of the book series Market Wizards and then, having run upstairs to help, doing little more than instructing his charges to sell a bit of crude at a time and wringing his hands while they awaited the results.

Late that afternoon, Andurand retreated to his enclosed office, where he could see his traders through the glass. Up on a pedestal and also encased in glass was a miniature model of the black-and-white Bugatti sports car he'd purchased after Blue-Gold's first big year; it had arrived with a note from the manufacturer, saying "with compliments," and was one of the few personal adornments in his office. Andurand switched on his PC and made a few more calls, still searching for answers to crude's sudden sell-off. Crema and Paul Feldman, the company's financial officer, joined him; all three appeared baffled.

Andurand had seen bad days in the markets before, but this one shook him to the core. Crude was behaving in a way he'd never seen before—indiscriminate selling, for multiple hours without abatement.

The sheer price drop in crude contracts, in which BlueGold was so deeply invested, was reason enough for panic, but the nature of the sell-off was unnerving as well. Crude had begun the day in backwardation, a situation in which the future prices of oil contracts were lower as their expiration dates stretched farther out in the calendar. In a case like that, contracts connected to a longer-term time frame—which, in BlueGold's case, were a series of Brent and West Texas contracts tied to whatever prices were in December 2013—would almost always remain steady while the nearer-term futures dropped precipitously in price. But that wasn't happening today. Everything was falling at the same time.

BlueGold's large position in the market had by then become a handicap. The moves it made, or even rumors of them, could affect prices to a large extent. By selling large numbers of contracts to limit its losses before prices fell even further, BlueGold was inadvertently pressuring other crude contract holders to sell off as well, and, in the process, making prices even less favorable for itself. It was an infuriating paradox for the hedge fund that had exactly the sort of market impact that advocates of position limits like CFTC commissioner Bart Chilton had imagined—albeit with the effect of depressing oil prices rather than spiking them.

As Patel and Simkin sold off their crude positions that afternoon, reporters began calling the office, asking questions. Were things okay? Was BlueGold blowing up? The traders had no idea.

Patel was busy trying to extricate BlueGold from its crude holdings, and he didn't want to disturb his superiors with questions from the media. But his friends were sending worried texts as well. Around 4 P.M., he shut his cell phone off. They would all have to wait.

For the rest of the afternoon, Andurand, Crema, and Feldman were in and out of meetings, and Patel and Simkin sold as many Brent and West Texas contracts as they could. Each sale dragged down prices, but they had little choice other than to act before things got even worse.

Markets thinned out by about 7:30 P.M. in London, when it was 2:30 P.M. in New York, and little could be traded efficiently after that. BlueGold had managed to sell off more than $3 billion in positions, losing $500 million in the process. It was a massive amount to sell, maybe even suicidal.

"That was the scariest day ever of my career," Andurand says now. "That really froze me. Usually I know how to manage—the front goes down more than the back," he said, referring to the timetable used to discuss commodity contracts, in which the front is the nearer term and the back is the later, "and you can recover and go the other way if you need it."

But this time around, both ends of the horizon had been moving, with the front end at moments falling three or four times as much as the back, causing BlueGold to lose much more money than Andurand had anticipated.

"I thought, if the market's starting to act like that, then we don't know how to manage it," Andurand recalls. "It was a psycho market."

■

Patel and a research analyst stayed late that night, watching the markets and rechecking BlueGold's remaining positions. The firm had decided to hang on to some of its West Texas holdings as well as its back-end contracts, but there would still be more distressed selling in the morning.

Patel left Sloane Square around 11:30 P.M. and caught one of the last London Underground trains out to Zone 4, on the city's farthest outskirts. The ride home to Chigwell, his quiet town northeast of London, was an hour. He sat numbly through it.

When he walked into his house after midnight, his live-in girlfriend was irritated. "I've been trying to call you for hours," she said. "Where have you been?"

"It was a bad day," Patel muttered. He didn't have the energy for a confrontation, and he didn't like to talk about work at home anyway. Nobody outside of the commodity markets, he felt, could really understand the sheer terror that accompanied BlueGold's sort of risk profile.

Patel walked into his home office and turned on the PC to check the markets again. He was only twenty-seven, but he'd invested all his savings in BlueGold; the place was more than just a paycheck to him. Even though the markets were essentially closed, with only limited activity in Asia, he couldn't relax. He felt unable to disconnect.

His girlfriend had gone to bed after their argument, and he too tried to lie down. But he was too anxious to get any sleep. At 2 A.M., he put on his gym clothes and climbed onto the treadmill for a five-mile run.

■

When the alarm on his cell phone rang at 8:30 the next morning, Andurand thought he'd had a terrible nightmare. Crude had dropped precipitously and BlueGold had lost a bundle. He glanced at his BlackBerry, which lay on the nightstand. Oil in the Brent market was down another $5 to the $106 range, a full $15 from where it had started Thursday morning. Andurand hadn't dreamed the carnage after all.

He went through his usual laid-back morning routine, checking the BlackBerry as he went. Brent dropped to $105 at one point. He was glad he had sold so much off the prior day. Meanwhile, he still had a company to manage. He fired off a note to Patel and BlueGold's analyst, telling them he'd be in very shortly and that things would be okay.

By the time Andurand reached the office, Brent had recovered some, and was now down only $1.50 or so on the day. That was a relief. The BlueGold team just couldn't be sure how long the respite might last.

Andurand and his traders examined their positions. They had sold off a chunk of their near-term exposure, but still had a number of December 2013 crude contracts.

Andurand instructed the traders to sell more of the nearer-term exposure, along with some ancillary positions in copper and agricultural commodities, instruments that fit with an overall positive outlook on the markets. Copper, a base metal used in nearly every electronic device and a key import in China, was a good bet in a time of economic growth, and soft commodities like corn and wheat were also poised for potential price gains. But with the market in such a sour frame of mind, even in the absence of news, Andurand was taking no chances.

Halfway through the afternoon, BlueGold had sold off another $2 billion of its overall bet on a crude-price rise. But it still had $3.5 billion invested in the market, the bulk of which was tied to upward price moves in Brent and West Texas contracts. The traders pared their Brent contract holdings a little more, leaving the fund with about $3 billion remaining. BlueGold would bank on the good health of the West Texas crude market in Oklahoma for a little while longer.

■

Andurand and Slyusarenko had plans that weekend to go to Paris for a wedding-dress fitting, one of four visits that would be needed before the dress was finished. Despite all that had happened at BlueGold that week, Andurand opted to go.

Like Patel, he avoided talking much to his fiancée about what went on at work. Slyusarenko could see from his face that he was feeling anxious, and she told him she was sorry he was stressed. But there was no real discussion of the terrifying events that had occurred.

Andurand couldn't get the markets off his mind. He left London Friday night on the Eurostar, after the most bruising thirty-six hours of his career, only to wake up in another city to look at a piece of clothing worth many thousands of dollars. He found his thoughts going to strange places. Maybe the markets were being manipulated, he thought. Maybe the Federal Reserve had plans to spend gobs of money—tens of billions a day—to float the American economy, only to sabotage the price of oil. There was no evidence of that, but it could be true, he thought, and the U.S. just hadn't yet announced it. He was certainly losing his predictive touch.

■

Things did not improve that year. For the month of May 2011 alone, BlueGold marked losses of 23 percent, and in the seven months that followed, the fund avoided losses only once, leaving its annual performance deeply in the red. Politics in Europe, where the prime ministers of Greece and Italy had resigned amid fiscal crisis, and potential crisis in the Middle East, where Iran and Israel appeared primed for war, were muddying the picture. In the U.S. the markets had been rattled by the failure of MF Global, the commodity broker run by Jon Corzine, a onetime head of Goldman Sachs.

To curb BlueGold's exposure to additional losses, Andurand had set more conservative risk parameters that lowered the amount of money he could lose in a single day before he had to begin cutting positions entirely. He also reduced BlueGold's leverage and sold off peripheral positions.

Andurand and Slyusarenko were married that August in St. Petersburg before a hundred friends and family members. The bride, then four months from giving birth to their daughter, looked impossibly svelte in a fitted white lace column, which she'd purchased off the rack in London after abandoning the tailor-made Parisian version. She carried a simple sprig of white flowers and wore her long, brown hair in waves beneath a lace-edged tulle veil. Andurand, looking fit with his hair buzzed, wore a tuxedo and black tie.

Guests sipping cocktails after the ceremony were serenaded by the British singer Craig David, known for his soft brand of hip-hop; between courses at the formal dinner that followed, the Bolshoi ballet performed with a full orchestra in accompaniment. The capper was a live concert by Elton John, who was said to charge $1 million for private performances (that was the reported cost for the conservative talk-radio personality Rush Limbaugh, for whose wedding John had played the year before).

"It was over the top," remembers Andurand's mother, Danielle. For friends who couldn't make it to St. Petersburg in person, the groom hired a videographer to chronicle the event and showed the film at a London movie theater when he returned from a safari and whale-watching on his honeymoon in South Africa.

For Andurand, the wedding was a welcome distraction as his business was coming unhinged. "We continue to focus on the fundamentals of our markets in the context of the broad macro picture," Andurand and Crema wrote in their November 2011 investor letter, "and are patiently waiting for a clearer opportunity to express our view." By year's end, BlueGold was down 35 percent and its assets had diminished to $1 billion. Its directional bets on a crude-price hike were not working, and tension was brewing between the two partners.

Andurand and Crema had always maintained a professional atmosphere, but the two were never close friends. Crema was older, with grown children; Andurand was newly married and facing first-time parenthood. Andurand had always been a brash risk-taker, willing to make aggressive bets on broad oil-market moves, whereas Crema excelled more in the sort of comparative trading of two or more products with price discrepancies in their markets that Ruggles and Jennifer Fan preferred. Andurand understood the nuances of crude, and Crema understood refined products. Crema had more experience as a manager, and was closer to retirement. He appeared to some to be looking for a comfortable way to exit the business.

That winter, knowing their results would be terrible, the partners agreed to split. Initially, Crema appeared willing to be bought out of BlueGold, with Andurand taking over on the first day of 2012. But they couldn't agree on a price. Crema wanted a big payout if he was to leave, but refused to pay Andurand anything to leave himself.

While the partner drama unfolded in private, the rest of Blue-Gold's team carried on as usual. Andurand and Crema had paid Christmas bonuses out of their own pockets, and, despite the fund's negative returns, employees seemed calm. Paul Feldman, BlueGold's CFO, had taken time off for a two-week vacation in Australia on that holiday; when he returned early in the new year, he was surprised to hear that Andurand and Crema were at odds. "You would never think anything was wrong," Feldman remembers. "No one in the organization had any inkling."

As the partners hashed it out, Andurand tried to restructure BlueGold's portfolio. He reduced risk yet again and searched for investments in some of the more regional markets in Europe. It was a halfhearted effort. Some days he felt depressed and couldn't drag himself to work until midafternoon. He reasoned that he was working when he was at home, and that he deserved some time with his baby daughter, born in London shortly before Christmas. Unfortunately, though, his confidence was blown.

Unable to agree on terms, Andurand and Crema finally stopped negotiating—just in time for the usual first-quarter visits from investors who wanted to hear their plans for the year. These were the loyal clients who had stayed with BlueGold despite the downturn, and they deserved honest information. But with their own decisions unmade, the partners felt they had little choice but to field questions about the fund's future without divulging that it might not have one.

Three months into 2012, they decided to simply close. Neither Andurand nor Crema was willing to walk away for the money being offered, so it seemed easiest to just liquidate BlueGold, turning its existing positions into cash and returning what they generated to investors. They announced their plans on April 5, with their portfolio down 3 percent for the year. Andurand then took off for the Caribbean to vacation with his new wife and daughter, having not yet spoken to all of BlueGold's clients personally.

Investors were furious. Those who had come through in March and heard nothing of the problems felt especially duped. One later griped that conversations with Andurand had always been too light on crude markets and heavy on irrelevant topics like kickboxing.

"I fielded a few of those calls," says Feldman. "We kind of just kept to the line that we couldn't announce anything until there was something to announce. It did create a bad feeling."

■

The unwinding of the firm was almost as painful as the decision to do so. Andurand continued coming to work to oversee the sales of BlueGold's positions and field the occasional phone call. But things were very slow. Where it had previously bustled with activity, the Sloane Square space by May was essentially a collection of half-packed boxes and a sprinkling of staff without much to do.

The business was now almost penniless too. After nearly all the trading positions were sold for cash and the investors' money returned, the founding partners wound up with just $2 million that they shared according to their ownership stakes: 53 percent for Andurand, and 42 percent for Crema (the other 5 percent went to some minority partners who had since left the company). But because of a handful of equity positions that couldn't yet be sold off, a shell of the company remained intact.

To have a place to continue working, Andurand rented a temporary office five minutes from his house in Knightsbridge. He also secured a new trading space at 100 Brompton Road—the same address where BlueGold had been in its infancy—and began renovating the third floor. He wanted to open up a new hedge fund on his own. Maybe he'd even hire a feng shui expert, he mused, to advise him on the décor in hopes of bringing better luck. A fish tank was supposed to help, he'd heard. (Glencore's office building in Mayfair had two.) He planned to bring his chief financial officer, risk manager, and investor-relations head along with him.

As he mulled his next steps, Andurand kept busy with side projects. He had a mixed track record outside of trading. He'd lost $3 million on a friend's movie project about a ballroom love story. The $13 million investment he'd made in a yet-to-be-developed French ski resort had languished. And he spent $20 million building a high-end resort in Koh Samui, an island in the Gulf of Thailand. In the meantime, he was focused on a touring kickboxing league he had recently put $20 million into, convinced that the underappreciated sport was poised for massive future returns. "Worst case," he said, "I lose 60 percent. Best case I make 100 times my investment."

That July, the Andurand family decamped to Sarrians, a small town in the south of France, for a month's holiday. Provence was in full bloom. Lavender and sunflowers dotted the fields, fresh tomatoes and zucchini filled the local markets, and the chirps of *les cigales,* or cicadas, were everywhere.

It was Andurand's first extended hiatus in five years, and he planned to spend it in high style. His rented villa, a fifteen-bedroom monstrosity a mile or two outside of town, had been booked months in advance for £150,000—not including the £50,000 broker's fee. It came with a full household staff, a tennis and volleyball court, gardens, and a 25-meter pool—the same length Andurand had struggled with as a college swimmer in Toulouse. A long gravel driveway led to the square cul-de-sac that fronted the house, behind which was a comfortable sitting room and spacious kitchen. A staff prepared meals and kept things tidy.

Thinking he might drive his luxury car around the relatively serene roads of Provence, where accidents and vandalism were less likely than in London, Andurand had shipped his Bugatti to the outdoor garage at Sarrians, which had space for numerous vehicles. Once there, however, he worried about the impact of the gravelly local roads on his low-slung car, and opted to drive his Porsche Cayenne instead.

Only a week into the trip, Andurand was restless. His kickboxing consultants were calling and e-mailing constantly with issues. He and Slyusarenko were unhappy with the cook at the house, who prepared dishes like salads and lamb chops without flair. They were also miffed at the château's owner, an elderly man who was staying nearby while Andurand and family used his larger house and who visited almost daily—as did the owner's large, lame dog, a chocolate lab that liked to sun itself by the burbling outdoor pool. The office area wasn't properly equipped, and Andurand lacked adapters to power his British-made gadgets in France. Even the inexpensive outdoor furniture bothered him.

Andurand couldn't help but miss trading. Since shuttering BlueGold, the crude market had entered free fall, with Brent contracts trading as low as $88 after having been priced at $125 as recently as March. It was the most pronounced swoon in prices in several years, and one that Andurand swore he had seen coming.

"Just after I closed, oil went down 30 percent, and I'd been short for months at BlueGold," he said while reclining by the pool one evening. "Where demand is flat and supply is going up 1.5 to 2 million barrels per day, and Iran is threatening to blow up the world, you need to cut production. You should only get excited," meaning, poised for a rise in crude prices, he added, "if you're going to have a long, ongoing war."

■

He spent the next few months preparing to launch his new hedge fund. Depending how well the fund-raising went, he was willing to put up to $100 million of his own money into the business, but he hoped some of his old investors would support the new venture. To help attract them, he had offered to forgo his own cut of the new fund's profits until they made back any money they'd lost at BlueGold—a move known in the hedge-fund business as transferring the high-water mark. It was a tough standard to meet, but money managers at Citadel, the large Chicago fund group, had recently done it, and Andurand figured he could too.

Over lunch at Ladurée, the tearoom at Harrods, in late September 2012, he appeared tanned and rested from a recent vacation along the Italian coast. He had already secured a single $100 million account for his new company, Andurand Capital, he explained, and planned to start trading that cash within a couple of days.

The oil market had had a volatile week, with a sharp move downward that took traders by surprise. Andurand, however, had not been following the news of late and had no theories yet on what had happened. He said he'd probably read the latest crude research over the weekend in preparation for Monday.

"I need to start making some money again," he said with his most modest smile. A few months later, he was back in front of a terminal on Brompton Road.

Pierre Andurand, the French commodity-trading wunderkind who successfully predicted both the top and the bottom of the crude-oil market in 2008, only to lose his nerve after a big setback in 2011.

Glencore founder Marc Rich, whose vision for more efficient crude-oil trading reshaped the entire commodity market in the 1970s and 1980s, during which time he was indicted for racketeering, tax evasion, and trading with the enemy.

Alex Beard, the mercurial head of Glencore's oil division who helped navigate the firm through the financial crisis of 2008 and 2009. He was rewarded during the company's 2011 IPO, which valued his personal stake at £1.7 billion.

Glencore CEO Ivan Glasenberg, whose interest in commodity trading was piqued after he overheard two men doing an international candle-wax transaction, on the day his company's shares were listed in Hong Kong. Glencore's IPO valued it at an impressive $59 billion.

Jennifer Fan, the math prodigy who was hired as an index trader on Morgan Stanley's commodity desk at age twenty. Her bet on gasoline prices generated $3 million after Hurricane Katrina clobbered the Gulf of Mexico.

John Mack, who as chairman and CEO of Morgan Stanley worried about aggression and greed on his bank's commodities team—characteristics that eventually led to trouble. At some point, I've got to crush these people, he had thought.

Gary Gensler, who says he was "blessed" to be the CFTC's chairman for five years, addressing a throng of reporters after a Washington, D.C., speech in 2010. Gensler was one of the staunchest advocates for regulatory reform after the commodities bubble burst.

Bart Chilton, the plainspoken CFTC commissioner who argued passionately for limits on speculative commodity trades, looked wary as his colleague Scott O'Malia, who disagreed with his views, spoke at a 2013 agency meeting.

Delta Air Lines CEO Richard Anderson (left) helped pull the troubled carrier out of bankruptcy and then got the top job. He and Delta president Ed Bastian (right) pushed for smarter commodity hedging, which led to the hiring of trader Jon Ruggles to help manage their $9 billion in fuel costs.

Once a silver trader on the Comex, Gary Cohn used his market savvy to arrange an aluminum position that earned hundreds of millions—and helped make him a partner at Goldman Sachs. As president and chief operating officer, he kept commodities a focus.

Jon Corzine, the onetime governor and senator who helped negotiate major deals at Goldman Sachs—including its 1999 IPO—was sued by the CFTC for failing to supervise employees at the futures broker MF Global, where $1.2 billion in customer money went missing.

A former white-collar defense litigator, David Meister raised the CFTC's enforcement unit out of obscurity, bringing a rash of manipulation cases against industry players that resulted in a series of nine-figure fines. His investigative targets included JPMorgan, UBS, MF Global, Jon Corzine, and Jon Ruggles.

Bloomberg/Getty Images

Xstrata CEO Mick Davis (center) walking out of the November 2012 shareholder meeting in Zug, Switzerland, at which his company's $70 billion takeover by Glencore was finally approved. Brett Olsher, the Goldman banker who tried to bring order to a raucous merger process, is on the left, and Bill Vereker, the Nomura banking chief who advised Xstrata's independent shareholders, is on the right.

Goldman Sachs

Jeff Currie, Goldman's chief commodities analyst, realized at a fall 2012 meeting of London hedge-fund managers that the popularity of his asset class had finally fizzled.

8

GOLDMAN SACHS

During the summer of 2011, officials at the London Metal Exchange got an unexpected complaint from The Coca-Cola Company. The amount of physical aluminum in storage was piling up, said a representative of the soda maker, and, along with it, so was the expense of buying the metal for beverage containers.

The culprit, as Coke saw it, wasn't simple supply and demand—in fact, there was plenty of aluminum sitting in warehouses. It was the shrewd tactics of Goldman Sachs, the bank that owned a network of metal-storage facilities in the Detroit vicinity, where waiting times for extracting aluminum were longer than ever. Every day those metal bars sat idle, Goldman's warehouse company effectively drove up the premium amount that aluminum producers could charge for delivering supplies to beverage-packaging factories, a cost that amplified the expense of the actual metal and, thus, the prices Coke and others paid for soda cans.

"The situation has been organized artificially to drive premiums up," said Dave Smith, Coke's head of strategic procurement, at an industry conference that June. "It takes two weeks to put aluminum in, and six months to get it out."

Smith, a midlevel executive, was speaking somewhat out of turn. Despite its complaints with the warehousing system—which industry participants considered to be a market of last resort when aluminum supplies were tight—Coke had tried to keep its concerns about Goldman behind the scenes. More than a year earlier, eight players had complained privately to the London Metal Exchange, or LME, the obscure London metals bourse that set the benchmark price for aluminum, zinc, copper, and other important nonprecious, or base, metals that were key in manufacturing. The U.S. warehousing system that the exchange oversaw was so inefficient that it was hurting corporate profits, they had argued.

The Midwest premium, the regional U.S. rate for getting metal from a seller to a buyer, was a cost imposed on Coke and other manufacturers in addition to the cash, or spot price of aluminum, which was by then bouncing back from its lowest levels in some time. Aluminum prices had increased 13 percent since the beginning of 2010, when Goldman had paid half a billion dollars to acquire Metro International Trade Services, the metal storage business based in Romulus, Michigan. Bought relatively cheap at a time when commodity prices were low, Goldman took on Metro as a way to broaden its suite of physical commodity holdings, which had become an important complement to its derivatives trading in London and the U.S. Around the same time, it had also bought coal-mining assets in Colombia.

In addition to the revenue those investments offered it, they presented Goldman with the possibility of a free look at what was happening on the physical side of commodities through ground-level operations. Tweaking existing contract trades in a commodity based on feedback from colleagues who worked in the physical markets was by then commonplace in banking. "We had pipeline capacity all over the place and we would call up and say, 'How's gas flowing this morning?'" remembers a trading manager who worked for years at one of Goldman's competitors. If flows were weak, he added, "We'd go, 'Oh, we're not going to get the pop we thought, so let's reposition.'" Still, Goldman spokespeople consistently denied that employees familiar with Metro's business operations shared information about it with internal traders.

Goldman wasn't the only one dipping into the physical commodity world, a cornerstone of companies like Glencore, which called it the "industrial" business. JPMorgan, never much more than a rounding error in Wall Street's commodity business before, spent $1.6 billion that year for a significant portion of the European company RBS Sempra Commodities. The deal brought JPMorgan a firm called Henry Bath & Son, a two-century-old metal warehousing company that was the late 1800s' answer to Glencore, a copper shipper, seller, and storer with immense market power and global reach. The same year as the Metro and Henry Bath acquisitions, Glencore itself bought the metal-warehousing division of Pacorini Group, the Italian commodity trader, whose storage locations spanned the globe from the Netherlands to Hong Kong. In fact, nearly all the world's private warehouses were being snapped up at the time by large multinational commodity companies. Broadly speaking, the bet was that metal traders would stock up on physical product while prices were relatively low and hold their stocks until the market improved, generating steady rental incomes for the warehouse owners in the process.

The new metal-warehouse owners quickly proved right—and had huge stacks of metal bars to prove it. The nine hundred thousand tons of aluminum Metro stored in its Detroit facilities when

Goldman bought it in 2010 were growing daily. Meanwhile, incentive fees Metro paid to hedge funds, physical commodity traders and other tenants—usually one or two hundred dollars per ton each year—encouraged them to leave the metal there for longer periods. The longer the waits for aluminum, the more Alcoa and other producers of the metal, such as the Russian company Rusal, could charge Coke and other aluminum users; they knew the bottler couldn't afford to wait months or a year for warehouse metal, so it was forced to pay up for open-market transactions instead.

In 2011 Coke was joined publicly in their complaint by Novelis, a company that provides rolled aluminum to the manufacturers that make beer cans, aluminum foil, cars, and consumer electronics. By then, LME officials had already been studying the economics of storage. Their survey found that queues were indeed growing, and that commodity buyers were unhappy. With waits for aluminum from Detroit stretching as long as seven months, the LME that July mandated a new minimum "load-out" rate, or the pace at which the metal was required to leave storage facilities, of three thousand tons—double what it had been before.

For the aluminum buyers, it was a pyrrhic victory. While the new requirement was double what it had been before, stockpiles in Detroit were nevertheless on their way to 1.5 million tons and a sixteen-month queue for removal.

■

For Goldman Sachs's president, Gary Cohn, the aluminum warehousing trade was a bit of déjà vu. Two decades before, in the early 1990s, he had moved to London to help expand Goldman's commodities business, a onetime New Orleans coffee trader that was known as J. Aron & Company. While in London, Cohn stumbled upon a lucrative aluminum trade that involved storing huge amounts of the metal until prices in the market allowed him to sell at a profit.

Cohn had already discovered some blind spots in J. Aron's existing business. Having started his career as an independent silver trader on the raucous floor of New York's Commodity Exchange, or Comex, a place made famous by the Eddie Murphy movie *Trading Places* in 1983, Cohn had some experience with trading floors. J. Aron, which Cohn had joined in 1990, had a long history with contracts on precious metals, commodities it had traded for years. But in contracts with which it had little prior experience, such as cattle and hogs, Cohn and his colleagues—who had just launched the Goldman Sachs Commodity Index in 1991 to track eighteen different raw materials—were wading through new and uncertain territory. (Ownership of the Goldman Sachs Commodity Index transferred to Standard & Poor's in 2007; the index is now known as the S&P GSCI.)

Shortly after the GSCI began trading, Cohn arranged to purchase cattle in Colorado to test out the physical commodity underlying one of the contracts the index was now buying on a regular basis. As part of their experiment, Cohn and his boss flew in a small plane over their cattle's ranch to inspect the goods—only to find the animals starving to death as they stood stranded in several feet of snow. Eyeing the scene, Cohn's boss told him to sell the physical cattle positions the minute he got back to New York. Cohn agreed it was a bad trade, and the suffering of the animals left a minimal impression.

Metals were also somewhat virgin territory. The LME was the home market for two of the GSCI's components, aluminum and zinc, and Goldman was giving big-volume orders to its brokers there monthly, as customer contracts on these commodities were rolled forward and replaced by new ones. But after examining the prices that Goldman was getting on its LME roll trades month after month, Cohn—who had little contact with the London floor traders except over the phone from New York—worried that he was getting fleeced.

J. Aron was "the low-hanging fruit," he recalls. LME traders were "just waiting for me to come in and roll my contracts. These guys [were] buying yachts off me."

Cohn, who was planning an early 1992 move to London, threw himself into the LME's world, where base-metal prices were established through five-minute buy-and-sell sessions in a red-seated inner circle on the trading floor known as the Ring. It was a more stately version of his beloved Comex pits, with traders using elaborate hand signals and multiple phones and speaking in British, rather than Brooklyn, accents.

As Cohn studied the LME's base-metals markets, he noticed something strange going on with aluminum, which was one of its most active futures markets: it was in deep contango, a situation in which the future price of aluminum was far higher than its cash price. This meant that GSCI investors were constantly paying extra money simply to stay in the same futures trade as they replaced their existing near-term contracts with new ones each month.

Commodity traders in the futures markets were using contracts, as opposed to actual, physical stocks of copper, aluminum, or oil, to express their view of the future price of raw materials. In other words, they were buying or selling bets on what they thought would be the price of aluminum down the road rather than actual, physical metal slabs. But every futures contract had an expiration date, and as that date neared, the holder had a choice:

either take physical delivery of the aluminum, or roll the contract forward and replace it with a similar futures contract dated farther out.

When markets were in backwardation, meaning the commodity contract connected to prices in the near future was cheaper than the present, or spot, price, the only cost to the roll was the fee the investor paid Goldman for changing the contract over from one month to the next. But when the market was in contango, the investor was paying not only the brokerage fee, but also the difference in price from, say, January futures to February futures—a figure that, in a deep contango scenario, was growing ever higher.

The aluminum markets were at a crossroads then. Oversupply around the world had depressed prices. The Soviet Union had just collapsed, and Russians were eager to amass hard currency in exchange for commodities (a dilemma that traders like Marc Rich & Co. helped them solve by buying aluminum on the cheap and reselling it to users who didn't particularly need it). An international squabble was developing over how to handle the problem, and the price of aluminum was spiraling.

Cohn realized it would be cheaper to take delivery of the aluminum than roll a futures contract forward. But doing so would mean breaking a long-held tradition of leaving the logistics of transporting bars of metal and barrels of oil to the professionals who actually used them. Sourcing and shipping a commodity like crude oil was elaborate enough that many futures traders would never bother with it. And storing metal until somebody else wanted to turn it into cans or cars was also a highly nuanced endeavor with its own rulebook.

He dove into the world of metal storage and financing, visiting warehouses and researching metal insurance. "I spent a month sort of due-diligencing a trade that took me thirty seconds to figure out," he says.

Convinced of the potential profits, he took the idea to one of J. Aron's senior managers, Lloyd Blankfein. Blankfein, a former gold salesman, was dubious.

Cohn was insistent. He had thought through every issue, he told Blankfein, and this was a "riskless" opportunity. Cohn would hedge every potential problem he could find—interest rate movements, currency movements, anything that could hurt the trade's performance—and would definitely make money. Blankfein told him to run an experiment using no more than $300 million, a substantial portion of the firm's $4 billion in capital during that period.

The following Monday, Cohn bought $100 million worth of physical aluminum—about a hundred thousand tons. Even with all the homework he had done, and despite his boasts to Blankfein, he honestly expected the potential profits to vanish as a result of a sudden physical price drop, a surprise hike in storage fees, or some other unforeseen complication. But the following day, nothing had changed much, so he bought another $100 million of metal. The next day, he bought another $50 million. By Friday, when the spread, or difference, between what he would have spent to roll the contract forward and what he was actually spending to store the metal was still intact, he knew he was on to something.

A few months later, Cohn relocated to the UK. There he secured Goldman a membership on the LME, and eventually, a seat on the board. He continued taking physical delivery of aluminum, stockpiling it in storage facilities in the Dutch city of Rotterdam. He also began calling the firm's aluminum-producer clients, seeing if they wanted to sell down their physical inventories; many were happy to oblige. Goldman Sachs was relieving them of excess metal and helping them to free up cash without tipping off the rest of the market. Meanwhile, its physical aluminum holdings offset the futures it sold in the markets, giving Goldman what amounted to a neutral position.

For more than two years, Goldman built enormous caches of aluminum. Its hoard helped prompt the biggest aluminum price rally the market had seen since 1988. During the years when Cohn was purchasing the commodity, physical market prices nearly doubled—amplifying the value of J. Aron's stockpiles and creating over half a billion dollars in profit to Goldman over several years.

To be fair, a number of factors worked in Cohn's favor, including aluminum production cuts that finally occurred after an industry agreement in early 1994. But to some, Cohn's trade and the resultant impact looked like a corner, that is, an amassing of a physical supply of a commodity intended to jack up its prices. In this case, the stockpile was technically legal. But it still may have helped prompt a price run-up that ultimately benefited the party who was a contributor to the price movement in the first place.

Cohn says he understands why the term "corner" might be used. But throughout the period where Goldman was building up its aluminum store, "we were more than happy to sell it," he says. "We were making cash aluminum available every day." It was an argument he would air again twenty years later under different circumstances.

Late in 1994, a few months after his thirty-fourth birthday, Cohn made partner at Goldman Sachs, joining the ruling 2 percent echelon of a 9,600-employee firm. Around the same time, he also received a strange complaint: the metal masses in Rotterdam had grown so extensive that their reflection of the sun was creating confusion for local air-traffic controllers. Airport officials asked Goldman if it could throw a tarp over its aluminum stash to make navigating the local skies a little easier.

Cohn was promoted further at Goldman, eventually becoming chief operating officer and president of the firm. Along the way, he helped secure Goldman's spot as a top commodities franchise on Wall Street, second only to Morgan Stanley in breadth and prominence (in industry rankings, they do-si-doed). He promoted the GSCI, encouraged smart house trading, and reviewed Goldman's forays into physical commodities, from wind energy to iron ore.

But at a time when the banking community was already smarting from the financial crisis of 2008, commodities created additional headline risk. Goldman bore the brunt.

■

At the time Goldman bought Metro International Trade Services in 2010, Metro was a low-profile company focused on delivering, stacking, storing, and eventually shipping out hundreds of thousands of tons of base metals every day. The company had been around since 1990, when a couple of entrepreneurs bought a single warehouse in Long Beach, just south of Los Angeles. Business was lean, with small tonnages shipping down from metal producers in the Pacific Northwest, and the owners eventually turned to the Midwest, which had a healthier flow of customers. It was the period before Cohn's lucrative aluminum trade for Goldman, and Russian smelters were still very active.

Toledo, Ohio, had long been the Midwest's metal-storage hub, but Metro's owners established a beachhead in Detroit, which had the advantage of rail and water access. Metal ingots were extremely heavy, requiring numerous train cars or barges to deliver them from producers like Alcoa directly to Metro's warehouses. By the late 2000s, a single day's haul required seventy-five trucks. Detroit soon became a destination for aluminum, as well as lead and zinc in smaller amounts. The Los Angeles area warehouse became a copper facility, and warehouses in New Orleans sprung up to house copper and zinc, much of which was shipped in from South America.

In 2008, when the financial crisis hit Detroit's automakers, Metro spotted a chance for further expansion—into abandoned commercial facilities whose builders had gone belly-up. Toward the end of 2009, Metro bought a huge building in Chesterfield, Michigan, a half-hour's drive north of Detroit, that had once been a Visteon Corporation plant, before the auto-parts maker filed for bankruptcy (though Visteon later emerged from Chapter 11 in 2010). It would become the largest warehouse in the entire LME system, with 714,000 square feet, mostly of storage space.

By 2010, Metro was storing one to two million tons of aluminum, zinc, and lead in its Detroit corridor, and had leases with about two dozen clients. But, thanks to the restrictive LME rules and the market's growing penchant for storing metal stocks, Metro's rental fees—about 40 cents per metric ton per day—were generating more than $100 million in revenue each year.

When The Coca-Cola Company, a longtime investment-banking client that had recently hired Goldman to advise it on a $12 billion acquisition, initially complained about the escalating storage costs of aluminum and slow delivery times, the firm tried to assuage its concerns. The trouble was the LME system, Goldman argued, which was inefficient and needed updating. Goldman itself was simply following the rules.

Truthfully, shipping out even three thousand tons of aluminum per day was a huge undertaking. One day in September 2012, a few months after the LME had doubled the minimum load-out rate, the eighteen Metro workers in the Chesterfield plant were very busy. Train boxcars sat with their doors open on the tracks that ran inside the building as workers loaded slabs of metal into them. Because the aluminum was so heavy, the stacks in each car were surprisingly low, filling up only a fraction of the space. Beeping forklifts breezed by as drivers picked up the bars specified by individual warrants, or certificates of ownership, for metal holders who wanted their wares transferred.

Rental fees had risen by that point to about 45 cents per ton per day, generating some $200 million per year in revenue on Detroit aluminum stores alone. Nonetheless, the premiums at work in the Midwest market made the ownership lucrative, explained a Metro executive, especially when aluminum markets were in contango.

"The ownership of metal is a control game," he said, adding that the markets were easy to squeeze because there were so few units in circulation. Metro's typical customer was a hedge fund, the executive said, that bought physical aluminum from a producer like Alcoa, shorted it through the futures markets as it was being shipped to the warehouse, and then took ownership of the warrants on the aluminum once they arrived in Detroit. (It was much the same principle that worked for Glencore's oil marketers, who sourced crude oil from producers in far-flung locations and then shorted crude through the futures market as they waited for the physical shipments to arrive, albeit with more complicated storage and financing fees tacked on at the end.) Then the aluminum-owning hedge fund could sell its warrant to another party, who might wait for aluminum spot prices to rise, locking in a profit.

The LME's increased load-out rate had done little to assuage Coke and other aluminum users. Premiums had gone from about 6.5 cents in 2010 to 11 cents by then, and would rise to a record of nearly 12 cents by the summer of 2013.

While Metro was thriving, Goldman's commodity traders were grappling with a major setback. In 2010 a powerful Dodd-Frank provision known as the Volcker Rule, after former Federal Reserve chairman Paul Volcker, had essentially promised to make the sort of house trading that had launched the careers of Jennifer Fan and Pierre Andurand illegal, forcing the firm to divest itself of some of its most successful trading desks. Although only five or six people had traded commodities strictly for the house at any given time, they had historically contributed as much as 20 percent of the Goldman commodities unit's revenue—a substantial amount to forgo.

The commodity traders who remained were now focused almost exclusively on the client flow business: the volume-driven endeavor of designing and handling hedging or index trades on behalf of others. Most physical commodity acquisitions were now difficult or even verboten as a result of laws governing bank holding companies to which Goldman was now subject. Metro and the Colombian coal assets had passed muster, but new investment ideas, including an iron-ore purchase commodity traders were keen on, kept getting turned down by Goldman management. Traders and some commodities bankers in London, eager to pursue more entrepreneurial opportunities, felt handcuffed.

Isabelle Ealet, who had befriended Gary Cohn in the early 1990s and given young Andurand his break in commodities in 2000, was by then cohead of the firm's entire securities division, the only woman to have ever won the title. By 2012, aware of the angst over failed physical-commodity purchases, she allowed two of her employees to explore selling Goldman's physical assets—Metro, its network of coal mines, and a few smaller investments. Morgan Stanley was already in talks to sell its commodity division to a sovereign-wealth fund; perhaps there was another market opening at the time.

When word got back to Cohn, he called Ealet on it. "You're wasting your time," he told her. Despite the limitations, commodities was an important focus for Goldman, he added. The business wasn't going anywhere.

■

September 2013 was the five-year anniversary of the financial crisis, and the major commodity players on Wall Street were still enjoying a unique set of regulatory advantages. Under U.S. laws, Goldman Sachs and Morgan Stanley were allowed to hold assets like refineries and mines that their competitors couldn't. Goldman's lawyers believed the firm could hold on to Metro and the coal mines at least until 2020. But their opponents, noting that their emergency transformation into bank holding companies in September 2008 had grandfathered some of their commodities businesses—a situation that JPMorgan, Citigroup, and others did not share—believed they should be selling the assets sooner.

That July, Goldman was the subject of a tough story on the front page of the Sunday *New York Times*. Citing multiple sources within Metro as well as a person "with direct knowledge of the company's business plan," the piece quoted forklift drivers describing days spent shuffling aluminum ingots from one Detroit-area warehouse to another, despite cries in the broader market that the metal queues were overlong. The implication was clear:

Goldman was moving aluminum within its own system as an end-run around the LME's load-out requirements in an effort to juice profits from storage fees.

Days later, during a Senate Banking Committee hearing, aluminum users testified to the problems of long waits for metal and concurrently rising premiums on aluminum. "Aluminum is our single biggest price risk," said Tim Weiner, global commodities risk manager for the beer company MillerCoors, because bank holding companies "have created a bottleneck which limits the supply." He cited as the culprits Goldman's outsized presence in the Detroit aluminum market and the lack of regulatory oversight at the LME. MillerCoors's rivals, Weiner added, shared its concerns. A number of senators expressed their outrage over the conditions that Weiner and the *New York Times* had described and, within weeks, Goldman received subpoenas from the CFTC.

Amid the backlash, Goldman higher-ups held a conference call to discuss their counterattack. But even within the firm's top ranks, there were misunderstandings about the complex warehousing business. One fundamental question they were discussing was: if aluminum prices had fallen 40 percent in recent years, how could buyers be complaining about climbing prices? (The answer was that it was the premium charged for aluminum delivery, not the actual price of aluminum, that buyers were complaining about. And anyway, as industry blogs later pointed out, aluminum prices had only fallen 28 percent during the years they were referencing.)

John Rogers, who oversaw Goldman's press and government affairs, suggested the company put Cohn forward as a public spokesman. "We've got the guy that's basically done more in storage than anybody else," said Rogers. "Why isn't he involved?"

Over the next week or so, Cohn and others called aluminum users to discuss their problems with the waits for metal. Goldman knew full well that most of those buyers didn't participate directly in the Metro warehousing system, which was largely the domain of hedge funds and miners like the privately held Swiss company Xstrata. But if it was aluminum they needed, Goldman told them, it would happily source aluminum on the spot market and provide it—at competitive market prices—in exchange for the user's pre-existing spot in the Metro queue. It was the same principle Cohn had articulated in defending his long aluminum trade from the early 1990s against accusations that he had created a corner.

When nobody took Goldman up on its offer, the whole outcry looked like a bluff. Armed with a list of ideas for improving the LME system, Cohn hurriedly booked a television interview and went on CNBC to discuss the matter. "We feel horrible for consumers if they can't get the metal," he explained. "We don't believe that to be the fact." Despite the firm's offer to provide immediate aluminum to users who needed it, "not a single person" had taken Goldman up on the idea, Cohn noted.

The following month, Goldman and the LME were sued for violating U.S. antitrust laws in the Detroit warehouses. A parallel Justice Department inquiry was soon under way.

9

THE DEAL

Goldman Sachs, as it turned out, was much more than just a commodity trader. It also advised some of its competitors in the business about raising cash through the bond and stock markets and undertaking mergers and acquisitions as part of its investment-banking business.

Glencore was not an advisory client. Nonetheless, in September 2011, a Goldman banker named Brett Olsher found himself playing armchair psychiatrist to an unhappy Ivan Glasenberg at a sushi restaurant in London.

Glencore had just undertaken its IPO in May, and now a mining CEO whose company Glasenberg wanted to buy was reluctant to talk seriously about a merger. "We've taken the company public," Glasenberg told Olsher in his somewhat nasal South African English. "We've done everything he wanted." Yet Glasenberg admitted he wasn't confident that he could convince Mick Davis, the head of Xstrata, to negotiate in earnest.

Olsher listened intently. The tall, nattily dressed financier had spent the last fifteen years in London advising mining companies.

Two and a half years before, he had worked on a controversial cash-raising deal for Davis in the thick of the 2008 financial crisis.

Arguably, it was awkward for Olsher to be holding a merger conversation, however preliminary, with his client's expected buyer. But Olsher, who was once dubbed the "man of steel" by a London newspaper for his knowledge of the metals business, prided himself on maintaining a good rapport with executives like Glasenberg, even if he often sat on the opposite side of the bargaining table.

"It's going to get done," Olsher said reassuringly. Davis, he added, was ready to talk to Glasenberg about a combination at some point. "I think it needs a year, though," Olsher added. After all, the Glencore IPO, which had established a public currency, or valuation, for the company for the very first time, was still very recent.

"I don't believe you," Glasenberg said.

It was a rare impasse for the indefatigable CEO. To Glasenberg, every day was groundhog day, as one associate put it: a new opportunity to make a trade. Known for his rigorous exercise regimen and round-the-clock travel, Glasenberg was routine-bound, tactical, and usually got his way.

But the year—in fact, the decade—had not played out quite the way he'd expected. There had been multiple failed attempts to woo Mick Davis, starting as early as 2001 and happening again as recently as Glencore's IPO preparations. In between, there had been the near-death experience of the 2008 financial crisis and the decision to go public in hopes of bringing greater stability to the company.

Those things had worked out well enough. But the fifty-four-year-old Glasenberg was weary of the constant reinvention that running a commodity trader required. Every January, he complained to associates, he had put on his figurative accountant's visor and started from scratch, trying to figure out how Glencore would make profitable transactions in the new year. He believed that until the company owned more industrial assets, like mines and processing centers, that created more consistent revenue, the firm would again and again face that cumbersome perennial challenge.

Some insiders had an additional theory: that Glasenberg wanted to see Glencore rank among the top-tier commodity and metal players, alongside $100 billion companies like BHP Billiton and Rio Tinto. (Glasenberg scoffed at the idea, preferring to play the greed card rather than admit to corporate vanity; as a huge shareholder himself, he'd say, the only thing he cared about was having fat returns.) Glencore had plenty of marketing expertise and a small but respectable beachhead in the physical mining, storage, handling, and drilling of raw materials. Until it increased its global presence with a transformational deal like an Xstrata merger, however, the top tier would be out of reach.

■

Glencore had gone public on May 19, 2011, just weeks after Andurand lost hundreds of millions in the Brent crude market drop. The market's initial reaction to Marc Rich's former company was modest, with the stock trading up only a few points in the first few days amid light trading. Still, the stock's debut had at least one of its shareholders' desired effects: making billionaires of Glasenberg, Alex Beard, and several others, and valuing the company itself at an impressive $59 billion.

The IPO also unlocked almost four decades of secrecy. Glencore's sixteen-hundred-page prospectus revealed a heft in certain commodities larger than some market participants had ever guessed. By its own estimates (exact figures on the market share of other players to compare to were impossible to come by), it was one of the world's largest players in crude oil and refined products, the very largest in the business of seaborne steam coal, and one of the biggest producers of sugar. In the trading of metals and minerals, it was equally fearsome, handling nearly a quarter of the market for cobalt, 14 percent of the market for nickel, and 13 percent of the market for zinc. Glencore operated fifty offices in more than forty countries, which were depicted on colorful maps.

Glencore's numbers were impressive too. For the prior year, it reported overall revenue of nearly $150 billion—nearly four times what Goldman Sachs had generated and about 40 percent of what the far larger energy company ExxonMobil made—and a net income of $1.6 billion. Its assets, or properties of value, both tangible and otherwise, amounted to $80 billion—considerably less than a typical oil major or a large depositor, but twice the size of a large futures broker like MF Global and plenty big enough to qualify as a systemically important entity under Dodd-Frank.

It was also a company laden with liabilities, both financial and legal. Prominent on the list of "risk factors" was Glencore's exposure to "fraud and corruption due to the nature," the documents stated, of its "business and operations." Glencore had long been the target of human-rights activists, who accused it of a wide range of corrupt practices, from bribery and tax dodges to hatching backroom deals with violent dictators. Glencore denied most of the assertions, brushing them off as the critiques of nongovernmental agencies that still associated the company with Marc Rich—a figure that many of the younger generation, even within the company, unapologetically considered to be a sleazeball. Nonetheless, headline damage was a constant threat.

During his pre-offering roadshow, Glasenberg was struck by how little investors knew about his company. Coiffed, trim, and reserved-looking in his pressed suit and conservative tie, he was more approachable than many money managers had expected, and his company's story often surprised them. Many regarded Glencore as a high-tech gambler that considered the world's raw materials mere chips on the table. Glasenberg tried to assure them that his company traded real, physical assets and used commodity contracts only as a hedge on short-term exposure. He likened Glencore to a logistics company such as FedEx or DHL.

Two of the investors intrigued by his pitch were Sheikh Hamad bin Jassim bin Jaber Al Thani and his deputy, Ahmad al-Sayed, who ran the Qatar Investment Authority, an $80 billion state-run investment piggy bank known on Wall Street as a "sovereign-wealth fund." Having made investments in a number of luxury brands and high-end buildings in London, Qatar was looking for new opportunities in the commodity sector, where it was rich in natural gas but little else. Thinking Glencore could be the logical next step, Al Thani considered a major preoffering investment. However, he wanted a discount, and Glasenberg, noting that providing IPO discounts to cornerstone investors was against stock-exchange regulations, had to tell the sheikh that a discount would not be possible.

■

In the normal course of business, Glasenberg and Davis had always spoken at least twice a month. Glencore did considerable marketing work for Xstrata, including transporting and selling about a third of Xstrata's products, among them most of its nickel and cobalt. Glencore also advised Xstrata on its coal and copper marketing. On one of their regular phone calls not long after the Glencore IPO, Glasenberg raised the merger idea anew.

"Mick, you've got to start talking again," he said. "Let's talk."

Davis hesitated. Generally he and Glasenberg got along fine. But doing a deal together was a totally different matter—and, in Davis's experience, an extremely unpleasant one.

The Xstrata chief had first run across Glasenberg in college in Johannesburg, where Davis, then a lecturer, had taught some of Glasenberg's friends. In 2001, the two reconnected when Glencore recruited Davis to run Xstrata, the renamed version of a small mining entity then in its portfolio. The job was a step down for Davis, who had been the chief financial officer of the huge miner Billiton before its $28 billion merger with BHP. But he had been passed over for the top position at the merged company, and spotted an opportunity in Xstrata. His new business went public in 2002, leaving Glencore, which had entrusted it with some lucrative coal assets, with its one-third stake.

In the years that followed, Xstrata made some forty different acquisitions, including the purchase of Mount Isa Mines (MIM), a copper and zinc operation in Queensland, Australia, and the Canadian nickel miner Falconbridge. Largely on the success of those deals, its share price rose dramatically, pleasing both its public and private shareholders. Suddenly Davis, who had undertaken the MIM deal above some Glencore objections, looked like a deal-making genius.

In 2007, Glasenberg approached Davis about combining their two companies, but their talks failed to generate anything. The executives couldn't agree on a price for the deal, and Xstrata's other shareholders were cool to the idea. Afterward, Xstrata's buying spree continued, this time around with less obvious success.

Xstrata management continued thinking about its corporate future. In 2008 the company was approached by the Brazilian mining giant Vale about a purchase, valuing it at $85 billion—a deal that could have produced a 1,400 percent return for Xstrata's original shareholders and made Davis and his lieutenants phenomenally wealthy. But Glencore, whose approval was crucial, objected.

Two and a half years later, Davis was still stewing over the lost opportunity. He was convinced Glasenberg had crushed the Vale deal at least partly out of spite—not that Glasenberg, who maintained that Vale's chief had never made a serious offer for Xstrata, particularly cared. Reputation was important to Davis, perhaps more so than for Glasenberg, who knew that many associates considered him and his team to be a bunch of hard-driving bullies. A father of three and an observant Jew, Davis had other interests apart from mining and metals. He devoted a good deal of his free time to religious philanthropy in London, where he chaired the United Jewish Israel Appeal of Great Britain (Glasenberg was also an observant Jew). A large, paternal-looking man, sometimes referred to as "Big Mick," Davis believed in taking extended holidays and traveled often to his homes in Israel and Cape Town, where he often spent parts of December and January. A passionate fan of the game of cricket, he had once spent three hours explaining its inner workings to Brett Olsher on a long plane ride, sketching its structure on a pad as he spoke. Nevertheless, he was known for his middle-of-the-night e-mails and his blunt approach to work.

Reluctant as Davis was to rekindle merger talks, he faced few options. Glasenberg, he knew, would never sell Glencore's stake back to Xstrata. And given what had happened with Vale, a third-party takeover was also unlikely. So Davis effectively had two alternatives: he could continue with the uneasy alliance that Xstrata and Glencore already had, but with Glencore now public and competing for the very mining assets Xstrata might want to buy; or he could try to work out a deal to combine more comfortably with Glencore.

"Mick," says a longtime associate, "is a very black-and-white guy." He "fast-forwards to the end, and then he works his way back from that as to what are the items on the critical path." So when Glasenberg suggested a meeting with an investment banker named Michael Klein as a way of initiating some shuttle diplomacy, Davis agreed.

Klein had an appropriate CV for the role. Not only had he worked with numerous well-heeled investors, including private-equity firms and the sovereign-wealth fund in Abu Dhabi, a sister city to Dubai in the United Arab Emirates, but he had also advised the UK on its financial-crisis bailouts and, as a senior executive at Citigroup, had helped keep its corporate culture smooth in the aftermath of mergers there.

Both Glasenberg and Davis had met Klein during his Citi days in London, but he had never personally been hired by either one of them. Now Klein, a short, retiring advisor known for his self-deprecating jokes, was running his own eponymous firm in New York. If Davis trusted Klein—and Glasenberg suspected he would—perhaps the three of them could get a more fertile dialogue going.

That summer, Davis met one-on-one with Klein. They hit it off, and within months Davis and Glasenberg were talking terms. Naturally, price was important to both parties, especially given that Glencore would offer new shares of its own equity to existing investors in Xstrata. Arguing that its own stock was undervalued,

Glasenberg was initially only offering a price ratio of 2.6 of its shares for every single share of Xstrata, which would have included no premium for Davis's investors. But since theirs was a world of big-boy toys, like mines and oil rigs near hot petroleum finds and dominance over hazardous global transportation routes, and since both men were incredibly wealthy already, the bigger point of contention between Glasenberg and Davis was over control of the combined companies.

Glencore and Xstrata had performed solidly as partner companies, and "both sides believed that their impact was individually quite critical," says someone briefed on the discussions the two CEOs held. But as the autumn wore on it became clear that ultimately, it was Glasenberg's inability to cede control that had flummoxed merger talks in the past. The only way to take the talks forward, the Glencore chief realized, was to call the deal a merger of equals. It was a rare strike of humility for the aggressive South African coal trader, who in private circles made scant effort to conceal his feelings of superiority to Davis.

Despite his tireless work ethic and enviable empire-building skills, Glasenberg had after all inherited a powerful company from his predecessors, Marc Rich and Willy Strothotte. By contrast, Davis had created a cohesive and friendly corporate culture, almost from scratch, that had weathered numerous acquisitions and still remained intact. Moreover, he was willing to step down after two or three years, once a merged Glencore-Xstrata was on solid footing. Glasenberg for a time could make a powerful second-in-command, and, with his large personal stake in the company, he was guaranteed a strong voice—not that those who knew him would expect anything less.

Glasenberg was warming to the idea of being a temporary

number two, but was not without his doubts, and some of his friends in the industry warned against the demotion. For one, his old friend John Mack, whom he had met in the early 2000s, was against it. Mack had left Morgan Stanley after failing to jell with Philip Purcell, the Dean Witter chief who had taken the top role after his brokerage had merged with Morgan. Years later, Mack returned after Purcell was ousted by some of the investment bank's old-liners. "Once you've been a chief, it's hard not to be a chief," Mack now warned Glasenberg.

But Glasenberg was determined to make the Xstrata accord, and over dinner with Klein at London's St. James Club in November 2011, they shook hands on a new, and costlier, deal. Investors would receive 2.8 shares of Glencore for every share they owned of Xstrata, and Davis would be CEO at the outset. Convinced the effort was a real one this time, the two signed additional nondisclosure agreements as they headed into the final, most detailed, discussions. Beyond the broad speculation that Glencore was keen to buy all of Xstrata, nothing had yet leaked.

That fall, Glasenberg was spending a lot of time in London, where he worked out of Glencore's fifth-floor boardroom to avoid wasting money on a partially used office. His thriftiness was an oddity at the well-heeled commodity firm, which also skimped on things like telephone services in its Baar headquarters, where callers would occasionally encounter busy signals when the person they were calling was on the other line—an anachronism in a world where voice mail had been ubiquitous for years. Over coffee with a couple of Bank of America investment bankers in November at the Landmark Hotel, Glasenberg sounded far more confident than he had with Olsher a couple of months before.

"We're going to get it done this time, because we're both

public," Glasenberg explained. But he couldn't resist some tough talk. If the originally conceived deal didn't work out, he told the bankers, he would find a way to outmaneuver Xstrata. Glencore would go into the public market and buy more shares of Xstrata if that was what it took, Glasenberg added, to expand Glencore's controlling stake. "By hook or by crook, he was going to get it done," remembers a banker who was at the meeting.

The detailed talks proceeded, with the complex process of reorganizing the company and establishing financial packages for management now of foremost importance. Davis and Xstrata chief financial officer Trevor Reid felt strongly that their shareholders wanted consistent leadership, and that they should be paid well for the work of blending the companies. Pay packages and perks on par with those of other mining executives would therefore be required. Organizationally, Glasenberg wanted his traders—whom he considered peerless in the business—to be kept separate from the mining engineers and other senior workers at Xstrata, some of whom he considered to be easily replaceable. For its part, Xstrata had some pointed questions about Glencore's trading operations, including why the margins in it appeared to be shrinking.

Things dragged a bit over the holidays, as Davis retreated to Cape Town for his customary winter vacation—a multiweek sojourn that Glasenberg, who often told investors they wouldn't catch him lying on a beach, found risible. But Davis was responsive throughout the holiday, and gradually the final details of the arrangement were put in place.

On February 7, 2012, Glencore and Xstrata announced their plans to build a $90 billion corporation. It was a breathtaking deal that turned the combined entities into the fourth-biggest natural-resources company in the world, they boasted.

The pact created "a new powerhouse," Glasenberg stated in a press release that day. To assist with the effort, a half-dozen investment banks were hired. Morgan Stanley and Citi would represent Glencore, and Goldman, Deutsche Bank, JPMorgan, and Nomura would represent Xstrata.

Some Xstrata investors immediately objected. "This is a fabulous deal for Glencore, it's probably a great deal for the Xstrata management, but it's a poor deal for Xstrata's majority shareholders," said one key money manager at the time. Another prominent investor openly agreed.

The more vocal institutions controlled less than 6 percent of Xstrata's public shares. But it was a meaningful portion, considering that a 16 percent no-vote had the power to scuttle the whole merger (the 34 percent Glencore owned couldn't be voted, and neither could additional shares in Xstrata management's hands). Meanwhile, behind the scenes, another powerful player was joining their number: Qatar Holding, the investment subsidiary of the Qatar Investment Authority, the sovereign-wealth fund that was run by Ahmad al-Sayed, the young lawyer Glasenberg had met—and disappointed—while marketing the Glencore IPO.

Noting the relatively cheap price and rumors of a potential combination with Glencore, Qatar Holding had been buying shares of Xstrata for several months, amassing a 3.6 percent stake by the middle of March. Separately, the sovereign-wealth fund was talking to executives at Morgan Stanley about purchasing a minority stake in the bank's commodities unit, which was by then a far less robust facsimile of the place where Jennifer Fan and Jean Bourlot had once traded. Despite the flight of talent, Morgan still had attractive physical and paper assets, however, and was primed to sell itself in case commodities trading became too unwieldy to continue under the much-feared Volcker Rule, the aspect of the Dodd-Frank Act meant to rule out house trading at banks.

When Qatar's position in Xstrata was first disclosed in February, Spiro Youakim, a senior mining banker at the investment advisor Lazard, spotted an opening. Despite what he considered a solid relationship with Xstrata, Youakim had not won one of the four banking spots advising the miner on its merger, so Lazard was free to work with a third party. Youakim began calling on the Qatari investment managers from London, eventually reaching al-Sayed directly. "You should buy more stock. It's very cheap," he told the investor. Al-Sayed heard him out, but was noncommittal.

Youakim, however, was encouraged. "I'm going to do some work on this," he told colleagues. "Who's with me?" One young female vice president volunteered.

In the months that followed, the two barraged Qatar Holding with research and phone calls on Xstrata, its sector, and how the combined companies might perform. There was an opportunity to demand a higher price from Glencore, Lazard's bankers argued, that would benefit Xstrata investors greatly. Al-Sayed was intrigued, but if he were going to be more active as an Xstrata shareholder, he also wanted a traditional British banker. So Youakim, a Lebanese and a devout Catholic, brought in his colleague Nicholas Schott.

By early April, Qatar's stake had risen to 5 percent of Xstrata's public shares, making it the miner's third-largest shareholder after Glencore and the U.S. money-management firm BlackRock, which owned just a fraction more than Qatar did. Keen to figure out what was going on, Davis and his lieutenants flew to Doha and presented their pitch for the merger at Qatar Holding's offices. Would Qatar be supportive of the deal? they asked.

"We're not trying to get in and out. We've built a big stake and we may go even further," one of the fund's officials said. The team indicated support not only for the merger, but also for the idea of Davis running the combined companies. They mentioned also that Glasenberg had come calling before his IPO—and signaled that their interest in a discounted stake had been rebuffed.

The Xstrata executives flew home relieved. Unbeknownst to them, Qatar had already hired Lazard to represent it.

■

But Xstrata soon had another nettlesome problem: the plummeting price of coal, of which it was the world's biggest single producer. Plagued by oversupply in Europe and general negativity in the market, which was expecting a fall in price, coal had dropped 9 percent from the day the Glencore-Xstrata merger was announced, and was now trading at a one-and-a-half-year low. The downturn raised questions among Glencore shareholders about whether 2.8 shares was too expensive a price tag.

And while investors were mulling that, they were hit with a bigger bombshell: the details of the sweetheart retention packages that had been created for Davis and his top managers. On top of his usual salary, bonus, and other perquisites, Davis was slated for annual compensation totaling $15 million per year for three years, plus the use of a private jet. Overall, an astonishing total of seventy-three senior people at Xstrata were guaranteed "retention awards" that amounted to as much as or more than they were being paid already. Altogether, the pay packages would cost $260 million.

The disclosure occurred at an exceedingly awkward moment. Encouraged by British business secretary Vince Cable, who was seizing on the public ire over high executive pay, some institutional investors in London's financial center, known as the City, were fighting back more aggressively against hefty compensation deals. The British bank Barclays and the advertiser WPP had seen their compensation plans opposed by shareholders in annual votes, and the chief of the insurer Aviva had even been forced to resign.

The movement, nicknamed the "shareholder spring," seemed to embolden already leery Xstrata investors. The head of equities at Standard Life, for instance, used the popular BBC "Today" radio show to deliver a stern warning. The Glencore merger was "in jeopardy" over the pay packages, he argued. A second Xstrata shareholder was even tougher: "Xstrata should be under no delusions," he told the London *Telegraph*. "It can run without Mick Davis at the helm."

Davis and his colleagues were surprised. Of course, they were the ones who had insisted on the retention packages, and they could just as easily have agreed to stay on for less money. But they had built the company and felt they were worthy of the compensation packages; it was just the timing that was unfortunate.

They also began to suspect Glencore of encouraging the humiliating press reports. For one thing, the reporters who were calling the Xstrata media representatives were eerily well informed. "I can't prove anything," says one of the advisors who worked with Xstrata, but Glencore team members "were very effective in using something causing significant outrage"—namely, the national furor over corporate compensation levels—to escalate in a way that damaged Xstrata.

Thras Moraitis, the head of corporate strategy at Xstrata, was as upset as his superiors about the public beatings they were taking. Some of his press officers wanted to counter the publicity by planting embarrassing stories on Glencore. Moraitis refused. "Our instinct is to fight this, but I'm not going to let you do it," he told his group. "If we go out toe to toe," he said, "this merger will collapse."

From his perch in Goldman's Fleet Street office, Brett Olsher, now one of Xstrata's top advisors on the deal, was thinking exactly the same thing. In his fifteen years of banking, few deals had ever been subject to quite such mean-spirited jockeying. Something, he felt, had to change.

Olsher invited all the deal's bankers to huddle over strategy. On the Xstrata side, Goldman and Nomura, whose chief of banking, William Vereker, was advising the independent stakeholders, were in control. JPMorgan and Deutsche Bank were Xstrata's brokers, the ones handling the investor relationships. On the other side, advising Glencore, were bankers from Morgan Stanley and Citigroup.

They met in Goldman's tenth-floor conference center, where china and sea-kelp-scented soap created an elegant atmosphere. Meeting rooms were so private that their doors were fitted with covered peepholes.

At the appointed time, Olsher addressed the group. "Look, we can keep going the way we're going, or try to get a deal done for these two guys," he said, referring to Glasenberg and Davis. "Why don't we compare notes" on what shareholders were saying, he suggested, "and where we have different views, let's get to the bottom of them."

The bickering started almost immediately. "Shareholders are very angry with the MIAs," said one of the Glencore bankers, referring to the compensation agreements, known as management incentive arrangements in Xstrata's corporatespeak. "You need to restructure them."

The Xstrata bankers said that wasn't what they were hearing. In any case, they added, the team needed to press forward. "This is the deal that our clients have agreed to," Olsher said. "So let's talk about how we can jointly go out and get this deal across the line."

Much of the group was unconvinced. "It was a bullshit meeting," one of the other participants recalled. Realizing they were getting nowhere, Olsher and Vereker began setting up meetings with investors themselves.

■

Throughout the compensation tussle, Qatar Holding had been largely silent. Davis had by now been to Doha more than once, meeting with Al Thani—who in addition to running the mother company, was also Qatar's prime minister—as well as with Ahmad al-Sayed. Qatar had repeatedly assured Xstrata of their support for the merger, but Davis had his doubts. Early that summer, with a July 12 merger vote drawing near, he asked Glasenberg what he thought.

"Are you sure the Qataris are there?" Davis said.

"Absolutely," Glasenberg replied, describing himself and al-Sayed as good chums. "We instant-message each other all the time," he said.

But on June 26, 2012, Glasenberg was working in the boardroom on Berkeley Street when al-Sayed called to give him a heads-up that Qatar Holding had had a change of heart about the deal. After careful consideration, Qatar had decided to oppose the Glencore-Xstrata merger on its announced terms, asking for 3.25 new Glencore shares for every old Xstrata one instead of the expected 2.8, al-Sayed explained. A press release was soon to be issued.

Holy shit, Glasenberg thought, standing in the hallway where he'd gone to take the call. Opposition from Qatar, whose stake in

Xstrata was 10 percent at last check and could now be even larger, would be a total nightmare. His mind whirled, then snapped back into its familiar, stoic, place. He would figure it out somehow.

"Okay, Ahmad," he said. "You want to play? Fine. Do it." They hung up.

Glasenberg then threw together a conference call with his top executives, where he was so incensed he could barely describe the situation in polite terms.

"We've got this shit," he sputtered to Alex Beard and his counterparts, explaining al-Sayed's demand for 3.25 shares. "The guy wants more."

The partners discussed it. The new ratio seemed pretty rich, they felt, maybe too rich to accept. If they stood their ground and the Qataris opposed the deal, that would squelch the combination they'd planned on. But Glencore still had a large blocking stake and could try yet again at some point. In the meantime, no one else could win Xstrata without Glencore's support.

Davis and his colleagues were perversely thrilled. Qatar's unexpected opposition not only created the possibility of greater wealth, but it also underscored the value of Xstrata and its management. So that all sides could digest the new proposal, the July merger vote was put off to early September.

■

July and August were a period of reflection for Glasenberg. Ever since that day in the Johannesburg boardroom when he had overheard two men conducting an international candle-wax trade, he'd had a passion for trading. To him, it was a game of nuance, of finding just the right angle and using leverage to push his agenda. But he had to think it through, and he had to come prepared.

He was loath to raise the price for Xstrata, especially when its business looked so weak. Struck by softening markets for coal, nickel, and zinc, the miner's profits for the first half of the year had fallen 42 percent, forcing it to trim spending. It was hardly the environment in which to sweeten a takeover deal, Glasenberg thought.

He had already tried logic with al-Sayed. "You've got to do this deal, because if you don't, the share price of Xstrata falls," Glasenberg had argued after the June 26 announcement. "You're going to look bad" if that happens, he added.

"Fine," al-Sayed replied, as if to challenge him.

Unfortunately for him, Glasenberg had no leverage. His opponent wasn't some thinly capitalized hedge fund who would be squeezed out of his Xstrata position if forced to wait long enough. It was an enormous sovereign-wealth fund, basically a bottomless pit of money. A meeting with Al Thani, who could overrule al-Sayed, was going to be essential.

Then Michael Klein suggested a surprising go-between: Tony Blair. The former British prime minister was widely respected in the Middle East, where among other things he was working with Palestine to prepare it for statehood. Since leaving Downing Street, Blair had opened a consulting firm, and would surely be willing to help smooth relations between Qatar, Glencore, and Xstrata.

Glasenberg was willing to try it. During a trip to New York in early August, he met with Blair and Klein and articulated the deal's latest snag.

After hearing Glasenberg out, Blair seemed amenable to the task. "I think I can help," he said.

Later that month, Glencore posted its own first-half decline in profits: 8 percent. Revenue had risen despite the fall in major commodity prices, and the marketing arm continued to perform. On a call with investors, Glasenberg was intransigent on the subject of Xstrata, insisting he would not change his terms. If the deal "doesn't happen," he said, "it's not the end of the world." He criticized the Qatari investors, saying Glencore was the more attractive of the two companies.

Privately, Glasenberg theorized that al-Sayed's move was an elaborate payback for not giving the Qataris discounted shares of Glencore eighteen months earlier. Qatar Holding had bought Xstrata shares as a cheaply valued entry point to a combined Glencore-Xstrata, he believed, but the miner's subsequent stock spiral had cost the sovereign-wealth fund billions. Now it was attempting to make back the lost money with a higher share ratio from Glencore.

On September 4, 2012, Davis, Trevor Reid, and Thras Moraitis flew back to Doha for yet another sit-down with Qatari officials. With the all-important shareholder vote just three days away, the Qatari fund managers told them that Glencore had not budged.

"We're standing our ground," one of the officials said, not acknowledging al-Sayed's recent conversation with Glasenberg. "Ivan hasn't talked to us yet, and we're not going to come to him."

"He's a trader," Davis said. "He'll come and see you at the last minute."

■

Glasenberg, of course, had talked to his partners about raising the bid. Paying the full 3.25, they felt, was a nonstarter. But perhaps they could meet the Qataris in the middle. The sovereign-wealth fund now had a position in Xstrata north of 12 percent, and with other dissenting shareholders tied to at least an additional 4 percent of the company's shares, meaning that at least 16 percent of investors were in opposition, the deal was almost certain to fall apart without a sweeter offer. The question was what that offer should be—and what terms Glencore could extract in return.

Glasenberg's objective was clear: to run the combined companies himself. "If we're going to pay a bit more, we're going to run the show," he argued to his fellow executives. They agreed.

Meetings for shareholders of both Glencore and Xstrata had been scheduled for the morning of Friday, September 7 in Zug. Glasenberg had been trying to arrange a meeting for himself, Al Thani, and Blair for some time. But the Qataris didn't avail themselves until the very last minute.

Late on Thursday, the day before the vote, Glasenberg went over to the luxurious Claridge's hotel in Mayfair, London, not far from Glencore's office. Michael Klein, Tony Blair, and Michel Antakly, who had become Glasenberg's most trusted banking advisor, were with him. Nicholas Schott, Spiro Youakim, and others were huddled in a meeting room nearby.

A collection of rooms had been booked upstairs, where the Qatari contingent, including al-Sayed and Prime Minister Al Thani, was situated. They kept the group waiting for a while.

Eventually, Glasenberg and Klein were summoned. The Glencore CEO made his final offer: to pay 3.05 shares for every Xstrata share—just a tick more than the median point between the original offer and Qatar's counter—but only, Glasenberg said, "if we control the company."

Some discussion followed, punctuated by side conversations in a corner of the room. The 3.05 ratio wasn't what Qatar was demanding, but it was an improvement on the original rate.

However, scuttling the deal had its risks too. Qatar had made significant investments in the UK, including the luxury department store Harrods and a huge skyscraper in London called the Shard, as well as a number of public companies. If Qatar caused the Glencore-Xstrata pact to fall apart, Blair argued to Al Thani, it might hurt British investors and their impression of the other country in general.

Qatar came around. The sovereign-wealth fund would accept Glasenberg's revised price—but wouldn't explicitly sign off on the governance changes.

"Work out the details with Mick," al-Sayed said.

Glasenberg was satisfied. He left Claridge's, went over to the London Arts Club for a drink with one of Glencore's coal customers, and caught a 4 A.M. flight back to Zug, where he went for an early-morning jog.

■

Throughout the midnight summit at Claridge's, Mick Davis and Trevor Reid were holed up in their respective apartments in Zug. Brett Olsher and Bill Vereker, who had flown in for the shareholder meetings, were staying in hotels nearby, preparing documents for the anticipated vote. Frequent calls from Klein kept them closely apprised of what was happening in London.

By early morning, it was clear that something had broken the impasse, although the final details were yet to be determined. At 7 A.M., Olsher and Vereker arrived at their client's office for a scheduled meeting with Davis and his team. Shortly thereafter, Glasenberg arrived, and he and Davis disappeared together.

"I've reached an agreement with the Qataris," Glasenberg told Davis once they were alone. "We've raised our ratio to 3.05."

"Hallelujah," said Davis. "Now we can get this deal done."

"But there's a small wrinkle," said Glasenberg. In exchange for the added premium, his partners at Glencore, he said, "want me to run the company."

Davis frowned. "Fine," he said. "If that's the way you guys want it, put it in writing, and I'll take it to my board."

In a matter of hours, the Glencore-Xstrata merger had gone from a combination of equals to a takeover.

■

The shareholder meetings planned for that day didn't come off very well. Faced with a last-minute change of some significance, both boards postponed their deal votes so investors would have more time to consider the new terms. ("Bloody hell," one shareholder grumbled as Xstrata chairman Sir John Bond read out the new details.) On November 19 the deal was approved—minus the Xstrata retention packages. Qatar, in an effort to maintain some neutrality, abstained.

To Xstrata management, Glasenberg's eleventh-hour deal with the Qataris had come as an initial surprise. But on reflection, as Davis himself had predicted, it had an air of inevitability. Xstrata brass hadn't been so naïve as to think the Glencore boss would be comfortable in the number two spot forever. But they believed that for two years he would.

For a number of months after the deal's approval, Davis continued running Xstrata. Regulatory approvals were still pending, and until the pairing had passed muster with antitrust officials, integration could not occur.

It was an awkward time. One day in January 2013, Davis and Trevor Reid, Xstrata's chief financial officer, were dining at the upscale Royal Automobile Club in London when Youakim spotted them from across the room. Eager to say hello, the banker approached their table and congratulated Davis on the completion of the deal.

Davis exploded at him, saying he'd blown the deal. He attacked Qatar Holding, the share-ratio negotiations, and the work Lazard had done.

"You gave the wrong advice to your client," he fumed. "Because of you, a lot of people are going to leave Xstrata."

10

THE REFORMER

Far removed from Glencore and Xstrata and unlikely to ever have sway over them, either separate or together, CFTC chairman Gary Gensler was busy reforming a beleaguered agency.

In early 2011, just as Glasenberg began courting IPO investors, Gensler had named a new top lawyer, a new chief cop, a new corps of advisors, and a new head of public relations from the staff of Barney Frank, the Democratic congressman after whom the Dodd-Frank Act was named. The act, passed only six months earlier, had been a life-altering event for workers at the CFTC, who were now beavering over dozens of new rules to govern the trading of basic commodity contracts and more complex private market agreements known as swaps.

Tight legislative deadlines and a new organizational structure that divided the agency's policy makers into small teams were making the CFTC more productive. But the idea that its small and underfunded staff could fend off the overwhelming influence of the Wall Street lobbying apparatus was still optimistic.

So Gensler adopted a blunt, catch-all approach to regulation. He insisted that swaps, the $600 trillion market that was responsible for much of the damage caused to banks and insurers during the financial crisis but was still barely regulated, be traded more publicly and better tracked. On three separate occasions he proposed strict limits on the size of commodity trades, having his legal staff write and rewrite voluminous filings for the *Federal Register*. He gave countless interviews, speeches, and congressional testimonies, stocking the CFTC Web site with links to documents providing exhaustive accounts of his positions.

Though Gensler was polished and diplomatic in public, thanking his hosts and staff graciously before railing against the latest regulatory blind spots or Wall Street chicanery he had uncovered, he could be curt in private. Asked his opinion by a bank executive on the Volcker Rule, a critical tenet of Dodd-Frank which intended to outlaw self-interested trading by financial firms, at one point he said, "I know what you guys want to do. You want to keep doing all your sneaky stuff." Knowing that, the CFTC and its fellow regulators planned to give the industry strict limits, he explained, and "cut you down."

Banking industry denizens made a show of being appalled by that sort of rhetoric—and some actually may have been, given the scarcity of such threats in Washington's regulatory circles. Financial lobbyists were used to overseers like Securities and Exchange chairman Christopher Cox, a former corporate lawyer who had been out of reach at a birthday party the night JPMorgan's emergency purchase of Bear Stearns was being finalized in March 2008 and was attacked roundly for missing the warning signs at that poorly managed, overly indebted bank that prompted the financial crisis. Or like Walter Lukken, the CFTC chairman who had issued a press release defending commodity speculation mere weeks after convening a task force intended to make a thorough study of the issue. After relinquishing their government posts, both officials had taken private-sector jobs representing the firms they had once regulated.

Gensler met frequently with industry representatives, fielding their suggestions, but paid little heed, ultimately, to what they wanted him to do. When his patience thinned, he sometimes resorted to mockery. Athanassios Diplas, Deutsche Bank's head of global systemic risk and an active member of the International Swaps and Derivatives Association, met with the chairman some eighty times in a two-year period after the passing of Dodd-Frank, prompting an amused Gensler to call Diplas his stalker. "You'll find him behind a bush at my house," Gensler would say of the boisterous Greek risk supervisor when other people were in the room. In a meeting with dozens of banking-industry officials gathered to discuss one of the swaps rules, Gensler did it again. "You know Diplas," he said, gesturing to the risk manager after a lively debate about one of the CFTC's proposals. "He's my stalker." Gensler even told the joke in a private meeting with regulators from the German securities supervisor BaFin, Deutsche's primary watchdog. One of them called Diplas afterward, sounding alarmed that there might be a seed of truth to the joshing. "Do you know what Gensler's saying about you?" he asked.

■

By early 2011, Gensler had relocated from Baltimore to Chevy Chase, Maryland, to be closer to the office. His two elder daughters had gone off to college, leaving only his youngest still living at home. Every morning, he got up early, let out the family's two yellow Labs, Chloe and Alice, and tried repeatedly to awaken his sleepy teenager, who was slow to get out of bed. Once she was up and dressed, he made breakfast and drove her to her private high school in northwest Washington before he drove to work at the CFTC's offices near the K Street lobbying corridor. After school, Gensler's daughter would get herself home, followed by her father by eight o'clock on most nights.

Since he wasn't much of a cook, Gensler often ordered Thai delivery for dinner or threw together something easy like pasta. Then he'd sit in the living room while his daughter did her homework and return some late-night calls. Long talks with his speechwriter or head of enforcement were common. Some of Gensler's daughter's classes were by now over his head, but he pitched in occasionally, impressing himself at one point by naming all the U.S. presidents before an important American history test.

Hobbies like running were hard to keep up. Gensler's favorite six-mile loop from Chevy Chase to Rock Creek Park, the hilly, wooded enclave that abutted some of the tonier residential neighborhoods of Maryland and the District, was only possible on the weekends. If he had to travel for work, a scenario he strove to minimize, his daughter often stayed with neighbors who could drop her off at school in the morning.

In business, Gensler's family life was omnipresent. He'd cut off conversations late in the day, muttering that he had to get home to his daughter even if he couldn't resist taking one more meeting with an aide right afterward. He spoke, eyes glistening, of his late wife Francesca and how she was still with him every day. In what sounded like an outtake from a old-fashioned political stump speech, he likened the need for "common sense" regulation in the contract markets to the need for traffic lights and policemen to protect his daughters while driving on public roads. It was as if Gensler, who spent so much time enervating the opponents of reform, was in fact driven by a core sense of mission on the job, so deeply rooted that Washington's self-interested culture simply didn't bother him.

CFTC commissioner Bart Chilton's quixotic attacks on commodity speculators continued. In January 2011, at one of the CFTC's regular public meetings, four out of the five commissioners agreed to move forward with a proposal on position limits. (In the interim, surveillance staff would use position points—the idea that had put Chilton into a huff at the December meeting—to monitor trading and potentially to request less risk-taking.) But commissioners Dunn, Sommers, and O'Malia still had their doubts.

Without clear evidence that speculators actually harmed commodity markets, Dunn said in his written remarks at the meeting, "position limits are a cure for a disease that does not exist or at worst, a placebo for one that does." Sommers, who cast the dissenting vote, largely agreed.

Intellectually speaking, they had a reasonable point; it was certainly the approach that Wall Street was using to pooh-pooh the measure. But waging professorial debates about the necessity of a new rule mandated by Congress was not their job.

The Dodd-Frank Act's language on position limits, which they were now required to impose, was unambiguous. The essential passage of Title VII, a portion called Section 737, stated that the CFTC was to place limits on the size of commodity contract positions held by any one person at a given time.

The trouble for advocates like Chilton and Berkovitz, the lawyer who had led the five congressional inquiries into the impact of speculation on commodity prices, was that the academic research on their topic was both limited and anecdotal. It was hard to prove a mathematically demonstrable link between futures trading and the resultant prices, however obvious the correlation might seem. Berkovitz and his colleagues on Levin's subcommittee believed it, Chilton believed it, large corporations befuddled by big swings in commodity prices that affected their core costs believed it, and even Andurand and Patel, who had seen how their sale of billions of dollars of crude-oil contracts at BlueGold seemed to exacerbate a market downturn, believed it. In short, everyone to some extent believed it. But in a market like commodities where higher risk-taking fashioned higher returns, and where cowed regulators had created massively profitable banks and hedge funds, the fact that there was no proven, causal relationship between speculation and prices was a wedge that imparted considerable leverage to Wall Street.

Ironically, an Atlanta-based hedge-fund trader named Mike Masters was one of position limits' most outspoken advocates. During the middle of 2008, when oil and other commodities were reaching their record prices, he had testified to Congress about the relationship he discerned between a rise in speculative activity in commodity trading and major price moves in commodities. As a trader focused mostly on stocks, including a handful of airlines, like Delta, that were hurt by rising oil prices, Masters had no inside knowledge of commodity trading. But he could spot patterns between stocks and other economic gauges, and he felt the harmful effect of commodity index positions on their underlying markets, which he had tracked using his own market data, was indisputable.

In 2010, concerned about the misconceptions surrounding commodity speculation, Masters seeded a think tank in Washington called Better Markets. There a staff economist named David Frenk was studying the impact of the Goldman Sachs Commodity Index's monthly "roll" period. But Masters's whole line of thinking, at least as it pertained to the massive price spikes that preceded the 2008 financial crisis, was relatively new.

Shortly after the commodity position limits proposal's late-January debut in the *Federal Register*, the CFTC faced an onslaught of complaints. Critics from Morgan Stanley and Goldman Sachs to Cargill and the International Swaps and Derivatives Association blasted the intended curbs, complaining they were ineffective, undermining, and unnecessary. The Futures Industry Association echoed Dunn's language, calling the limits "a 'solution' to a nonexistent problem." Large commodity index fund managers were equally annoyed. The proposal would "hamper" the ability to "prudently" manage investments, argued U.S. Commodity Funds. Over time, more than fifteen thousand comment letters were dispatched.

For the rulemakers, the attacks were wearying, and Chilton, whose mere appearance could often cause chatter, had become a polarizing character. He and his wife spent most of their time in Hot Springs Village, Arkansas, where their daughter and grandson lived, making him hard to pin down. When he was in Washington, which was only about one week per month, he was often rushing in from, or out to, some sort of media appearance, to the irritation of colleagues hard at work on interpreting the finer points of swap-trade finalization or what size caps to put on a bundle of natural-gas contracts.

"It's not where you are, it's what you do" is Chilton's self-described motto. His long-winded speeches and homespun lingo—small investors who bought commodity contracts through indexes were "massive passives"; traders who used sophisticated algorithms to game the public markets with light-speed transactions were "cheetahs"—worked well on television, but less so in high-level policy meetings with commodity-market academics and lawyers. Now, some of the internal disputes were becoming more personal.

In early March, MSNBC commentator Ed Schultz, host of *The Ed Show*, who had become a strong advocate for commodity position limits, lambasted Dunn's opposition to the proposal. Chilton, who was booked that night on Schultz's show as a guest, tried to downplay the breach between himself and his colleague, using sterile, respectful responses.

It was an embarrassing juxtaposition for both commissioners, who despite their more academic ruffles were in fact friends and golfing buddies whose relationship went back thirty years. Dunn, who had been lobbying for days to get involved in the *Ed Show* discussion, was irritated. He had already left a blistering voice mail for one of the show's producers saying that if Schultz were going to attack him, he could at least have "the decency" to interview him. Now Chilton was being portrayed as an angel of reform, fighting the dark magic of Wall Street and disciples like Dunn. "Nice hatchet job Bart did on me last night," Dunn griped to an agency staffer the day after the interview. Privately, he suspected Gensler and Chilton of having shut down Lukken's 2008 study on speculators—which had never been finished—and boxing out the economist who asserted they had no impact on commodity prices. But, this being Washington, a bastion of passive aggression, unlikely alliances, and conflict-ridden friendships, Dunn never confronted Chilton about it, other than to say mildly that the study should never have been killed. At sixty-six he had his own private life to return to in Harpers Ferry, West Virginia, and was eagerly awaiting the appointment of a new Democratic commissioner so that he could resign.

Over the months that followed, a final vote on the limits, now past their immense public-comment period, was delayed repeatedly. Chilton continued simmering, pondering his political odds. On October 18, under pressure from Senator Carl Levin, who had threatened a hearing on the missed deadlines, the CFTC finally held another vote. David Frenk, the Better Markets economist, published his white paper on the Goldman Sachs Commodity Index that very same day, finding that the index's monthly "roll" period—in which existing near-term contracts were changed out for new ones as they neared expiration—contributed to steeper contango, or an upward bias in commodity prices, distorting the markets.

As anticipated, O'Malia and Sommers opposed the new rule, with the latter describing the curbs as a setup for an "enormous failure." To the surprise of some, however, Dunn dispiritedly cast a favoring vote, saying position-limits were a congressionally mandated obligation, even if they were, in his view, a "sideshow." Since the Democrat Mark Wetjen was soon to be confirmed as his replacement, it was Dunn's last significant move as a CFTC commissioner. Six days later, after seven years at the agency and a brief stint as its acting chairman, Dunn stepped down.

■

Enforcement, or the policing of contracts like futures and swaps, had never been at the top of Gary Gensler's to-do list, which was dominated by the policymaking aspects of the job. The CFTC had a small team relative to the Securities and Exchange Commission and the Justice Department, and commodity contracts had never grabbed the public's interest in the same way that stocks had. Regulating the swaps market, a global, $600 trillion industry, and imposing position its, which had captured the attention of important Democrats in Congress, seemed more important priorities.

But the more time he spent observing the industry's behavior in the various contract markets—known overall as derivatives because they were derived from simpler products like stocks and commodities—the more objectionable Gensler felt it was. The swindle that first captured his attention was the handling of an internationally regarded interest rate known as LIBOR, the acronym for the London Interbank Offered Rate, in London, which had little to do with commodities. But his sudden enforcement zeal spurred a crackdown on misconduct and sleaze in the contract market for raw materials.

Late in 2010, Gensler hired David Meister, a trim, antsy father of two teenagers, to run the forgotten enforcement division. Meister was a partner at the prominent New York law firm Skadden, Arps, Slate, Meagher & Flom, where he represented securities firms in white-collar crime cases. His hiring process had been vintage Gensler. After a couple of more formal meetings with his potential boss at the agency's offices, Meister had been summoned to a third sit-down in a lobby restaurant of Manhattan's Waldorf Astoria hotel. To keep Meister occupied during some down time, Gensler brought along a twenty-five-year-old CFTC speechwriter, with whom Meister chatted for three or four minutes about where he was staying in New York and other innocuous topics. Gensler later boasted that he had subjected Meister to a job interview with an inexperienced young aide and that Meister had been shocked that Gensler considered that interchange to be part of the interview process.

Meister, however, had more substantive concerns. To do the CFTC job, he had abandoned, at least for the three or four nights a week he slept in the crummy studio apartment he'd rented in Washington's DuPont Circle district, a cozy life in suburban Westchester and a well-compensated perch at a law firm that paid partners millions of dollars per year. A former assistant U.S. Attorney in Manhattan, Meister was familiar with the Spartan offices and low-tech systems that characterized a government job. In the past, though, he had at least operated from one of its better-reputed offices, the Southern District of New York, where the miscreants included mobsters, terrorists, and white-collar criminals like Marc Rich who actually feared facing consequences for their actions. At the CFTC, Meister was now running a division that had lacked a permanent head for two and a half years and was known mainly for its exposure of small-fry Ponzi schemes and other retail fraud matters. Overall, it was really petty stuff.

Since enforcement matters hadn't even been listed on Gensler's mental Post-it Note at the outset, he told Meister that if he joined the CFTC, the entire oversight program would be his to run, without undue interference from the boss. To Meister, accustomed to the groupthink of a private law firm, that was an attractive proposition. At forty-seven he worried he was aging out of some of the higher-ranking opportunities in government, so if he wanted another significant crack at law enforcement, this would have to be it. He convinced his family that the job was important to him, and vowed to be back in Westchester as often as the job would allow so that he wouldn't miss out on too much of their lives.

Early in January 2011, Meister took a late-Sunday shuttle from La Guardia to Ronald Reagan Washington National Airport to report for his first week of work. He attended Gensler's weekly 9 A.M. senior staff meeting, then scheduled an all-enforcement personnel gathering for the next day. He was concerned about making a solid initial impression on his 175 employees, many of them career government attorneys whom he presumed might be tempted to dismiss him as a fast-talking jerk lawyer from New York.

Later that week, he addressed the group, some of whom were watching via videoconference from Kansas City, Chicago, or New York. "We're going to make a lot of decisions on this job," he said. "Some of the decisions will be good ones, some will not." But in every case, Meister added, "I'm going to have your back."

Meister explained his basic calculus when it came to litigation, which was that the staff should bring cases it "ought" to win, not only the ones it suspected it would definitely win. "At times you're going to lose," he said. But Dodd-Frank, by lowering the legal standards required to bring certain cases and allowing the CFTC to pursue certain cases that had been beyond its purview in the past, would be a boon. No one asked any questions.

Meister began meeting individually with some of the enforcement lawyers and reviewing the cases already in progress. He earmarked the more promising ones and opened a computer file dedicated to what he called "high-impact" litigation. There were about two dozen—a number that would fluctuate over time, but would always be the focus of the greatest manpower.

One case that immediately interested Meister involved potential manipulation in the crude-oil market. The CFTC had gathered evidence suggesting that a pair of experienced crude traders, both of whom had worked previously at BP, dumped physical oil positions at times in order to drive down the price of oil contracts in the West Texas Intermediate market. There's a "shitload of money to be made shorting," or betting on a fall, of WTI crude, one of the traders wrote in a late-2007 e-mail, if someone were able to manipulate physical stores of oil in that market in such a way that an unexpected surplus occurred. The traders, who worked at two small firms known as Arcadia and Parnon, eventually did that, the evidence suggested, generating $50 million in profits.

The Arcadia crude-oil case had been under investigation for more than two years, moving along at the CFTC's usual low metabolic rate. Meister saw promise in it. Manipulation cases, which had been relatively rare at the agency, were always high-impact, in his view, and this one dealt with a particularly crucial period in the crude markets. He asked his team to fast-track the inquiry and set a deadline for bringing charges that was several months away. On May 24, the agency actually filed suit, levying another big public shock.

■

Gensler's embracing of enforcement was uncannily well timed. Late in October 2011, not long after the position-limits proposal had received its narrow approval, it emerged that MF Global Holdings, the large futures broker run by the former politician and Goldman Sachs head Jon Corzine, was in dire trouble. Citing poor financial results and overexposure to the European debt crisis, on October 24 the ratings agency Moody's downgraded the quality of MF Global's debt to just above junk status, meaning that the company was closer to default, or not repaying its creditors, than it had been before. That day, with rumors circulating about bad bets that Corzine had made in the bond markets, MF Global stock fell slightly.

October 25 was much worse. Spurred to action by the downgrade, MF opted to report quarterly earnings early, and the results were terrible. The company's shares fell a whopping 48 percent, and word soon trickled out that Standard & Poor's, a competitor of Moody's, was considering lowering MF Global's credit rating to actual junk, a move that would place it in the riskiest echelons of corporate borrowers, those who were most likely to walk away from their debts.

During the CFTC's weekly division-head meeting that Wednesday, senior staff discussed MF Global's situation as the commissioners listened from across the conference table. Ananda Radhakrishnan, the agency's head of risk, promised that MF Global would be a top focus until matters were resolved. The staff of both the clearing and swaps divisions said they would get in touch with the company.

It was the very least they could do, considering what a major issue MF Global could be for the CFTC. In the U.S., the firm was the eighth-largest futures broker and the biggest one not owned by a major bank. MF contributed a sizable portion of the volume on stateside exchanges like the Chicago Mercantile Exchange, but it also had a significant presence on the London Metal Exchange and other foreign markets. Moreover, many of its customers, who together accounted for more than $7 billion in funds, were small farmers and other mainstream commodity hedgers who used the futures markets to preserve businesses from catastrophic events. It was just the sort of constituency the CFTC was created to defend.

Gensler went to see the CFTC's newly appointed head of swaps, Gary Barnett, after the meeting. "Just make sure you send staff on site" at MF Global, he said. "They've got one role: to make sure customer money is secure." Barnett dispatched monitors to the brokerage's New York and Chicago offices within twenty-four hours.

Over the next several days MF, like Bear Stearns and Lehman Brothers before it, was pounded by negative rumors, causing its stock to drop precipitously. By the end of the week, the company had lost two-thirds of its value, and was looking for a suitor who could salvage it from bankruptcy.

Central to the market's concerns was the notion that Corzine, who had made his name as a bond trader at Goldman during the 1990s, had gotten in over his head with overoptimistic bets on European credit. Just as an ailing Greece was requesting a second bailout package to help pay its mounting debts, Corzine was betting on the health of larger economies like Spain and Italy, believing the European Union would never let them fail. He had a rational point, as time would prove. But that didn't prevent him from being socked with huge margin calls, that is, demands from his Wall Street creditors for additional cash in order to keep his original trades in place as the markets moved against him. On October 28, Corzine directed his back office to resolve about $175 million of overdrafts in MF's accounts. To pay those off, $200 million was moved from a customer money account into a firm account in a chain of events that later stoked controversy.

That Jon Corzine could preside over such a grand failure seemed shocking. He had run Goldman Sachs and the state of New Jersey. His brains and knack for persuasion had served him in scenarios with much higher stakes. In 1998, he had collaborated with Goldman's rivals on Wall Street to construct a bailout package for the failing hedge-fund Long-Term Capital Management that saved the stock markets from a potentially devastating disruption, and his ability to convince his fellow partners of the need for more permanent bank funding had cemented Goldman's plans for an initial public offering, which would be held in 1999. (That IPO, which had been accompanied by his ouster from the firm, also made Corzine $400 million.) His accomplishments as governor during a period of global recession and state fiscal crisis were far fewer, but even there, his reputation was for inertia, not political brinksmanship.

But the European bond bets at MF Global were the culmination of a decade of reckless behavior during which Corzine had abandoned his first marriage and had begun an affair with a New Jersey union official, had been critically injured in a highway car crash while not wearing a seat belt, and was televised guffawing about getting drunk the night Lehman Brothers filed for bankruptcy. Having taken over a much smaller version of MF in 2010, Corzine had fired fourteen hundred people and branched into an array of new businesses, aiming to make MF Global a far bigger force in the markets at a time when swaps and commodities had become part of the trading mainstream.

Now, flustered by the breakneck pace and unanswered questions about MF's business, the handful of banks interested in a distressed purchase of the gravely ill brokerage soon backed away. Interactive Brokers, a Connecticut securities firm that planned to buy MF, was the last to back down. It did so during a harried Sunday night in which a reported $900 million in customer money could not be located on MF's books.

At 2:30 A.M. on Halloween, the phone rang at Gensler's house. It was a CFTC staffer telling him that the deal with Interactive Brokers was on ice. "A hole" had been found in the customer account, the staffer told Gensler. "Alright," said the chairman, incredulous at the timing of the call and the odd term being used to describe a large amount of missing public money. "What do I do?"

Gensler padded downstairs in his bathrobe. Over the pleas of the dogs Chloe and Alice, who wanted to be let out, he dialed into an open line for members of the Financial Stability Oversight

Council, the systemic-risk panel Dodd-Frank had created. By the time he was patched in, regulators from the SEC and the Fed were already being briefed. During Interactive's due diligence on MF's books, a $900 million to $950 million hole had indeed been located, regulators were told. Unable to get satisfactory answers, the buyer was likely backing away from the deal. MF Global's bad bond bets were now an international crisis.

Later that day, MF filed for bankruptcy protection, creating havoc in some commodity markets, where the prices of some major agricultural products slipped notably and crude-oil volumes were lower than usual. Customers of the bankrupt firm had been effectively barred from the markets, able only to close out existing positions rather than put on new ones. The situation lowered trading volumes and left many people unable to put on new trades.

By Tuesday, Meister and the FBI had launched investigations. The missing customer money soon dwindled to the $600 million range, according to reports at the time. That was lower than the initial estimates, but the gap was still huge—and mixing customer money with firm money in the brokerage industry was a cardinal sin. The true size of the hole, overseers would eventually learn, was actually $1.2 billion.

Gensler decided not to participate in the enforcement phase of the MF debacle. He knew Corzine only slightly, as one of the scores of partners at Goldman and, briefly, his boss in the bond division. In 1991 he had used Corzine's entry number to run in a marathon that Corzine hadn't planned to run. That was about the extent of his direct dealings with the former Goldman head, and, even then, the conversation had occurred through a secretary.

But this was Washington, where no whiff of political scandal was too faint to create an embarrassing narrative. Chilton had

had this proven to him the hard way over the exact same investigation. Ironically, the December before MF's failure, Corzine had come to Chilton's New York office to lobby for modifications to CFTC Regulation 1.25, which addressed the handling of customer funds at brokerages—the very area that later proved to be MF's weak spot. Chilton, who had arrived sweaty and late from a TV interview, had not promised anything, and was in fact chastised by Corzine, who was miffed over having been kept waiting on the night of an important Christmas party. But the mere occurrence of the meeting, and a follow-up phone call the next July, now appeared suspect. Chilton, who tended to publish his private meetings on the CFTC's Web site—even though not all of his colleagues did—felt he was being punished for his transparency.

■

At the same time that it was reconstructing what had gone wrong at MF Global, the CFTC was making a name for itself as a tougher enforcement agent. Its crude-oil manipulation case against Arcadia, Parnon, and the former BP traders was moving through the court system, and pivotal cases on LIBOR were well under way. Ten months into Meister's first year in office, the agency had brought ninety-nine different enforcement actions, a record number nearly double what it had accomplished the year before.

Unlike the SEC and the Justice Department, which had more accomplished enforcement arms with precedents to follow, Meister was making new rules as he went. Since there was no science to determining settlement fees, for instance, he often generated hefty fines through sheer will. "He pretty much knew that financial institutions weren't willing to fight the government and he could settle for a high amount of money," says someone who worked with Meister at the time. "They used to settle for thousands of dollars and David said, 'Well, how about $100 million?'" Soon he was getting multiple hundreds of millions for settlements.

MF Global remained a central focus, intensified by the fact that Corzine had refused to acknowledge any wrongdoing with the customer funds. The agency was piecing together a case that would go after both the company and its senior management for negligence and possibly worse. At the same time, the CFTC was investigating questionable trading practices by a senior hedging manager at Delta Air Lines who had been actively using a personal account to buy and sell crude-oil contracts and other futures products while in possession of direct knowledge of the large airline's hedging plans—plans that had the potential to move the market.

∎

The rancor over position limits had not subsided. Against the objections of industry trade groups who had sued the CFTC to halt their imposition, the curbs were slated to take effect in the latter part of 2012. But on September 28, the federal judge handling the court challenge threw out the CFTC proposal entirely, saying the agency had overstepped its authority in imposing the curbs without adequately justifying them first. The matter was remanded to the CFTC, which would be expected once again to conduct further study of its proposed rules and reassert them at a later point. In a mixed vote, the CFTC opted to appeal the decision, tying it up in court for many more months.

For Gensler, it was a humiliating setback. The decision was a blow to one of the agency's key policy initiatives, one at which both Gensler, and certainly Chilton, had thrown substantial political capital. Still, "it's just part of our democracy," Gensler later said.

His comment typified the strange optimism of a man who successfully navigated some of the most toxic political conditions in recent memory. By late 2013, Gensler had just weeks left in office and no clear plans for what he would do after he left the agency. But, sitting in a drab conference room in the downtown Manhattan office that the agency shared with the investment firm Brown Brothers Harriman & Co., he resisted murmurs that he had been eased out.

Tapping his penchant for naming long lists of the legislators and political staffers with whom he had worked, Gensler said he'd been asked to stay by "Pete Rouse, Tim Geithner, Jack Lew, Denis McDonough," and others, citing a former White House chief of staff, the past and current treasury secretaries, and the current White House chief of staff as examples of his supporters.

Even in those final days, Gensler remained ruthlessly efficient, using minutes freed up by a latecomer to hold an impromptu meeting with enforcement staff and, a bit later, abandoning other colleagues, who risked making him late for his train home that night, at the elevator. His impact had been broad. Since 2009 more than five dozen new rules and orders had been written as part of the agency's obligations under Dodd-Frank. About $410 trillion of the swaps market was now reporting into the CFTC's data banks, bringing never-before-seen scrutiny to the once opaque market for those off-exchange derivative trades. And that was only the policy front.

On the policing side, the CFTC's enforcement unit had continued reeling in major settlements, including a $700 million civil fine against the Swiss bank UBS for LIBOR manipulations, and additional nine-figure fines for others. The Arcadia case was still in court, having survived a motion for dismissal, and a landmark case against the onetime natural-gas trader Brian Hunter, whose outsize positions at the hedge fund Amaranth had caused a market crisis in 2006, was soon to be litigated. The CFTC had also filed suit against Jon Corzine, charging that he failed to supervise MF Global employees who squandered customer money in order to bail out his European trades. That case, which Corzine was fighting, sought to bar him from participating in the futures industry, the sort of punishment rarely meted out to a person of the former governor's stature in the markets.

Finally, position limits had been resurrected. On November 5, 2013, a little more than a year after the original proposal was vacated in court, the Commission approved an amended set of position curbs in a three-to-one vote, with only O'Malia dissenting. (Sommers by that time had left and had not yet been replaced, and Wetjen voted in favor of the proposal.)

This time, CFTC lawyers left no wiggle room in their rule filing. The new proposal went through the fine language of the Dodd-Frank Act pertaining to position limits, arguing that the "necessity" of the limits was not the agency's to prove and that repeated congressional studies conducted by Levin's subcommittee had already shown speculative activity to have a very tangible price impact on crude oil, among many other markets.

Nonetheless, the agency made a stab at justifying its proposals anyway. The position limits proposed on twenty-eight major commodity markets were needed as a "prophylactic" measure to guard against manipulative activity such as corners and squeezes, the rule filing stated. But they were needed also because "excessively large speculative positions may cause sudden and unreasonable price fluctuations even if not accompanied by manipulative conduct."

The filing was helped by additional academic research that had by then flowed into industry circles, as well as its own experiences. In a throwback to a prior era, it cited as examples supporting the need for tighter curbs on speculation, first, the Hunt brothers' infamous silver stockpiles of the late 1970s and early 1980s and, more recent, the natural-gas price volatility caused by the hedge fund Amaranth in 2006, both of which had made market participants wary of trading in such unnatural conditions. Unmentioned but present in the public mind were fears that spikes in the price of wheat and other foods had sparked revolution in the Middle East in 2011, and that commodity index investing had contributed to high agricultural costs and the resultant global food crisis in general.

Satisfied that his pet issue might finally come to fruition, Chilton announced his own plans to step down toward the end of 2013. He was writing a book on Ponzi schemes and eager to continue his television career. "It wouldn't surprise me in the least if it was challenged legally," Chilton said of the new speculative curbs, "but I think it's a bulletproof rule."

But in an interview with Bloomberg news, he eviscerated the industry lobbying that had undermined his efforts at reform. "The lesson for me is: The financial sector is so powerful that they will roll things back over time," he said. "The Wall Street firms have tremendous influence." To pummel distasteful regulatory measures, he added, with a classic Chiltonesque flourish, that bank lobbyists employed what he called the "D.C. Quadra-Kill," a four-pronged strategy that involved respectively squashing, defunding, negotiating, or, if all else failed, litigating until things turned in its favor. It was a depressing rant coming from one of the few voices, however glib at times, for reform.

Gensler eschewed such rants about Wall Street, preferring to keep his thoughts on the CFTC to broad policy successes. His musings on the future, while vague, included a notable passing reference to Hillary Clinton, a potential Democratic candidate for president in the next election. " 'You don't wake up every day wanting to read what they say about you,' " Gensler recalled Clinton once telling him at a gathering during her first White House primary race in 2008. " 'You do it because of the policy.' "

"It made sense," Gensler said that November afternoon in the Commission's New York office. "I'm not going to say that every day was great, but I'll say that every day was interesting." A mere two months later, he was packing boxes in his Washington office.

11

THE SIDE BET

Less than a year into his tenure at Delta, Jon Ruggles was upending the airline's broken hedging operations. His trade book had generated more than $400 million. His risky heating-oil bet had effectively funded executive bonus checks during a cash crunch. And he was modernizing the flyer's philosophy on trading in general.

Word of his achievements was circulating around Delta's Atlanta headquarters. At an officers and directors meeting, Ruggles and his team practically got a standing ovation for what they had contributed to the profit-sharing pool. Ben Bergum and one of his colleagues were promoted to a management-level role that, among other things, required them to speak to small groups of employees about how they did what they did. Ruggles's little third-floor conclave in the finance building, which had started with a handful of employees and a useless hedge book, now numbered twenty.

"The people in the group were like celebrities around the campus," Ruggles recalled. He made a number of motivational speeches about the hedge group's accomplishments. "Speaking to a group of two hundred flight attendants and saying we were winning the war on fuel, that's powerful," he remembers.

Ruggles and his wife, Ivonne, had by then settled into an expansive house in Atlanta. After nearly a decade of marriage, they were also expecting their first child late in the spring. But Ruggles found it hard to focus on his personal life. Having made Delta a far more active market participant, he was now working eighty-hour weeks and was racked with insomnia, often waking up several times a night to check energy prices in the overseas markets. It was early 2012, and Iran was threatening to close the Strait of Hormuz, a critical waterway for shipping crude from the Middle East. As a result, crude prices were on a sharp upswing, the kind of move that had the power to wipe out an airline's quarterly earnings.

Ruggles was ready for it. That winter, he had put in place a fresh trading position betting that crude contracts would linger in a range between $105 and $125. During a period where oil was trading in the low $110s for weeks, it seemed like a pretty wide berth.

Initially, it worked. For the first quarter of the year, as Brent crude popped 9 percent, the hedge book generated gains of $45 million, helping Delta to stay in the black. Toward the end of February, though, it even looked as if the $125 ceiling might not be high enough, as crude contracts moved into the low $120 range. In addition to the turmoil in Iran, which was fighting a trade embargo by countries in Europe, strife in Nigeria, a key oil producer, loomed large, lifting crude contract prices yet higher.

U.S. airlines were understandably jittery. Fuel now topped their list of expenses, and there was little sign of relief in the offing. Citing a respected energy-market research firm, the Federal Aviation Administration predicted that crude would remain above

$100 a barrel for the rest of the year, and ticket-price hikes appeared inevitable.

Southwest Airlines, which in an unfortunate bit of timing had removed most of its jet-fuel hedges late in 2011, reported a slight loss in April as it faced mounting crude prices with no contracts to reduce the added expense. Reviewing the company's performance at a town hall meeting in Dallas the following week, Southwest's chief financial officer singled out Chris Monroe, the unassuming executive who ran the carrier's hedging operation, as the person responsible for reversing those fortunes.

"If we can keep fuel in check—Mr. Monroe," she told hundreds of employees, pointing in his direction, "we'll be in good shape." Laughter erupted around the room, but the CFO appeared to be only half kidding. Employees were glancing across the cafeteria tables, which were dotted with Dr Pepper cans and other refreshments, to catch Monroe's eye in the back corner of the room. He smiled and shook his head; there was only so much that one man could do. Even at Southwest, hedging decisions were made by committee, and sometimes the group didn't move fast enough to mitigate the blow that erupting crude prices could deal.

Delta, which now had a quick-thinking fuel trader running its hedge book, seemed more insulated from such setbacks. But Ruggles, the company was learning, could also be a galvanizing figure. His unassuming face and conservative shirts and suits left an unthreatening first impression, and his chronic tardiness and midwestern plainspokenness were humanizing. He frequently told funny stories about himself—about his lack of friends, his trouble getting Ivonne to date him at first, his checkered educational track record—and relished sharing a juicy piece of industry gossip, often at another trader's expense.

But his spurts of intellectual arrogance and distaste for red tape of any sort could be unnerving. "He wasn't flashy like gold chains and white Porsches, he was more understated than that," remembers someone who worked with him at Bank of America in Houston. (By the time he got to Atlanta, Ruggles drove a silver Mercedes coupe.) "But he knew a lot about a lot," the person added, whether it was houses and fine art or the energy markets—giving him a cocksure approach to commodities that made some people uncomfortable. Plus, what Ruggles understood to be the standard risks of the game sometimes sounded harrowing to his colleagues—at least they had at Bank of America during the two years he'd worked there. "The fact that he was underplaying risk" in suggesting commodity deals to clients, a former coworker said, scared the pants off some of the traders.

Ruggles knew some of these perceptions were dogging him at Delta, particularly since the confrontation he'd had with Trey Griggs, the salesman at Goldman who had questioned his heating-oil position. To address any concerns about Delta's presence in the markets, Bergum and others put together numerous Power-Point presentations detailing their strategies. Delta management, which was closely vetting Ruggles's trades, also sent daily reports to directors that outlined the level of risk in the hedge book. Such briefings were commonplace on Wall Street, where firms like Goldman calculated its value-at-risk, or the amount of money it could lose in a given day during adverse market conditions, on a real-time basis. And although it was in a different industry, Delta's board, which later that year added George Mattson, a retired Goldman investment banker, was very involved with such matters.

In dealing with his bosses, Ruggles started noticing more push-back against the things he wanted to do. His efforts to establish a more lenient hedge policy for Delta, for instance, were not progressing. He was still subject to overruling by Paul Jacobson, the treasurer, who kept a close eye on the trading desk from his office nearby, and of course also by Edward Bastian, Richard Anderson, and the board. The scrutiny was making him paranoid. He suspected Goldman's team of criticizing his trading practices simply because it was receiving smaller commissions than in the past, now that Delta had IntercontinentalExchange accounts and unique trading relationships. Having a savvy hedger on their hands whose game plan wasn't entirely clear, he thought, annoyed the Goldmans, Morgan Stanleys, and JPMorgans of the world, sparking questions about his motives and for no good reason.

"We were always long" on crude, or betting on higher crude prices in the contract markets, Ruggles recalls, "though we were not always long in a linear way. The banks would have a hard time figuring out what we were doing." That, he presumed, was his biggest problem.

Through the first half of the year, Delta was moving ahead on its Trainer refinery purchase, which Anderson considered to be a key weapon for fighting runaway jet-fuel prices. By early April, CNBC had the story. The carrier was set to spend more than $100 million on the Philadelphia-area plant, it reported. The low price tag revealed what was in many ways an unattractive asset. The seller, ConocoPhillips, had stopped running the plant due to financial losses, and a major renovation would be needed before the facility could begin refining crude into more useful products again. Delta's rumored purchase was the first known instance of an airline making such an attempt, though others had considered it in the past.

In the energy-trading community, the reaction was brutal.

Delta executives would only delve into such a troubled business "because they're stupid," Edward Hirs, a professor of energy economics, told *Forbes*. Airlines had historically avoided refineries and other physical assets for good reason, he and other critics argued: they were expensive to operate and riddled with liability. Moreover, a sudden move against the refinery's owner in the crude or jet-fuel market could wipe out its profit margins. The whole undertaking struck many observers as either a foolish fantasy deal or a capitulation to the idea that it was a failure at fuel hedging. "They must have gotten burned on paper trades in the past," groused one commodities trader.

Ruggles, who was busy negotiating with BP and traders in Alex Beard's division of Glencore over crude supply contracts for Trainer, took the criticism in stride. He had been disappointed not to bring in a private-equity partner for the refinery investment, which was one of his original ideas for sharing the ambitious project's risk. But that failure had not hurt his confidence in the deal. He had a plan for optimizing the refinery's output that involved expanding its production of jet fuel and trading its other refined products, such as diesel fuel and kerosene, in exchange for additional jet fuel. Initially, Delta's crude would be shipped across the Atlantic from West Africa, a fairly costly trip, but within a few years, he figured, it would instead be coming from the Bakken shale formation in North Dakota, where huge stores of underground crude were now being harvested. In the meantime, he comforted himself that he'd worked at Conoco and another driller and knew how to bargain with suppliers to keep crude relatively cheap. And once the Bakken crude was more accessible, he figured, Delta's considerable expertise in physical logistics would help it move supplies quickly and cheaply.

On April 30, 2012, Delta announced the Trainer purchase with much fanfare: a $180 million deal to acquire the shuttered refinery with a $30 million contribution from the state of Pennsylvania, which was eager to see the plant's hundreds of jobs preserved. BP would provide the crude for processing, and Delta would trade diesel, gasoline, and other products to BP and Phillips 66 for additional jet fuel. Because the needed repairs that were part of the "turnaround" of the facility would cost $100 million, the refinery wouldn't begin producing fuels for at least several months, but Delta planned to start operations around Labor Day.

Anderson flew to New York to talk to airline analysts that day. He could hardly contain his excitement.

"We hit it at the bottom of the market," Anderson said in a television interview with CNBC. "Big ideas like this can create a lot of value for your shareholders," he added, pointing out that Delta's shares had risen 10 percent since news of the deal had first leaked.

"Commodities prices are at all-time highs, whether it's foodstuffs, metals, or energy," Anderson said. A case in point, he continued, was that even with the benefit of the Trainer deal, Delta's expected fuel costs that year were projected to be more than $12 billion, an all-time high.

On June 15 at Delta's annual meeting, Anderson stepped up the rhetoric. "It's our intention to begin to participate in the pricing function and put a lot of downward pressure on the cost of refining a barrel of jet fuel," he told a reporter. In light of its refinery purchase, Delta expected to soon become a seller of jet fuel, rather than a buyer, he said.

His comments did not sit well with the jet-fuel market, where whispers of manipulation began to make the rounds. Complaints reached the market-data provider Platts, which Delta had petitioned for participation in the so-called pricing window, an end-of-day period in which Platts collected bids and offers for various commodities, including jet fuel. Applicants were subject to review and were asked to adhere to a strict methodology.

Shortly after the annual meeting, Platts fired off a letter to Delta's internal lawyers complaining about the CEO's comments. The pricing window was reserved for legitimate traders only, the letter said, and Delta's CEO had given Platts reason to think it might engage in behavior that distorted the markets. Aware of the backlash, a Delta spokesman tried to soften Anderson's comments, telling another reporter at Reuters that the airline would produce and sell jet fuel only to itself. In fact, Monroe Energy, the company subsidiary that now owned the Trainer plant, was legally prohibited from selling jet fuel on the open market, the spokesman pointed out—making the CEO's remarks seem all the more absurd.

But the damage was done. The commodity business hated the refinery deal, Platts was threatening to shut Delta out of the pricing process, and the actual production of jet fuel was still months away. There was nothing to do but try to avoid more incendiary comments and wait. Anderson, who had been barraged by reporters wanting interviews and had wanted to proselytize his message of taking control of the markets, would have to let an article he'd penned for Delta's in-flight magazine be his last remarks on the subject for some time.

On May 19, 2012, Ivonne gave birth to a son in Atlanta. Ruggles, who was exhausted from work, had looked forward to the opportunity to rest at home with his wife and new baby, who had no grandparents in the area to help out during the sleepless nights that were no doubt coming. Ruggles had scheduled a couple of weeks off so the family could bond.

For Delta, however, the timing could hardly have been worse. Two days before Ruggles's son was born, crude experienced a pronounced drop, sparked by robust production from the oil-producing nations of the Middle East at a time when demand in the U.S. was at a fifteen-year low. The recession and unemployment were finally affecting fuel purchases, making an excess supply overwhelming at a time of muted demand, depressing prices. By early June, crude had crossed below $100, and was now significantly cheaper than the $105 level Ruggles had pinpointed earlier that year as the commodity's expected bottom price.

It was a rich irony: crude was now relatively cheap, but Delta's hedges were costing it money. To subsidize its trading, which relied on the extension of credit, the airline had to sell some of its more valuable contracts, which were options, or the rights to sell crude, at $105. But it wasn't enough. As oil got cheaper and cheaper, Delta's brokers started making additional margin calls, asking for more cash to fund the trades Delta had made. Over time, the company exhausted its credit lines with Goldman and others, and had to post hundreds of millions to them in cash.

At home with Ivonne and the baby, Ruggles received constant e-mails from his staff on the trading desk. Delta's senior executives were not happy, they reported. "It was the type of market where people were in a panic," Ruggles remembers. After more than two weeks of distractions, he cut his paternity leave short.

Instead of rushing back to manage the book, however, Ruggles was dispatched to Japan to meet some oil executives in Tokyo. It was as if Delta didn't want him around. Meanwhile, Jacobson and

Bastian took over the trading. Ruggles suggested leaving the original hedge book intact, arguing that even below the $105 level for crude, the level at which the commodity contracts were no longer effective at hedging crude prices, Delta wouldn't lose much money because the price of actual jet fuel would be more affordable. But senior management ignored his counsel, buying swaps, or private contracts, betting that the market would stabilize at about $100. "They doubled down when we should have gone the other way," Ruggles recalls. Eventually, with crude falling to $88, he says the resultant paper losses mushroomed to $700 million.

On the third-floor trading desk, the environment was toxic. The team was now caught in a war between Ruggles and his superiors. Some of Delta's board members, reviewing the details of the losses, appeared to be outraged. Ruggles says that at least one board member called and screamed at him, and there were threats that the entire book would be liquidated, or would have its trading positions sold and turned into cash. Bergum, who had started the year on such a high note, worried openly about his job security. "I didn't know if we were going to show up and get fired," Ruggles says he confided at a particularly bleak moment.

Still, the crisis was somewhat contained. Thanks to improvement in passenger revenue, Delta managed to make a profit for the second quarter, despite rising jet-fuel costs and a margin requirement of $350 million.

Around that time, Jacobson summoned Ruggles into his office for an impromptu conversation with Anderson via speakerphone. The CEO, knowing that Ruggles had been overruled by the decision to bet with $100 crude swaps, tried to reassure the head trader that ultimately the right decision had been made. "I know you gave up your profits from the hedge books, but don't worry about it," Anderson boomed over the speakerphone. "The airline's better off."

"Okay," said Ruggles. He was unconvinced.

∎

By that fall, Ruggles was struggling. He was sleeping poorly, eating junk food, and not seeing nearly enough of Ivonne and the baby. Delta management's handling of the hedge book that summer had infuriated him, and his job now, as he saw it, was to undo their mistakes as crude prices bounced upward, off their June lows. Anderson, Bastian, and Jacobson did not understand the options market, Ruggles fumed, and their approach was sophomoric. No wonder Delta had incurred hundreds of millions in paper losses on the book.

By September the Trainer refinery turnaround was largely complete, and test runs of the plant's refining systems were under way. Much of the refinery's laid-off staff had been rehired, and crude was on its way for processing. The public spats over pricing had also cooled, and Delta had even resolved its issues with Platts, the market-data provider, making the airline eligible to participate in the pricing window once its refinery went online.

Ruggles, however, was being frozen out. Delta management decided to operate Trainer at arm's length from its core business, with the subsidiary that owned the refiner reporting directly to Anderson. Supply arrangements were being handled by others, as were strategic plans. Just about the only thing Ruggles was permitted to do with the refinery that fall was discuss it at an industry speech in Las Vegas that October—and even there, he stuck largely to company talking points. Observers were impressed with his performance, but to Ruggles, it was little comfort.

There were other bad signs as well. Delta management was now balking at hires Ruggles wanted to make, and hinting that his bonus for the year would be less than he'd hoped for. Meanwhile, superiors continued making trading decisions he considered to be inane.

In late October, the East Coast was hit with torrential rain, heavy winds, flooding, and widespread power outages as a result of the severe weather event known as Superstorm Sandy. Numerous refineries around New York harbor were shut down, and many large tank "terminals" storing refined products like jet and auto fuel were flooded and taken offline. In New York City and many parts of New Jersey, which had been devastated by the storm, long gas lines formed. New York's governor ordered emergency fuel supplies, and New Jersey's imposed gas rations on motorists.

Delta's newly reopened Trainer facility, about one hundred miles away, was miraculously unharmed. But damage to the coastal pipelines had made fuel difficult to transport. Ruggles tried to negotiate deals to sell the Trainer product to competing airlines, but was undercut by colleagues. Meanwhile, an aviation-publication poll revealed that many jet-fuel market participants doubted whether Delta would achieve the desired annual cost savings or set a precedent that other airlines might follow.

Despite the troubles at work, side projects kept Ruggles busy. Ivonne was negotiating to buy a cosmetics manufacturer in northern New Jersey, so the two were searching for a home in Montclair, not far from the business she planned to help run. They had flown up to New York to catch a day of the U.S. Open annual tennis tournament, using seats provided by one of Delta's brokers, and made a family trip of the Las Vegas speech. And Ruggles was making money in his personal account, where he traded contracts on crude, heating oil, and several other high-volume energy commodities in an account registered under Ivonne's name.

Personal trading was common in commodities markets but not among corporate employees. Some companies, perhaps not thinking ahead about the nature of the work their hedgers performed, didn't explicitly forbid it. Guidelines for commodity traders, who weren't even required to have specific financial licenses, were loose compared to those that governed stocks and other products. As the debate in Washington over speculators demonstrated, many market participants considered arenas like crude, gold, and copper too liquid to be manipulated. At Bank of America, where employees were typically asked to hold investments for at least thirty days, company policy would have precluded Ruggles from trading in his personal account. But his superiors were unaware of the activity, say people with knowledge of his tenure there, and perhaps because his role was one that didn't directly involve investing client money, Ruggles largely escaped scrutiny.

Late in 2012, Delta received a subpoena from the CFTC, asking for trading records pertaining to either personal or corporate trading in which Ruggles had engaged. The company itself was apparently not a target. But its head of fuel was.

The implications of the subpoena were grave. As the architect of Delta's hedging strategy, Ruggles had been in regular possession of nonpublic information on what one of the world's biggest energy buyers planned to do in the markets. As Patel and Andurand had learned at BlueGold, a large enough sale in the crude market could knock prices down by as much as $2 or $3 per contract; anyone who had advance notice of such a sale could theoretically make huge profits trading ahead of it. And since Ruggles was trading some of the same products at home that he traded at work, the potential for using his corporate knowledge to make personal trades was omnipresent.

One of Delta's higher-ups called Ruggles, who was not in Atlanta when the request arrived. The CFTC had subpoenaed Delta's trading records, the executive explained, with an emphasis on obtaining information on what Ruggles had been doing. Management wanted to know what the inquiry was all about.

Ruggles replied that it was not a big deal. The CFTC had been looking at him for a while, he told Delta—at that point, it had probably been more than a year. He had a personal lawyer in Washington, and regarded it as his problem alone and nothing for the carrier to worry about.

Delta's lawyers reviewed the situation. It seemed strange that Ruggles wouldn't discuss the probe in greater detail, especially if he had known about it for a while. Surely he realized his job was on the line, they thought. Delta asked again that Ruggles return to Atlanta to brief the company's lawyers. When he did not respond, the company gave him an ultimatum: show up for a meeting by a certain date in December, or be terminated.

He never returned.

■

In Ruggles's mind, the CFTC probe had little bearing on his departure.

I had first spoken to him after the Trainer refinery deal's announcement in the spring of 2012, when I'd called to introduce myself. Mutual contacts had described him as the mastermind behind that deal, and having covered it for CNBC, I was curious to meet him. For a senior manager in a guarded corporate culture like Delta's, Ruggles was surprisingly receptive, and seemed to enjoy schooling me on the history and nuances of the crude contract markets with which he dealt. He had an offhand knowledge of a litany of fun facts, including the attempts to squeeze the Brent-crude market in the early 2000s and what Mexico's strategy was for hedging its exposure to crude oil prices in the coming year. He also told hilarious stories about his first stint as a contract trader in Trafi's London office.

That summer, Ruggles and I chatted frequently and met for lunch or coffee on a couple of occasions. I even met Ivonne a couple of times, once for tea with Ruggles and once for dinner with my husband. Ruggles had lots of views on how the Trainer facility should be managed, though I couldn't quite tell what his level of involvement was (and it turns out that it was nil at that point). Like Pierre Andurand, Ruggles evinced a remarkable combination of arrogance and anxiety, at times bloviating about his trading accomplishments and at others speaking in self-deprecating terms about his limitations. Throughout those six months while he was still employed at Delta, he seemed knowledgeable about what was happening on the airline's fuel desk.

Given all of that, I was surprised to hear of Ruggles's sudden departure from Delta in December of 2012. We connected a few days later, at which point he told me he'd had a "tantrum" on the trading desk and essentially walked out. In uncharacteristic fashion, however, he declined to explain why. I thought it strange that Ruggles would have abandoned a well-compensated perch at the airline that he had seemed during our short acquaintanceship to relish. But some of our mutual acquaintances told me Ruggles had a dispute with the airline over its hedge book, and I had no reason to doubt them.

By late January 2013, Ruggles was ensconced in a large

Montclair, New Jersey, colonial, for which he had paid $956,000 in cash. Ivonne was working at the cosmetics factory she now owned, and their son was zipping around in a walker with wheels, trailed by a young Thai au pair, on the snowy morning I drove out to their house to visit.

Relaxed in jeans and a button-down shirt, Ruggles spoke of his relief at having exited Delta and of excitement over his job search in New York. He said he was talking to at least one brokerage firm, as well as some private-equity shops that wanted to do more in commodities.

I brought up my book project. In light of Ruggles's abrupt job change, I was concerned that he'd want to back out of the interviews he'd agreed to while he worked out the terms of his departure with Delta. But he was undaunted by the job change and assured me that with limited exceptions, he'd happily speak to me on the record about his work.

"The way I think about markets is just completely different from everybody else," he said. "And I have a view on most days, the market's going to tell you what it's going to do. Today, two news stories are out there, the first is Iranian—the Fordow news—is it confirmed or not confirmed?" he went on, referring to disputed reports that an Iranian uranium-producing bunker had weathered explosions. "My hunch is, it's probably already happened, but nobody seems to care. The Americans came in and saw the headline and kind of bid it up, so all before nine in the morning, it went up really quickly, and since then it's been going down. And that's the opinion of the day, it's going to be a bearish day."

He chattered on about market structure and his own history, including how he'd made his way to Delta. He grew more reserved when it came to describing his exit, saying he could not discuss it.

"I got really angry about the book," he said simply. It was positioned for a rise in crude, he added, and "they wanted to flip it."

Instead of addressing his situation, Ruggles offered a tour of his new home, a spotless, four-story building on a quiet suburban side street. The family was still settling in, and the house was minimally furnished, but the warm wood floors and fresh white walls were inviting.

Ruggles's home office was in a cozy attic space, under a window overlooking the street. Walking over to a pair of screens, he pressed the mouse button to move the cursor over some commodities charts highlighting the energy market's recent activities. He had been trading quite a bit lately, he said. The adjoining screen was open to his personal account, under the heading "Ivonne Ruggles."

■

Two months after that interview, I heard word that Ruggles had been forced out of Delta, not because of a hedging dispute but because of some federal investigation involving his wife. In late March, I called Ruggles and confronted him about the rumors.

Ruggles acknowledged having personally been under investigation by the CFTC at least since 2011, saying that the agency had "been watching me closely for probably a year and a half." But the probe had played "zero" part in his departure from the airline, he said. He talked about the issues that had arisen between Delta and Platts, and the blowback he had received at Delta from brokers like Goldman, which were allegedly concerned about its trading activities. He denied that the Justice Department, which was rumored to be reviewing his activities and Ivonne's role in them, was involved.

Ruggles was weirdly insouciant. When it came to regulatory

probes, "I don't care, it's par for the course," he said. I had surmised that Ruggles had hoped I simply wouldn't find out about his trouble with the CFTC and that it wouldn't bear a mention in my book, but it seemed that perhaps he simply didn't care either way. His involvement in the world oil business as a London trader, a McKinsey consultant who had worked for foreign clients, and a senior trader at Delta would no doubt make him a person of interest to the U.S. government, he said: "That's going to be a part of my life for the rest of my life in this business."

He clammed up after that.

12

THE POP

Goldman's respected commodities analyst, an Oregon-born Anglophile named Jeff Currie, was meeting clients at London's Mandarin Oriental hotel when it hit him that the boom he had been profiting from for years might finally be over.

It was October 2012 and London Metal Exchange week. Hosted by the historic bourse, hundreds of metals traders were in London for a series of seminars on the market they covered: a spectrum of base, or nonprecious, metals that ranged from aluminum to zinc. Currie's team at Goldman covered all the major markets, and with a large collection of current and potential clients all in the same place at once, he had arranged a breakfast information session to showcase his research.

On the morning of the gathering, Currie ran through his usual outlook, stopping to field the occasional question as he went. But something in the room, he realized, was off.

It wasn't the attendees. Some of the commodity world's biggest personalities were in the room, traders whose profit-and-loss statements had been the subject of glowing press just a few years ago. It was their performance and their mind-set that had changed.

Instead of entertaining wild stories of how they had beaten the market, Currie was hearing about the difficulty the managers were having in hitting up investors for new money. Suddenly he was feeling more like a shrink than a market advisor.

Given what had actually happened to commodity contract markets, it was understandable. The Goldman Sachs Commodity Index had traded sideways for two years in a row, ending each year neither up nor down and removing the big commodity-price moves that had helped generate returns in years past. Tired of trading the markets or weighed down by losses, names like Centaurus and BlueGold, the two best-performing funds in commodity-trading history, had summarily folded, along with countless lesser-known rivals. Survivors like Clive Capital and John Paulson's dedicated gold fund were struggling with sharp reversals. Glancing around the room, Currie noted that the collective assets under management were the lowest they had been in the decade or so that commodity-focused hedge funds had even existed. No wonder, he thought, when the average commodity fund that year was on track to lose almost 3 percent.

In fairness, Currie thought it wasn't all the managers' fault. "It's not so much that the commodities story itself is over," he said after the London meeting, "as it is that the other asset classes," or groups of investment instruments, like stocks or bonds, "have a better outlook."

Currie had prepared a chart showing that the era of cash, oil, and gold as favored trades had effectively ended. Despite the commodity supercycle, a theory still being thrown around at the time that argued for a protracted period of high commodity prices, he felt that the potential for returns was now far better in stocks. During the 2000s, as commodities were raging toward their all-time high, stocks were up only slightly. But the Fed's easy-money policies, the centerpiece of which was a recurring $85 billion monthly asset-purchasing program intended to stimulate the economy, had helped the stock market recover from the financial crisis. Investments in simple stock indexes like the Dow Jones Industrial Average and the Standard & Poor's 500 stock index were now creating the sort of gains in stock-trading hedge funds that the commodity players had once generated: 15, 18, even 20-plus percent, simply by taking old-fashioned positions in publicly traded companies.

As of this writing late in 2014, more than two years after he made it, Currie's proclamation about stocks seems obvious. Day after day in the period that followed, the stock markets hit all-time highs, zooming past historically significant levels for the first time ever. Bonds, which along with commodities had been a darling of post-recession investing, were suddenly unwanted, as investors shied from treasury notes and safe corporate bonds with terrible returns. Investing in treasuries, the respected stock investor Leon Cooperman said repeatedly, was like walking in front of a steamroller to pick up a dime. Even the market for junk, or likely-to-default, bonds and risky European credit, usually a lucrative sandbox for sophisticated investors, was too crowded to enter at reasonable prices. Desperate for better yields on their money, too many traders had already piled into them.

In order to invest in stocks, mutual funds, or pension funds, endowments and hedge funds had to locate some cash, and, in many cases, that involved dumping out of commodities. Around the time of Jeff Currie's breakfast meeting, two years since the last time the average commodity hedge fund had made a profit, money managers were doing just that.

The California Public Employees' Retirement System, also known as Calpers, which had made the commodities world seem palatable to small investors with its initial investment of $450 million in 2007, hastened the exodus. Ironically, Calpers had never actually made money on commodities, even though it bought them during years of solid returns—and had in fact lost, on average, 8 percent of it per year. Other major pensions, including the Illinois Teachers' Retirement System and the California State Teachers' Retirement System, uncertain of the value of commodities investments, opted out too.

Critics of commodities as mainstream investments, such as Better Markets economist David Frenk, believed the whole pitch had been a mirage. Some blamed the investment banks for flogging commodities indexes that, given the cost of rolling contracts forward every month or two, were simply too expensive to hold when the price of raw materials wasn't rising. Those embedded costs, the critics said, had effectively ruined the GSCI, the Dow Jones–UBS, and other commodity trackers in a world where the degree of contango, the scenario in which commodity contracts tied to future prices were pricier than current commodities, wasn't big enough to bury them. It was unfortunate that Calpers and others had failed, they said, but, in a way, it was justified, because the pension funds had become the dumb money and it was time to get smarter about regular people's cash.

"I'm not a fan of the indexes," said Jeff Scott, chief investment officer at the $74 billion financial firm Wurts & Associates, which had used commodities as a portfolio hedge over the years, as the rotation got under way.

"In this space, it has to be a thoughtful, probably active-manager approach," he added. "Do we need to have lean hogs in the portfolio? That may not be the best thing. And a lot of stuff is packaged together that we don't need."

Scott, who was implementing other tools in his investment mix in order to curb the risk of inflation—one of those problems for which you want positions that aren't correlated to the stock market, like commodities—had a point. But the trouble with commodities ranged far beyond simple performance numbers. Because of actual misdeeds and regulatory clampdowns to ward off expected future ones, the raw-material trading industry itself was getting a bad name. The failures of the Peregrine Financial Group, the Iowa futures brokerage that filed for bankruptcy in 2012 after its founder made off with more than $215 million in customer funds, and of MF Global, which had been ordered by the courts to make harmed customers whole, had eroded trust in U.S. contract trading overall. Dodd-Frank had made house trading at banks nearly impossible and made "swap," or private contract, trading more cumbersome, and stood to make futures trading less profitable. Even with Gensler on his way out, the CFTC was winning greater respect in commodity circles, and other regulators, like the Federal Energy Regulatory Commission, or FERC, and the Justice Department, were taking on higher-profile trading investigations too.

In 2013 JPMorgan was charged by FERC with manipulating regional power markets in the U.S. by using elaborate pricing schemes. The bank was fined $410 million on its civil violations alone, and the U.S. Attorney in Manhattan continued to investigate possible criminal actions in the matter. In the throes of the FERC settlement talks, JPMorgan announced plans to sell off its physical commodities business altogether. Morgan Stanley too, beset by trader departures and dwindling revenue, was in on-and-off talks with suitors to buy its commodities division. Just before Christmas 2013, Morgan Stanley announced plans to sell its oil and gas assets to the Russian producer Rosneft, where Morgan's former chief executive, John Mack, was a director. The CFTC inquiry into Ruggles's personal account continued, with no clear resolution pending. (About a year after his departure from Delta, Ruggles told me he had given up trading; he had landed a job consulting with the energy business at the private-equity firm the Carlyle Group.)

Meanwhile, the exposure of Goldman's aluminum-warehousing practices spurred multiple government probes as well as a private lawsuit accusing it of anticompetitive behavior. In November 2014, a two-year investigation by the Senate Permanent Subcommittee on Investigations, the bipartisan panel chaired by Carl Levin—the Democratic lawmaker who had published numerous studies on the U.S. commodity markets—became an embarrassing spectacle for the bank. In a scathing, 400-page report published by the subcommittee, Goldman was repeatedly criticized for its handling of the Metro metal-storage business, where it reportedly engaged in "merry-go-round transactions," moving client aluminum from one Detroit-area warehouse to another in order to jack up revenue from holding the metal even as buyers of it faced long waits and higher surcharges in the U.S. markets. In a reporter briefing the day of the report's release, Levin was blunt in his depiction of Goldman's behavior: "Goldman's warehouse operations were being manipulated to lengthen the queue," he said, noting that the questionable metal deals had occurred at a time when the firm was also expanding its own trading in aluminum and aluminum-related financial products.

Levin was inferring that Goldman's commodity traders might

have benefited from insider knowledge of what was happening in Metro's physical-metal business, a brand of behavior that, while not inherently illegal and, in fact, widespread on Wall Street during the 2000s, the firm had long denied. The report noted that sensitive information about Metro's business—including details that might have been of value to metal traders—had been shared over the years with fifty Goldman employees, including some with oversight of the commodity-trading business. In addition, the report explained, Metro's board of directors was stacked with Goldman officials, some of whom were closely involved with commodities trading and investments.

The firm was adamant that its behavior was above board. Early in the week of a two-day Senate hearing on the matter, Goldman released its own position paper on the aluminum-storage issues and held its own advance briefing with reporters. A central finding in the Senate panel's voluminous study was that Metro had arranged side deals with a handful of clients—including Glencore and Red Kite, a closely-held British metal-trading hedge fund—to create the metaphorical "merry-go-round" of metal, effectively lengthening the wait for aluminum in the U.S. overall by clogging up the available ground transport systems for short-term financial gain. But the firm insisted that pushing up aluminum prices in the U.S.—something that occurred against the backdrop of falling aluminum prices on the benchmark exchange—was never its aim. "The queues were the result of metal owners' independent, financially-motivated decisions to remove metal that had been placed in Metro's warehouses," Goldman's own report stated. "Like any other landlord, Metro was merely competing for tenants."

Levin's two-day hearing on Metro and other bank commodity

holdings emphasized the systemic risks that owning oil tankers, pipelines, coal mines, and other physical raw-material operations brought to the American financial industry. The Senator was adamant that those assets be sold to more appropriate operators, whose brushes with disaster wouldn't risk another U.S. taxpayer bailout. Goldman, as it turned out, was already on it; months before the Senate hearings, it had announced plans to sell Metro.

While Goldman may have been singled out for the most public humiliation as commodities went out of vogue, some of its European counterparts faced unpleasant brushes with infamy, too. In Europe, Tony "Chocfinger" Ward's cocoa corner had embarrassed the industry, and Glencore's IPO had inadvertently invited a period of painful new scrutiny. Just a few years after the U.N. oil-for-food scandal and Trafi's toxic-waste incident in the Ivory Coast, the physical commodity traders were again seen as mercenaries who left damage in their wake.

They could shrug off the tabloid rich lists and accounts of their children partying with celebrities (the subject of an anonymous gossip item in the *New York Post* involving Ivan Glasenberg's daughter), but the more substantive allegations resonated. During its negotiations with Xstrata alone, Glencore was the subject of two astonishing documentaries: "Stealing Africa," an account of its Zambian copper-mining business that highlighted how the country actually lost money by providing electricity to miners like Glencore while they in turn siphoned out $3 billion in revenue; and a BBC documentary that revealed child laborers working on Glencore mining property in the Democratic Republic of Congo. Glencore fought the allegations, arguing that it never employed minors and that the children depicted in the documentary were associated with local squatters, but the revelations kept coming.

∎

The secret club, for the most part, held firm, fueled by its own finances, its prominence in the industry, and, to some extent, its raw talent. Bank ownership would come and go, regulatory priorities would change, and investors might occasionally walk away. But even forty years after Marc Rich had monopolized the crude-oil trading market, there still weren't that many players with whom to share the spoils. A global presence in numerous commodity-trading markets was a rare thing indeed, a recipe for making money if you knew what you were doing. And a true knack for wagering on the price vicissitudes of crude, copper, or cotton remained a profitable skill in almost any environment—especially when only a handful of individuals in the world could really do it well and on a large scale.

Andurand is a case in point. Early in 2013, he opened his new firm, Andurand Capital, and settled the remaining legal issues with Dennis Crema amicably. He even sent me an e-mail saying what a nice guy his former partner was and that he hoped their relationship would come off well in this book. The first six or so months at the new fund went terrifically for Andurand. Settled in Knightsbridge and employing some of the very same staff—including Neel Patel and Paul Feldman—that BlueGold once had, Andurand Capital generated more than 50 percent returns as of midyear, betting rightly on the inefficiencies in the market for Brent crude contracts compared to their West Texas Intermediate siblings.

The young Frenchman was back in the press, chatting about kickboxing and crude-oil spreads, being mentioned as the husband of a stunning former model, and generally succeeding at a time when others failed. By the fall, however, that bet on the spread, or gap, between Brent and West Texas crude had shaved off some of those gains. Still, Andurand was ahead. By the end of 2013, he was up 24 percent, and was managing more than $200 million. His onetime rival, Jean Bourlot, was less fortunate; at the same time Andurand Capital was preparing investor presentations to highlight its maiden year, Bourlot's London-based hedge fund, Higgs Capital, was shutting down. So, for that matter, was Arbalet Capital, the fund Jennifer Fan had opened in 2012. She soon joined the hedge fund Millennium Management as a commodity trader there. She was thirty.

Like Andurand, former Xstrata head Mick Davis was a success story. Late in 2013, just months after the rancorous Glencore deal had been finalized, he announced an initial funding round of $1 billion for his new mining venture, X2 Resources. Backed by two respected investors, Asia's Noble Group and the private-equity firm TPG, Davis was predicting mining gains at a time when the company he'd just left had written down $7.7 billion, largely on losses related to Xstrata assets. His impressive reputation, it appeared, had preceded him—and investors were willing to provide him with an influx of cash to use. Not surprisingly, Brett Olsher helped advise on the deal.

ACKNOWLEDGMENTS

What you have just read is the result of a three-year undertaking that was made possible by an array of sources, associates, and friends who are too many in number to name here. The shortlist follows.

My job at CNBC introduced me to the commodities world with stories on key players in natural gas, agriculture, and crude-oil trading. Once I latched on to the topic, Mark Hoffman and Nik Deogun generously encouraged my efforts, allowing me time for travel and writing. Many thanks to them, as well as to Nick Dunn, Lacy O'Toole, and especially my indefatigable producer, Dawn Giel, for their ongoing support. Thanks as well to Mary Duffy, Brian Steel, Jim Cramer, Robert Frank, Phil LeBeau, David Faber, Mary Thompson, Gennine Uliasz, and Max Meyers for their encouragement, and also to Mary Ann Lateano-Fox and Patty DelVecchio for their help with my author photo.

Bob Barnett, my lawyer and longtime friend, offered great counsel as always.

Adrian Zackheim, my past and current publisher, was stalwart. Through numerous calls, lunches, and the occasional emergency huddle on Hudson Street, we made a game plan. Emily Angell offered encouragement when it was most sorely needed. The tireless Allison McLean had a marketing plan from day one. Will Weisser was a consistent advocate, Joe Perez and Chris Sergio designed a smashing cover, and Jesse Maeshiro helped push the book across the finish line. Liz Hazelton, Jacqueline Burke, Brittany Weinke, and Linda Cowen also provided essential help in the final throes of the process.

Within the world of commodity trading, my rabbis are many. Some of my best sources, of course, can't be named. But here is a partial list of people whose knowledge and assistance were deeply appreciated: Dwight Anderson, Bill Bagley, Jeff Christian, Jeff Currie, Billy Dunavant, Buck Dunavant, David Frenk, Andy Kelleher, Herman Kohlmeyer, Doug Leslie, David Lilley, Mike Masters, Jason Mraz, Neel Patel, Craig Pirrong, Beau Taylor, Eli Tullis, Chris Wibbelman, and Trevor Woods. In addition, Stuart Burns, Chris Grams, Miriam Heywood, Brookly McLaughlin, and Michael Southwood went above and beyond in sharing research and other insights.

I must of course thank Pierre Andurand, Bart Chilton, Gary Cohn, Jennifer Fan, Gary Gensler, and Jon and Ivonne Ruggles, who spent considerable time telling me their personal stories; in some cases, they also made colleagues and family members available to talk to me. And to those traders, bankers, hedge-fund managers, investors, farmers, analysts, and academics who haven't been named: You know who you are, and I thank you.

In the course of researching this book I had the good fortune to stumble upon an exceptionally smart, diligent, and, perhaps most important, cheerful researcher: Krista Dugan. The book's tight time frame and technical bent made her job that much more difficult, and she handled it all with aplomb. Many thanks, Krista.

I'm grateful to my friends in faraway places, who made the field reporting much easier. Thanks especially to Cassell Bryan-Low, Niels Bryan-Low, Jonny Horsman, and Bruce Orwall, who made London feel like a second home. (Honorable mention also goes to Triyoga, the Arsenal Football Club, and Blakes Hotel.)

I was shameless in asking for practical advice, and my friends and former colleagues magnanimously indulged me. Thanks to Dana Cimilluca, who provided invaluable insight on the Glencore-Xstrata deal; Sheelah Kolhatkar, who gamely read the manuscript and commiserated with me over our mutual juggles in court, at Starbucks, and in many other settings; and Chris Stewart and Andrew Goldman, who read semifinalized chapters and provided suggestions for improvement. Sarah Ellison, Leigh Gallagher, and Mike Siconolfi talked me out of numerous reporting (and personal) crises. Thanks also to my comrades Greg Ip, Charles Duhigg, and Bethany McLean.

Before all those people came the unsinkable Peter W. Kaplan, who died the weekend I finished writing this book. Peter gave me my first crack at reporting while I was still in college, and was the only newspaper editor willing to hire me once I graduated. His curiosity, tenacity, and love of good prose have inspired me ever since. I will miss him dearly, but I've tried to keep in mind the advice he shared from one of his own mentors, Clay Felker: Never hold your best stuff.

Finally, but most important, thanks to the friends and family who believed in me throughout the project, among them Gretchen Drobnyk, Erin Greenwell, Lauren Grodstein, Glenn Kenny, Merissa Marr, Jodie Morse, Julian Pritchard, and Claire Rush. Thanks to Joy Villas Barimbao and Agnes Dziedzic, who helped keep things together on the home front, and to my parents, Pat and Joe Kelly, for

ACKNOWLEDGMENTS

inspiring me to do journalism and write books (and, many years later, for babysitting my kids so I could finish them). Thanks finally to my stepdaughter, Laney, and my son, Zack, for indulging my hobby; to my favorite boy, Bogart, for always being there for a hug; and to my husband, Kyle, for absolutely everything: cooking, caring for the children, brainstorming, editing, and providing emotional support. And most of all for my baby, Josie, for parting with me during such a tender time and still somehow turning out a mama's girl. This book is especially for you.

NOTES

1. THE BUBBLE

1 **hovering in the low $120s:** Prices for ICE's Brent crude futures and CME's Light Sweet Crude, or WTI, futures are used throughout the book. Crude-oil pricing data was provided by each respective exchange.

5 **maintains a minor presence:** "The Composition of the Cent," *United States Mint*, https://www.usmint.gov/about_the_mint/fun_facts/?action=fun_facts2.

5 **cigarette lighters:** "Cerium," *Royal Society of Chemistry*, http://www.rsc.org/periodic-table/element/58/cerium.

5 **movie-projection bulbs:** "Cerium," *Making Science Make Sense* (Bayer US), http://www.bayerus.com/msms/msms_science_fun/PeriodicTable/cerium/index.aspx.

6 **More than three thousand years ago:** Irving Finkel, curator, British Museum, London, e-mail correspondence, July 16, 2013.

6 **trading of commodities:** Edward J. Swan, *Building the Global Market: A 4000 Year History of Derivatives* (Amsterdam: Wolters Kluwer, 2000).

6 **Dutch traders who exchanged tulips:** Mike Dash, *Tulipomania: The Story of the World's Most Coveted Flower & the Extraordinary Passions It Aroused* (New York: Crown, 2000).

6 **Commodity trading came to the U.S.:** Swan, *Building the Global Market*.

6 **500 million:** Extrapolated from data in Galen Burghardt, "FIA Annual Volume: Data," *Futures Industry*, March 2004, http://www.futuresindustry.org/fi-magazine-home.asp?a=910.

6 **2 billion:** Extrapolated from data in Galen Burghardt and Will Acworth, "Volume Trends: Decline in the West, Surge in the East," *Futures Industry*, March 2010, http://www.futuresindustry.org/files/css/magazineArticles/article-1448.pdf.

7 **about $800 billion:** Claudio Borio et al., eds., "International Banking and Financial Market Developments," Bank for International Settlements, *BIS Quarterly Review* (December 2004), p. A99, http://www.bis.org/publ/qtr pdf/r_qt0412.pdf.

7 **More than $13 trillion:** Claudio Borio et al., eds., Bank for International Settlements, *BIS Quarterly Review* (December 2009), p. A103, http://www.bis.org/publ/qtrpdf/r_qt0912.pdf.

8 **"supercycle":** Bilge Ertan and Jose Antonio Ocampo, "Super-cycles of Commodity Prices Since the Mid-19th Century" (working paper, United Nations Department of Economic and Social Affairs, New York, 2012), http://www.un.org/esa/desa/papers/2012/wp110_2012.pdf.

8 **"Peak Oil":** The term refers to a theory, first put forth in 1956 by scientist M. King Hubbert, which argued that oil production in the U.S. would reach its highest point in the latter half of the twentieth century and would decline thereafter. In the 2000s, the concept of Peak Oil took on new meaning, defining a generalized fear of running out of oil, and the global consequences that would bring. See M. King Hubbert, *Nuclear Energy and the Fossil Fuels* (Shell Development Company Exploration and Production Research Division, 1956), http://www.hubbertpeak.com/hubbert/1956/1956.pdf. For a succinct discussion of how "Peak Oil" played in the public's mind in the 2000s, see Daniel Yergin, "There Will Be Oil," *Wall Street Journal*, September 17, 2011, http://online.wsj.com/news/articles/SB10001424053111904060604576572552998674340.1.

10 **John Arnold . . . philanthropist:** Leah McGrath Goodman, "When a Billionaire Trader Loses His Edge," *Fortune*, May 4, 2012, http://finance.fortune.cnn.com/tag/john-arnold/.

15 **the resultant $4 per gallon price of gasoline:** Jad Mouawad, "Congress Looks for a Culprit for Rising Oil Prices," *New York Times*, June 25, 2008, http://www.nytimes.com/2008/06/25/business/25oil.html?_r=0.

15 **where members of Congress held forty hearings:** Ibid.

15 **their own records showed:** U.S. Commodity Futures Trading Commission, *Staff Report on Commodity Swap Dealers and Index Traders with Commission Recommendations*, Washington, D.C., September 2008, http://www.cftc.gov/ucm/groups/public/@newsroom/documents/file/cftcstaffreportonswapdealers09.pdf.

16 **grain prices were causing revolution:** Troy Sternberg, "Chinese Drought, Wheat, and the Egyptian Uprising: How a Localized Hazard Became Globalized," *The Arab Spring and Climate Change: A Climate and Security Correlations Series* (Center for American Progress, Stimson and the Center for Climate and Security, February 2013), http://climateandsecurity.files.wordpress.com/2012/04/climatechangearabspring-ccs-cap-stimson.pdf.

16 **commodity indexes like the GSCI were to blame:** David Frenk and Wallace Turbeville, "Commodity Index Traders and the Boom/Bust Cycle in Commodities Prices," posted October 18, 2011, http://papers.ssrn.com/sol3/papers.cfm?abstract_id=1945570.

16 **2 percent on a single day:** Matt Whittaker, "Traders Flee from Gold after Goldman News," *Wall Street Journal*, April 16, 2010, http://online.wsj.com/news/articles/SB10001424052702303491304575187840789262772#printMode?KEYWORDS=Paulson+gold.

2. THE SPECULATOR

25 **French oil and gas company Total:** Telis Demos, "Goldman's Commodities Queen," *Fortune*, September 25, 2008, http://money.cnn.com/2008/09/24/news/companies/Goldman_demos.fortune/index.htm.

25 **Singapore was a big oil processing center:** "Singapore Overview," *U.S. Energy Information Administration*, http://www.eia.gov/countries/cab.cfm?fips=SN.

32 **China Aviation Oil (Singapore) Corporation Ltd.:** Wayne Arnold, "Failed China Fuel Supplier Waited Too Long for Help," *New York Times*, December 4, 2004, http://www.nytimes.com/2004/12/04/business/worldbusiness/04losses.html?pagewanted=print&position=&_r=0.

34 **up to 10 percent of active, or "open," contracts:** David Cho, "A Few Speculators Dominate Vast Market for Oil Trading," *Washington Post*, August 21, 2008, http://online.wsj.com/news/articles/SB10001424052748704285104575491981967381818.

36 **close to 10 percent apiece:** "World Economic Outlook, April 2008: Housing and the Business Cycle," *International Monetary Fund*, p. 81. http://www.imf.org/external/pubs/ft/weo/2008/01/pdf/text.pdf.

36 **the most severe winter weather in fifty years:** John Liu and Li Xiaowei, "China Tries to Restore Power; Storms Forecast to Ease," Bloomberg, February 4, 2008, http://www.bloomberg.com/apps/news?pid=newsarchive&sid=a44nuzlAd5Xo&refer=home.

37 **poor government planning:** Jane Louis, "Lights Out in SA, but Gold and Platinum Glow Bright," *Hard Assets*, January 28, 2008, http://www.resourceinvestor.com/2008/01/28/lights-out-in-sa-but-gold-and-platinum-glow-bright.

37 **"Peak Oil":** M. *King* Hubbert, *Nuclear Energy and the Fossil Fuels* (1959), and Daniel Yergin, "There Will Be Oil" (2011).

40 **nuclear weapon in Iran, or labor strikes in Nigeria:** Jad Mouawad, "Oil Prices Take a Nerve-Rattling Jump Past $138," *New York Times*, June 7, 2008, http://www.nytimes.com/2008/06/07/business/07oil.html.

40 **"This whole industry" . . . 1850s:** Jad Mouawad and Diana B. Henriques, "Why Is Oil So High? Pick a View," *New York Times*, June 21, 2008, http://www.nytimes.com/2008/06/21/business/21oil.html?pagewanted=all.

42 **Companies like Marathon Oil:** "Even Big Oil Feels the Price Pinch," *New York Times*, DealBook blog, July 31, 2008, http://dealbook.nytimes.com/2008/07/31/even-big-oil-feels-the-price-pinch/.

42 **Ikea and DuPont:** Larry Rohter, "Shipping Costs Start to Crimp Globalization," *New York Times*, August 3, 2008, http://www.nytimes.com/2008/08/03/business/worldbusiness/03global.html?pagewanted=2.

43 **American International Group:** Adam Davidson, "How AIG Fell Apart," Reuters, September 18, 2008, http://www.reuters.com/article/2008/09/18/us-how-aig-fell-apart-idUSMAR85972720080918.

43 **WTI experienced a record pop:** "Record One-Day Jump in Oil Price," *BBC News*, September 22, 2008, http://news.bbc.co.uk/2/hi/7630513.stm.

3. THE FIRM THAT MARC RICH BUILT

47 **$4 billion in bank lines:** Glencore Third Quarter Investor Update, November 12, 2008, p. 10, http://www.glencorexstrata.com/assets/Uploads/ 200811120800-Investor-presentation.pdf.

47 **Marc Rich:** Daniel Ammann, *The King of Oil: The Secret Lives of Marc Rich* (New York: St. Martin's Press, 2009). Much of the information in this chapter related to Marc Rich and the history of Marc Rich & Co. is drawn from Ammann's work.

47 **first to take advantage:** Ibid.

48 **a €7.5 million house:** David Robertson, "Superbright, Disarmingly Quiet: The Stealth Approach to Wealth," *The Times*, May 21, 2011, http://www.thetimes.co .uk/tto/news/uk/article3027294.ece.

48 **"investment banking times three":** Eric Onstad, Laura MacInnis, and Quentin Webb, "Special Report: The Biggest Company You've Never Heard Of," Reuters, February 25, 2011, http://www.reuters.com/article/2011/02/25/ us-glencore-idUSTRE71O1DC20110225.

49 **$87 million apiece:** Ann Davis, "Commodity King: Aggressive Swiss Giant Rides Resources Boom," *Wall Street Journal*, July 31, 2007.

50 **record profits of $6.1 billion through price levels:** Saijel Kishan, "Glencore 2007 Profit Jumps to Record $6.1 Billion," Bloomberg, March 11, 2008, http:// www.bloomberg.com/apps/news?pid=newsarchive&sid=aS_wQurA8Kuo& refer=latin_america.

52 **for €900,000:** Jane Baird and Natalie Harrison, "Glencore Credit Derivative Spreads Widen Sharply," Reuters, October 21, 2008, http://uk.reuters.com/ article/2008/10/21/glencore-cds-idUKLL27496720081021.

54 **an independent commission report:** Paul A. Volcker, Richard J. Goldstone, and Mark Pieth, "Manipulation of the Oil for Food Programme by the Iraqi Regime," *Independent Inquiry Committee into the United Nations Oil-for-Food Programme*, October 27, 2005. Glencore's written response to the allegations can be found on page 196.

55 **fled the Nazis with his family . . . status in the industry:** Ammann, *King of Oil* and author reporting.

56 **at least $1 billion:** Kelly Phillips Erb, "Marc Rich, Famous Fugitive & Alleged Tax Evader Pardoned by President Clinton, Dies," *Forbes*, June 27, 2013, http:// www.forbes.com/sites/kellyphillipserb/2013/06/27/marc-rich-famous- fugitive-alleged-tax-evader-pardoned-by-president-clinton-dies/.

56 **South Africa . . . Rich's standing in it:** Ammann, *King of Oil* and author reporting.

57 **Rich sold his 51 percent stake:** David Henry, " 'King of Oil' Marc Rich, controversial commodities trader and former fugitive, dies at age 78," *Bloomberg News*, June 26, 2013, http://business.financialpost.com/2013/06/26/marc-rich -dies/.

57 **three grown daughters . . . making it to the hospital:** Ammann, *King of Oil*.

58 **upon his death from a stroke:** Erb, "Marc Rich, Famous Fugitive."

59 **a controlling interest:** Onstad, MacInnis, and Webb, "Biggest Company You've Never Heard Of."

59 **forced to sell:** Eric Onstad, "Xstrata Shareholders Approve $5.9 Billion Rights Issue," Reuters, March 2, 2009, http://uk.reuters.com/article/2009/03/02/uk-xstrata-idUKTRE5212JW20090302.

59 **candle-wax trade:** Javier Blas, "Commodities: Into the Spotlight," *Financial Times*, April 10, 2011, with additional reporting by the author.

4. THE BANKS

65 **once used by the energy company Texaco:** Elsa Brenner, "Morgan Stanley Seals Deal on Texaco Headquarters," *New York Times*, March 31, 2002, http://www.nytimes.com/2002/03/31/nyregion/in-business-morgan-stanley-seals-deal-on-texaco-headquarters.html.

65 **after the terrorist attacks:** Ibid.

66 **14 percent of their combined total fixed-income revenue:** "Coalition Index—2012," *Coalition Development Ltd.*, February 2013.

69 **a quarter of Goldman's pretax income:** Gregory Zuckerman and Susanne Craig, "To Weather Rocky Period, Goldman Makes Riskier Bets," *Wall Street Journal*, December 17, 2002, http://online.wsj.com/news/articles/SB1040074780804862913.

69 **$4 billion in trading profits:** Kate Kelly, "How Goldman Won Big on Mortgage Meltdown," *Wall Street Journal*, December 14, 2007, http://online.wsj.com/news/articles/SB119759714037228585.

70 **$9 billion write-down:** Morgan Stanley, "Morgan Stanley Reports Fourth Quarter and Full Year Results," news release, December 19, 2007, http://www.morganstanley.com/about/ir/shareholder/4q2007.pdf.

75 **a quarter of the country's crude-oil production:** Lawrence Kumins and Robert Bamberger, "Oil and Gas Disruptions from Hurricanes Katrina and Rita," *Congressional Research Service Report for Congress*, October 21, 2005, http://fpc.state.gov/documents/organization/55824.pdf.

76 **gas contracts rose 20 percent:** Jad Mouawad, Simon Romero, et al., "Gas Prices Surge as Supply Drops," *New York Times*, September 1, 2005, http://www.nytimes.com/2005/09/01/business/01oil.html?pagewanted=all&_r=0.

76 **George W. Bush vowed to tap:** Ibid.

76 **John Mack, a veteran:** Gregory Cresci and Adrian Cox, "Morgan Stanley Makes Mack Chief Executive to Replace Purcell," Bloomberg, June 30, 2005, http://www.bloomberg.com/apps/news?pid=newsarchive&sid=aYfgRpHtthcE&refer=home.

78 **$3.2 billion on an order for a dozen:** Massoud A. Derhally and Andrea Rothman, "Emirates May Sell 30% Stake in Initial Public Offer," Bloomberg, November 13, 2007, http://www.bloomberg.com/apps/news?pid=newsarchive&sid=apCr91hDXFbc&refer=europe.

82 **was being criticized:** "Debt Crisis Puts Spotlight on Dubai World," *CBC News*, November 27, 2009, http://www.cbc.ca/news/world/debt-crisis-puts-spotlight-on-dubai-world-1.832960.

82 **two drunken British travelers:** Barbara Surk, "British Tourists Get Three Month Sentence in Dubai Sex-on-Beach Trial," *USA Today*, October 16, 2008,

http://usatoday30.usatoday.com/travel/news/2008-10-16-dubai-sex-on-beach-trial_n.htm.

5. THE REGULATORS

85 **demise of the energy trader Enron:** Richard Oppel and Andrew Ross Sorkin, "Enron's Collapse: The Overview; Enron Collapses as Suitor Cancels Plans for Merger," *New York Times*, November 29, 2001, http://www.nytimes.com/2001/11/29/business/enron-s-collapse-the-overview-enron-collapses-as-suitor-cancels-plans-for-merger.html.

85 **Its seminal report:** Permanent Subcommittee on Investigations, *The Role of Speculation in Rising Oil and Gas Prices: A Need to Put the Cop Back on the Street*, 109th Cong., 2d sess., 2006, S. Prt. 109–65.

88 **In 1975, it opened for business:** Emily Lambert, *The Futures: The Rise of the Speculator and the Origins of the World's Biggest Markets* (New York: Basic Books, 2011). Bagley was interviewed for this book in October 2013. Some of the details he recounted can also be found in Lambert's *The Futures*. Additional details on the Hunt brothers' soybean corner and the London options scandal can be found in the works below.

88 **a soybean-market manipulation by the Hunt brothers:** Harry Hurt III, *Texas Rich: The Hunt Dynasty from the Early Oil Days Through the Silver Crash* (W. W. Norton, 1982).

89 **a group of con men:** "Business: Options Scam in Boston," *Time*, January 30, 1978, http://content.time.com/time/subscriber/article/0,33009,945904-1,00.html.

90 **$4 per gallon:** Jad Mouawad, "Congress Looks for a Culprit for Rising Oil Prices."

93 **In 1990, he advised the National Football League:** Kurt Eichenwald, "Investment Bankers Play Football's Newest Position," *New York Times*, March 19, 1990, http://www.nytimes.com/1990/03/19/business/investment-bankers-play-football-s-newest-position.html?src=pm.

93 **major financial scandal:** Paula Dwyer et al., "The Lesson from Barings' Straits," *BusinessWeek*, March 12, 1995, http://www.businessweek.com/stories/1995-03-12/the-lesson-from-barings-straits.

93 **Barings Bank:** Richard W. Stevenson, "Young Trader's $29 Billion Bet Brings Down a Venerable Firm," *New York Times*, February 28, 1995, http://www.nytimes.com/1995/02/28/us/collapse-barings-overview-young-trader-s-29-billion-bet-brings-down-venerable.html.

95 **"murder boards":** A commonly used term in Washington. Insights into the origins of the term can be found here: William Safire, "On Language: Murder Board at the Skunk Works," *New York Times Magazine*, October 11, 1987, http://www.nytimes.com/1987/10/11/magazine/on-language-murder-board-at-the-skunk-works.html.

96 **Gensler's twin brother:** Mara Der Hovanesian, "The Gensler Twins: Identical? Don't You Believe It," *Bloomberg Businessweek*, November 17, 2002, http://www

.businessweek.com/stories/2002-11-17/the-gensler-twins-identical-dont-you-believe-it.

96 **hometown of Baltimore:** Hanah Cho, "Longtime T. Rowe Manager Robert Gensler to Retire," *Baltimore Sun*, April 13, 2012, http://articles.baltimoresun .com/2012-04-13/business/bs-bz-trowe-gensler-retirement-20120413_1_ research-analyst-money-manager-media-telecommunications-fund.

97 **first financial-services industry speech:** Gary Gensler, "Remarks of Chairman Gary Gensler Before the Managed Funds Association" (keynote address, Managed Funds Association Forum, Chicago, Ill., June 24, 2009).

98 **Kenneth Medlock and Amy Myers Jaffe:** Kenneth B. Medlock III and Amy Myers Jaffe, "Who Is in the Oil Futures Market and How Has It Changed?," The James A. Baker III Institute for Public Policy, Rice University, August 26, 2009, http://bakerinstitute.org/media/files/news/94bb2e2c/EF-pub-MedlockJaffeOilFuturesMarket-082609.pdf.

98 **immediately panned the study:** Craig Pirrong, "Have You Heard the One About the Baker Institute and the Oil Speculators?," Streetwise Professor blog, August 28, 2009, http://streetwiseprofessor.com/?p=2454.

99 **Energy users like:** Will Acworth, "CFTC Examines Position Limits," *Futures Industry*, September 2009, http://www.futuresindustry.org/downloads/Sep_09-Pos_Limits.pdf.

99 **proposed energy position limits in the** *Federal Register*: Commodity Futures Trading Commission, "Position Limits for Derivatives," *Federal Register* 76, no. 17 (January 2011): 4752.

100 **during a lunch:** Ian Katz and Robert Schmidt, "A Goldman Guy Turns on the Street," *Bloomberg Businessweek*, February 11, 2010, http://www.businessweek .com/magazine/content/10_08/b4167068042271.htm, plus additional reporting by the author.

102 **who had gotten his start at PhiBro:** Julia Werdigier and Julie Creswell, "Trader's Cocoa Binge Wraps Up Chocolate Market," *New York Times*, DealBook blog, July 26, 2010, http://dealbook.nytimes.com/2010/07/26/traders-cocoa-binge-wraps-up-chocolate-market/.

102 **nearly every bean:** Jack Farchy, "Hedge Fund Develops Taste for Chocolate Assets," *Financial Times*, July 16, 2010, http://www.ft.com/intl/cms/s/0/e50feefc-9120-11df-b297-00144feab49a.html#axzz2tnvm8YRW.

102 **had shot to their highest price since 1977:** Christopher Leake and Rob Cooper, "Choc Finger: Meet the Real-Life Willy Wonka Who's Just Bought an Incredible £658m of Cocoa Beans," *Daily Mail*, July 18, 2010, http://www.dailymail.co.uk/news/article-1295608/Choc-finger-Meet-real-life-Willy-Wonka-Anthony-Ward-whos-just-bought-incredible-658m-cocoa-beans-.html.

102 **published pictures of him:** Ibid.

102 **Ward's face on a pig's body:** Werdigier and Creswell, "Trader's Cocoa Binge."

102 **German Cocoa Trade Association:** Ibid.

103 **cocoa fell dramatically:** Caroline Henshaw, "Armajaro Releases Stocks as Cocoa Bet Melts," *Wall Street Journal*, December 16, 2010, http://online.wsj.com/news/articles/SB10001424052748704828104576021501880774790?mod=rss_markets_main.

6. THE HEDGER

106 **world's biggest consumers of fuel:** Hunter Keay (managing director, senior airline analyst, Wolfe Research), in phone call with author's researcher, November 2013.

107 **"out of control" and "silent killer":** Mary Jane Credeur, Mary Schlangenstein, and Paul Burkhardt, "United, Delta Profit at Risk on 'Silent Killer' Hedges," Bloomberg, January 31, 2011, http://www.bloomberg.com/news/2011-01-31/united-delta-profit-at-risk-from-silent-killer-in-fuel-hedges.html.

108 **considering making fare hikes:** Ibid.

109 **having cut six thousand jobs:** "Court Approves Delta's Emergence from Bankruptcy Protection," *New York Times*, April 26, 2007, http://www.nytimes.com/2007/04/26/business/worldbusiness/26iht-delta.1.5448309.html?_r=0.

109 **A Texas native . . . new chief executive:** Dan Reed, "Executive Suite: Delta Chief Takes Unlikely Flight Path," *USA Today*, February 14, 2008, http://usatoday30.usatoday.com/travel/flights/2007-10-21-delta-ceo-anderson_N.htm and author reporting.

111 **$1.2 billion:** Matt Cameron, "Airlines Use Aircraft as Alternative to Cash in Margin Calls," *Risk*, August 17, 2009, http://www.risk.net/print_article/risk-magazine/news/1530797/airlines-aircraft-alternative-cash-margin-calls.

111 **new record high each month:** Food and Agriculture Organization of the United Nations, "World Food Prices Reach New Historic Peak," February 3, 2011, http://www.fao.org/news/story/en/item/50519/icode/.

112 **twenty-six-year-old Tunisian fruit and vegetable vendor:** Kareem Fahim, "Slap to a Man's Pride Set Off Tumult in Tunisia," *New York Times*, January 21, 2011, http://www.nytimes.com/2011/01/22/world/africa/22sidi.html?pagewanted=all&_r=0.

112 **Facebook, Twitter, and other social media:** David D. Kirkpatrick, "Tunisia Leader Flees and Prime Minister Claims Power," *New York Times*, January 14, 2011, http://www.nytimes.com/2011/01/15/world/africa/15tunis.html?pagewanted=1&_r=0.

112 **Their ranks soon swelled to hundreds of thousands:** "Egypt Protests—Friday, February 4," *Guardian*, February 4, 2011, http://www.theguardian.com/world/blog/2011/feb/04/egypt-protests-day-departure-live.

112 **food prices were a particular stressor:** Sternberg, "Chinese Drought, Wheat and the Egyptian Uprising."

113 **which produced up to 1.6 million barrels:** International Energy Agency, "Efforts to Restore Oil Production in Libya Are Progressing Faster Than Anticipated," http://www.iea.org/newsroomandevents/news/2011/november/2011-11-15.html.

117 **David Becker:** Becker had been made a managing director at Citi at the relatively young age of thirty-four and would have eventually headed commodities there. But he was fired from the firm in 2004, and, two years later, he pleaded guilty to criminal charges that he falsely inflated commodities-trading profits in order to win a bigger personal bonus. He was eventually sentenced to fifteen months in prison. See United States Attorney for the Southern District of New York, "Former Head of Citibank Commodities Sentenced to 15 Months for Falsely Inflating Profits by up to $20 Million," news release, March 19, 2007, http://www.justice.gov/usao/nys/pressreleases/March07/beckersentencingpr.pdf;

and David Glovin, "Ex-Citigroup Trader Claimed 'Widespread' Wrongdoing," *Bloomberg*, March 2, 2007, http://www.bloomberg.com/apps/news?pid= newsarchive&sid=aVLH7JTz2EaE.

119 **Trafi also exposed Ruggles:** The raid Ruggles remembers came during a period when Trafi was under intense scrutiny by regulators in both the U.S. and abroad. The next year, Trafi would plead guilty in federal court to selling oil to U.S. companies under false pretenses—namely, that they were shipments legitimately obtained through the United Nations oil-for-food program, introduced in the 1990s to help Iraqis suffering from international trade embargoes. As part of its guilty plea, Trafi paid nearly $10 million in fines and penalties and forfeited another $10 million that had been frozen in a corporate bank account. See Harvey Rice, "Firm Pleads Guilty in Oil-For-Food Case, *Houston Chronicle*, May 26, 2006, http://www.chron.com/business/energy/arti cle/Firm-pleads-guilty-in-Oil-For-Food-case-1862731.php.

119 **Ivory Coast government:** Trafi's conflict with the Ivory Coast occurred in the summer of 2006 and involved the dumping of 400 metric tons of petrochemical waste from a tanker ship it had leased. For a cut-rate fee, Trafi hired a local sanitation company to handle the materials, and the company dumped the hazardous sludge in various locations near a major city, ultimately killing at least ten people and sickening thousands. In the initial aftermath of the event, the Ivory Coast's prime minister fired his entire government and Trafi co-founder Claude Dauphin served five months in jail without ever being charged. But most of the administration was later reinstated, and Trafi eventually settled the matter without admitting wrongdoing. See Lydia Polgreen and Marlise Simons, "Global Sludge Ends in Tragedy for Ivory Coast," *New York Times*, October 2, 2006, http://www.nytimes.com/2006/10/02/world/africa/ 02ivory.html?pagewanted=all. And "Trafigura Found Guilty of Exporting Toxic Waste," *BBC News Africa*, July 23, 2010, http://www.bbc.co.uk/news/ world-africa-10735255. For Trafigura's version of events, see http://www.trafig ura.com/media-centre/probo-koala/.

7. THE WILDERNESS YEAR

134 **$1 million for private performances:** Sean Michaels, "Elton John Performs at Rush Limbaugh's Wedding for $1m," *Guardian*, June 8, 2010, http://www .theguardian.com/music/2010/jun/08/elton-john-rush-limbaugh.

139 **Citadel, the large Chicago fund group, had recently done it:** Azam Ahmed, "Citadel Clears Its High Water Mark," *New York Times*, DealBook blog, January 20, 2012, http://dealbook.nytimes.com/2012/01/20/citadel-clears-its-high-water-mark/?_php=true&_type=blogs&_r=0.

8. GOLDMAN SACHS

141 **got an unexpected complaint:** Tatyana Shumsky and Andrea Hotter, "Wall Street Gets Eyed in Metal Squeeze," *Wall Street Journal*, June 17, 2011, http://on line.wsj.com/news/articles/SB10001424052702304186404576389680225394642.

141 **"The situation has been organized"**: Ibid.

142 **increased 13 percent**: Ibid.

142 **when Goldman had paid half a billion dollars**: Jonathan Leff and David Shepard, "Goldman to Resume Talks on Sale of Metals Warehouse Unit: Source," Reuters, November 18, 2013, http://www.reuters.com/article/2013/ 11/18/us-goldman-metro-sale-idUSBRE9AH0U120131118.

142 **coal-mining assets in Colombia**: Juan Pablo Spinetto, "Vale Sells Colombian Coal Assets to Goldman for $407 Million," *Bloomberg Businessweek*, May 28, 2012, http://www.businessweek.com/news/2012-05-28/vale-sells-colombian-coal-assets-to-goldman-for-407-million.

143 **nearly all the world's private warehouses**: Tom Vulcan, "Metals Warehousing: The Perfect Hedge and the Perfect Storm?," *Hard Assets Investor*, March 23, 2012, http://www.hardassetsinvestor.com/features/3567-metals-warehousing-the-perfect-hedge-a-the-perfect-storm.html, along with author's reporting.

144 **Their survey**: "Warehouse Study by Europe Economics," May 27, 2011. The study can be accessed at http://www.lme.com/news-and-events/notices/2011/ 05/11-141-warehouse-study-by-europe-economics/.

144 **1.5 million tons and a sixteen-month queue for removal**: David Kocieniewski, "A Shuffle of Aluminum, But to Banks, Pure Gold," *New York Times*, July 20, 2013, http://www.nytimes.com/2013/07/21/business/a-shuffle-of-aluminum-but-to-banks-pure-gold.html?_r=0.

145 **eighteen different raw materials**: Based on data provided by Standard & Poor's, the current owner of the index.

147 **The aluminum markets were at a crossroads then**: Ed Meir, senior commodity consultant for INTL FC Stone, in phone conversation, March 6, 2013, as well as author's reporting.

148 **the firm's $4 billion in capital**: Phillip L. Zweig, "Goldman Sachs' Spectacular Road Trip," *Bloomberg Businessweek*, October 31, 1993, http://www.business week.com/stories/1993-10-31/goldman-sachs-spectacular-road-trip.

149 **9,600-employee firm**: Phillip L. Zweig et al., "Where Does Goldman Sachs Go from Here?," *Businessweek*, March 19, 1995, http://www.businessweek.com/ stories/1995-03-19/where-does-goldman-sachs-go-from-here.

151 **40 cents per metric ton per day**: "Goldman to Buy LME Warehouse Firm Metro," Reuters, February 18, 2010, http://www.reuters.com/article/2010/02/ 19/us-goldman-metro-idUSTRE61I0ZH20100219 and author reporting.

151 **hired Goldman to advise it on a $12 billion**: FactSet.

152 **45 cents per ton . . . $200 million per year**: Dustin Walsh, "Aluminum Stores Grow at Warehouses," *Crain's Detroit Business*, July 30, 2012, http://www .crainsdetroit.com/article/20120729/SUB01/307299986/aluminum-stores-grow-at-warehouses.

153 **Premiums had gone from**: Based on proprietary data from CRU Group, provided by Michael Southwood, senior metals consultant at CRU.

154 **Goldman was the subject of a tough story**: David Kocieniewski, "A Shuffle of Aluminum."

155 **Goldman received subpoenas**: Jack Farchy and Thomas Braithwaite, "Subpoenas Issued over Metals Warehouse Probe," *Financial Times*, August 12,

2013, http://www.ft.com/intl/cms/s/0/b8917ace-037f-11e3-b871-00144feab7de. html?siteedition=intl#axzz2rGnkpzbz.

155 **if aluminum prices had fallen:** The 28 percent figure was confirmed independently with LME after first reading about it in commentary on MetalMiner. Lisa Reisman, "MetalMiner, Goldman Sachs Battle It Out over LME Aluminum," *MetalMiner,* July 31, 2013, http://agmetalminer.com/2013/07/31/goldman-sachs-metalminer-battle-it-out-over-lme-aluminum/.

156 **Cohn hurriedly booked a television interview and went on CNBC:** Gary Cohn, interview by Kate Kelly, *Halftime Report,* CNBC, July 31, 2013, http://video.cnbc.com/gallery/?video=3000187032.

156 **Justice Department inquiry:** Jamila Trindle and Tatyana Shumsky, "U.S. Probes Metals Warehouse Firms," *Wall Street Journal,* July 25, 2013, http://online.wsj.com/news/articles/SB10001424127887323971204578628232626155990.

9. THE DEAL

158 **"man of steel":** Martin Baker, "Ex-Goalie Scores in Metals," *Telegraph,* October 8, 2006, http://www.telegraph.co.uk/finance/2948607/Ex-goalie-scores-in-metals.html.

162 **before its $28 billion merger:** Anita Raghavan, S. Karene Witcher, and Andrew Trounson, "BHP, Billiton to Merge Operations to Create a Global Mining Giant," *Wall Street Journal,* March 19, 2001, http://online.wsj.com/article/SB984931118144036379.html.

163 **Vale about a purchase:** Rebecca Bream, "Vale Blames Delays in Xstrata Bid on Glencore," *Financial Times,* March 1, 2008, http://www.ft.com/intl/cms/s/0/fe1571ea-e701-11dc-b5c3-0000779fd2ac.html?siteedition=intl#axzz2rGnkpzbz.

164 **private-equity firms and the sovereign-wealth fund:** Mara Der Hovanesian, "A Dark Horse at Citi," *Businessweek,* November 28, 2007, http://www.businessweek.com/stories/2007-11-28/a-dark-horse-at-citi.

164 **advised the UK:** Michael J. de la Merced, "Former Citi Banker Earns Spot on Glencore-Xstrata Merger by Himself," *New York Times,* DealBook blog, February 7, 2012, http://dealbook.nytimes.com/2012/02/07/former-citi-banker-earns-spot-on-glencore-xstrata-merger-by-himself/?_r=0.

164 **helped keep its corporate culture smooth:** Mara Der Hovanesian, "A Dark Horse."

166 **Mack had left Morgan Stanley:** Landon Thomas Jr., "John Mack Is Back at Morgan Stanley," *New York Times,* July 1, 2005, http://www.nytimes.com/2005/06/30/business/worldbusiness/30iht-morgan.html.

167 **wouldn't catch him lying on a beach:** John W. Miller, "Glasenberg: We Don't Do Work-Life Balance," *Wall Street Journal,* MoneyBeat blog, May 3, 2013, http://blogs.wsj.com/moneybeat/2013/05/03/glasenberg-we-dont-do-work-life-balance/.

167 **February 7, 2012, Glencore and Xstrata:** Glencore & Xstrata, "Recommended All-Share Merger of Equals of Glencore International PLC and Xstrata PLC to Create Unique $90 Billion Natural Resources Group," news release, February 7, 2012.

NOTES

168 **"fabulous deal for Glencore":** Sarah Young and Eric Onstad, "Glencore-Xstrata $90B Deal Meets Shareholder Opposition," *Financial Post*, February 7, 2012, http://business.financialpost.com/2012/02/07/glencore-xstrata-90b-deal-meets-shareholder-opposition/.

168 **16 percent no-vote:** Lianna Brinded, "Timeline and FactBox: Glencore and Xstrata Merger," *International Business Times*, May 3, 2013, http://www.ibtimes.co.uk/glencore-xstrata-merger-shares-trading-qatar-sovereign-464122. Further details on the terms of the merger can be found at "Recommended All-Share Merger of Equals of Glencore International PLC and Xstrata PLC," Deal Circular, p. 48, http://www.glencorexstrata.com/assets/Uploads/Everest-Scheme-Circular.pdf.

168 **(the 34 percent Glencore owned):** Ibid.

168 **3.6 percent stake:** Jan Willem van Gelder and Barbara Kuepper, "The Financing of Glencore and Xstrata," Profundo Economic Research, Amsterdam, December 4, 2012.

168 **talking to executives at Morgan Stanley:** Kate Kelly, "Morgan Stanley, Qatari Fund May Do Commodities Deal," *CNBC*, July 20, 2012, http://www.cnbc.com/id/48241872.

169 **5 percent:** Dinesh Nair, "Qatar Builds Up Xstrata Stake Ahead of Glencore Deal," Reuters, April 9, 2012, http://www.reuters.com/article/2012/04/09/us-qatar-xstrata-idUSBRE83805320120409.

170 **oversupply in Europe and general negativity:** Vattenfall, "Commodity Markets at a Glance: April 2012," http://www.vattenfall.com/en/file/Commodity_Markets_at_a_Glance_April_2012_20780475.pdf.

170 **retention packages:** "Recommended All-Share Merger of Equals of Glencore International PLC and Xstrata PLC," Deal Circular, pp. 31–34. http://www.glencorexstrata.com/assets/Uploads/Everest-Scheme-Circular.pdf.

171 **The British bank Barclays:** Howard Mustoe, "Barclays Says 27% of Investors Voted Against Pay Package," Bloomberg, April 27, 2012, http://www.bloomberg.com/news/2012-04-27/barclays-says-27-of-investors-voted-against-executive-pay-plan.html.

171 **advertiser WPP:** Robert Budden and David Oakley, "WPP Suffers Shareholder Revolt over Executive Pay," *Financial Times*, June 12, 2013, http://www.ft.com/intl/cms/s/0/933c8ac2-d380-11e2-b3ff-00144feab7de.html#axzz2rGnkpzbz.

171 **chief of the insurer Aviva:** Marietta Cauchi and Vladimir Guevarra, "U.K. Pay Protests Oust Aviva Chief," *Wall Street Journal*, May 8, 2012, http://online.wsj.com/news/articles/SB10001424052702304363104577391282844502266.

171 **"in jeopardy":** David Cumming interview, "*Today*," BBC, quoted in Jill Treanor, "Xstrata-Glencore Tie-Up 'in Jeopardy' over retention packages," *Guardian*, June 25, 2012, http://www.theguardian.com/business/2012/jun/25/xstrata-glencore-tie-up-in-jeopardy.

171 **"Xstrata should be under no delusions":** Helia Ebrahimi and James Quinn, "Chiefs at Risk in Xstrata Merger," *Telegraph*, February 4, 2012, http://www.telegraph.co.uk/finance/newsbysector/industry/mining/9061755/Chiefs-at-risk-in-Xstrata-merger-talks.html.

173 **A press release was soon to be issued:** Qatar Holding, "Qatar Holding Seeks Improved Terms in Proposed Merger of Glencore with Xstrata," news release, June 26, 2012.

174 **10 percent at last check:** Chris Wright, "Sovereign Wealth Funds: Qatar Seals Its Kingmaker Role in Xstrata Deal," *Euromoney,* December 2012, http://www.euromoney.com/Article/3123638/Sovereign-wealth-funds-Qatar-seals-its-kingmaker-role-in-Xstrata-deal.html.

175 **had fallen 42 percent:** Half-Yearly Report 2012, Xstrata, http://www.glencorexstrata.com/assets/Uploads/xta-ir2012-en.pdf.

176 **"end of the world":** Josephine Moulds, "Glencore's Merger with Xstrata Close to Collapse," *Guardian,* August 21, 2012, http://www.theguardian.com/business/2012/aug/21/glencore-merger-xstrata-close-collapse.

176 **north of 12 percent:** Mirna Sleiman and Dinesh Nair, "Qatar Demands Respect with Muscular Xstrata Strategy," Reuters, September 6, 2012, http://www.reuters.com/article/2012/09/06/us-qatar-glencore-strategy-idUSBRE8850PD20120906.

178 **Harrods and a huge skyscraper:** Edna Fernandes, "How Qatar Bought Britain," *Daily Mail,* March 10, 2012, http://www.dailymail.co.uk/news/article-2113159/.

179 **"Bloody hell":** Anousha Sakoui, Javier Blas, and Helen Thomas, "Glencore Raises Stakes in Xstrata Deal," *Financial Times,* September 7, 2012, http://www.ft.com/intl/cms/s/0/0cfe770c-f8b3-11e1-b4ba-00144feabdc0.html#axzz2rGnkpzbz.

10. THE REFORMER

181 **$600 trillion:** Claudio Borio et al., eds., Bank of International Settlements: *Quarterly Review,* December 2011, Statistical Annex, p. A10, http://www.bis.org/publ/qtrpdf/r_qs1112.pdf.

186 **like Delta:** Kit R. Roane, "Mike Masters: The Making of a Maverick," *Institutional Investor,* September 1, 2011, http://www.institutionalinvestor.com/Popups/PrintArticle.aspx?ArticleID=2892271.

187 **Futures Industry Association echoed Dunn's language:** Futures Industry Association to David Stawick, Secretary of the Commodity Futures Trading Commission, March 25, 2011, http://www.futuresindustry.org/downloads/FIA_Position_Limits_Comment_Letter.pdf.

187 **The proposal would "hamper":** Ann Battle, Associate at Sutherland, Asbill and Brennan LLP, on behalf of United States Commodity Funds LLC, to David Stawick, Secretary of the Commodity Futures Trading Commission, October 21, 2010. In the absence of a working link at cftc.gov, the letter can be viewed at http://www.marketsreformwiki.com/mktreformwiki/index.php/Position_Limits_Regulation_-_Comment_Letter_-_United_States_Commodity_Funds_-_October_21,_2010.

189 **the CFTC finally held another vote:** Asjylyn Loder and Silla Brush, "Top U.S. Regulator Approves New Limit on Commodity Speculation in 3–2 Vote,"

Bloomberg, October 18, 2011, http://www.bloomberg.com/news/2011-10-18/cftc-votes-3-2-to-approve-new-limits-on-commodity-speculation.html.

189 **published his white paper:** Frenk and Turbeville, "Commodity Index Traders."

189 **"enormous failure":** Jill E. Sommers, "Opening Statement, Fifth Open Meeting to Consider Final Rules Pursuant to the Dodd-Frank Act" (Commodity Futures Trading Commission Public Hearing, Washington, D.C., October 18, 2011).

189 **"sideshow":** Michael V. Dunn, "Opening Statement, Public Meeting on Final Rules Under the Dodd-Frank Act" (Commodity Futures Trading Commission Public Hearing, Washington, D.C., October 18, 2011), http://www.cftc.gov/PressRoom/SpeechesTestimony/dunnstatement101811.

192 **both of whom had worked previously at BP:** Rex Dalton, "Oil Speculators: Civil Complaint Names Nicholas Wildgoose of Fairbanks Ranch," *San Diego Reader,* June 22, 2011, http://www.sandiegoreader.com/news/2011/jun/22/citylights2-Nicholas-Wildgoose-oil-speculators/?page=1&.

192 **"shitload of money":** Grant McCool, "Arcadia, Parnon Fight Oil Price Manipulation Lawsuits," Reuters, October 10, 2012, http://www.reuters.com/article/2012/10/11/oil-futures-lawsuit-idUSL1E8LB1KK20121011.

193 **$50 million in profits:** Commodity Futures Trading Commission, "CFTC Charges Parnon Energy Inc. Arcadia Petroleum Ltd., and Arcadia Energy (Suisse) SA with Price Manipulation in the Crude Oil Market," news release, May 24, 2011.

193 **just above junk:** Aaron Lucchetti, "Moody's Cuts MF Global Rating to Near Junk," *Wall Street Journal,* October 25, 2011, http://online.wsj.com/news/articles/SB10001424052970203911804576651462414325974?KEYWORDS=MF+Global+Moody.

193 **MF Global stock fell slightly:** Ibid.

193 **MF opted to report quarterly earnings early:** Peter Elkind with Doris Burke, "The Last Days of MF Global," *Fortune,* June 4, 2012, http://finance.fortune.cnn.com/2012/06/04/the-last-days-of-mf-global/.

194 **considering lowering MF Global's credit rating to actual junk:** Shira Ovide and Jacob Bunge, "S&P May Cut MF Global's Credit Rating to Junk," *Wall Street Journal,* Deal Journal blog, October 26, 2011, http://blogs.wsj.com/deals/2011/10/26/sp-cuts-mf-globals-credit-rating/.

194 **eighth-largest futures broker:** Jacob Bunge, "MF Global: What Would a Buyer Be Getting?" *Wall Street Journal,* Deal Journal blog, October 30, 2011, http://blogs.wsj.com/deals/2011/10/30/mf-global-what-would-a-buyer-be-getting/?KEYWORDS=MF+Global.

195 **two-thirds of its value:** Jacob Bunge, "MF Global Shares Hung Up in Limbo," *Wall Street Journal,* Deal Journal blog, October 31, 2011, http://blogs.wsj.com/deals/2011/10/31/mf-global-shares-hung-up-in-limbo/.

195 **Central to the market's . . . last-minute deal:** Aaron Lucchetti, Justin Baer, and Mike Spector, "Corzine Races to Save Firm," *Wall Street Journal,* October 31, 2011, http://online.wsj.com/news/articles/SB100014240529702045282045770080904280888540 with additional reporting by the author.

195 **On October 28:** *CFTC v. MF Global Inc., MF Global Holding Ltd., Jon S. Corzine, and Edith O'Brien*, 13 CIV 4463 (The District Court for the Southern District of NY, 2013), http://www.cftc.gov/ucm/groups/public/@lrenforcementactions/documents/legalpleading/enfmfglobalcomplaint062713.pdf.

195 **collaborated with Goldman's rivals:** Roger Lowenstein, "Corzine Forgot Lessons of Long-Term Capital," Bloomberg, November 1, 2011, http://www.bloomberg.com/news/2011-11-02/corzine-forgot-lessons-of-long-term-capital-roger-lowenstein.html.

195 **convince his fellow partners:** Craig Horowitz, "The Deal He Made," *New York*, July 18, 2005, http://nymag.com/nymetro/news/politics/12194/index6.html.

195 **$400 million:** Roben Farzad and Matthew Leising, "Corzine Lived Up to Risk-Taking Reputation at Helm of MF Global," Bloomberg, November 3, 2011, http://www.bloomberg.com/news/2011-11-03/corzine-lived-up-to-risk-taking-reputation-at-mf-global-before-bankruptcy.html.

196 **had abandoned his first marriage:** Ibid.

196 **been critically injured:** Bryan Burrough, William D. Cohan, and Bethany McLean, "Jon Corzine's Riskiest Business," *Vanity Fair*, February 2012, http://www.vanityfair.com/business/2012/02/jon-corzine-201202.

196 **guffawing about getting drunk:** Skybridge Alternatives (SALT) Conference, May 2011. On a panel moderated by the author. Video available at http://www.businessinsider.com/video-jon-corzine-talks-about-getting-drunk-2011-11.

196 **fired fourteen hundred people:** Burrough, Cohan, and McLean, "Jon Corzine's Riskiest Business."

197 **crude-oil volumes were lower than usual:** Christian Berthelsen, "MF Global's Ripples in Crude Oil Market," *Wall Street Journal*, Deal Journal blog, October 31, 2011, http://blogs.wsj.com/deals/2011/10/31/mf-globals-ripples-in-crude-oil-market/.

197 **effectively barred from the markets:** Mike Spector, Jacob Bunge, and Aaron Lucchetti, "MF Global Collapses as Books Questioned," *Wall Street Journal*, November 1, 2011, http://online.wsj.com/news/articles/SB10001424052970204528204577009473406903312.

197 **he had used Corzine's entry number:** Silla Brush, "Corzine Wasn't Too Close with CFTC Chief, Review Finds," Bloomberg, July 31, 2012 http://www.bloomberg.com/news/2012-07-31/corzine-wasn-t-too-close-with-cftc-chief-review-finds.html. The "confidential" memo referred to in the article above can be viewed at http://www.cftc.gov/ucm/groups/public/@freedomofinformationact/documents/file/participationmattersmfg.pdf.

198 **Parnon, and the former BP traders was moving through the court system:** This was still true as of February 2014. See Bob Van Voris, "Oil Probe Records Disclosure Won't Be Delayed, Court Says," Bloomberg, December 10, 2013, http://www.bloomberg.com/news/2013-12-10/oil-probe-records-disclosure-won-t-be-delayed-court-says.html.

198 **ninety-nine different enforcement actions:** Commodity Futures Trading Commission, "CFTC Releases Annual Enforcement Results," news release, October 6, 2011, http://www.cftc.gov/PressRoom/PressReleases/pr6121-11.

199 **Soon he was getting multiple hundreds of millions:** Commodity Futures Trading Commission, "CFTC Releases Enforcement Division's Annual Results," news release, October 24, 2013, http://www.cftc.gov/PressRoom/PressReleases/pr6749-13.

199 **threw out the CFTC proposal:** Bill Singer, "Dramatic Federal Court Ruling Vacates CFTC Positions Limit Rule," *Forbes*, September 28, 2012, http://www.forbes.com/sites/billsinger/2012/09/28/dramatic-federal-court-ruling-vacates-cftc-positions-limit-rule/.

201 **which Corzine was fighting:** Attempts by Corzine's attorneys to have the CFTC suit, as well as other claims against him, dismissed failed. See Jacqueline Palank, "Judge Rules Suit Against Corzine Can Move Ahead," *Wall Street Journal*, February 11, 2014, http://online.wsj.com/news/articles/SB10001424052702304104504579377141033786398.

201 **rule filing:** Commodity Futures Trading Commission, "17 CFR Parts 1, 15, 17 et al. Position Limits for Derivatives, Proposed Rule," *Federal Register* 78, no. 239 (December 12, 2013): 75680.

202 **he eviscerated the industry lobbying . . . until things turned in its favor:** William D. Cohan, "Angry Bart Takes His Parting Shot," Bloomberg, December 24, 2013, http://www.bloomberg.com/news/2013-12-24/angry-bart-takes-his-parting-shot.html.

11. THE SIDE BET

205 **Citing a respected:** FAA Aerospace Forecast Fiscal years 2012–2032, p. 35. http://www.faa.gov/about/office_org/headquarters_offices/apl/aviation_forecasts/aerospace_forecasts/2012-2032/media/FAA%20Aerospace%20Forecasts%20FY%202012-2032.pdf.

208 **CNBC had the story:** Kate Kelly, "Delta Eyeing ConocoPhillips Refinery for More Than $100 million," CNBC, April 4, 2012, http://www.cnbc.com/id/46883861.

209 **"because they're stupid":** Steve Schaefer, "Why Buying a Refinery Could Be a Disaster for Delta Airlines (Even with JPMorgan's Help)," *Forbes*, April 11, 2012, http://www.forbes.com/sites/steveschaefer/2012/04/11/why-buying-a-refinery-could-be-a-disaster-for-delta-air-lines-even-with-jpmorgans-help/.

210 **Phillips 66:** Effective May 2012, ConocoPhillips had split into two companies, and Phillips 66 was the name of the resultant entity that sold the Trainer facility to Delta. See Phillips 66, "Our History," http://www.phillips66.com/EN/about/history/Pages/index.aspx.

210 **in a television interview:** Kate Kelly, CNBC, May 1, 2012, http://video.cnbc.com/gallery/?video=3000087462&play=1.

210 **"It's our intention":** Paul Burkhardt and Mary Schlangenstein, "Delta CEO Says Airline to Pressure Prices as Jet Fuel Seller," *Bloomberg Businessweek*, June 15, 2012, http://www.businessweek.com/news/2012-06-15/delta-ceo-says-airline-to-pressure-prices-as-jet-fuel-seller.

211 **pricing window:** Platts, "An Introduction to Platts Market-on-Close Process in Petroleum," McGraw Hill Financial, http://www.platts.com/IM.Platts.Content/aboutplatts/mediacenter/PDF/Platts_IntrooilMOC.pdf.

211 **telling another reporter at Reuters:** Janet McGurty, "Delta Says It Won't Sell Jet Fuel on Open Market," Reuters, June 18, 2012, http://in.reuters.com/article/2012/06/18/us-refinery-operations-delta-monroe-idINBRE85H12W20120618.

213 **a margin requirement of $350 million:** Delta Air Lines, "Delta Announces June Quarter Financial Results," news release, July 25, 2012, http://ir.delta.com/files/earnings/2012/Delta%20Air%20Lines%20Announces%20June%202012%20Quarter%20Financial%20Results.pdf.

219 **Iranian uranium-producing bunker:** Phoebe Greenwood, "Mystery Over 'Explosion' at Iran's Fordow Nuclear Site," *Telegraph,* January 28, 2013, http://www.telegraph.co.uk/news/worldnews/middleeast/iran/9831282/Mystery-over-explosion-at-Irans-Fordow-nuclear-site.html.

12. THE POP

223 **Clive Capital:** While this was true in the relevant time frame, by September 2013, Clive Capital would also close. Jesse Westbrook and Chris Larson, "Clive Capital Fund Plans to Close after Two Years of Losses," Bloomberg, September 20, 2013, http://www.bloomberg.com/news/2013-09-20/clive-capital-fund-plans-to-close-after-two-years-of-losses-1-.html.

223 **on track to lose almost 3 percent:** Newedge CTA Index, Monthly Return, http://www.newedge.com/content/dam/newedgecom/internal_feeds/Newedge_CTA_Monthly_Report.pdf.

224 **like walking in front of a steamroller:** Bruno J. Navarro, "Leon Cooperman's Top Stocks for 2013," CNBC, January 2, 2013, http://www.cnbc.com/id/100349212.

225 **8 percent of it per year:** Ianthe Jeanne Dugan, "Pension Funds Cut Back on Commodity Indexes," *Wall Street Journal,* February 5, 2013, http://online.wsj.com/news/articles/SB10001424127887324761004578286172166045096.

226 **the Iowa futures brokerage that:** Jacqueline Palank, "Court Approves Distribution to Peregrine Customers," *Wall Street Journal,* December 18, 2013, http://online.wsj.com/news/articles/SB10001424052702304866904579266440192687088?KEYWORDS=peregrine+financial.

226 **of MF Global:** James O'Toole, "MF Global Ordered to Repay Customers $1.2B," *CNNMoney,* November 18, 2013, http://money.cnn.com/2013/11/18/investing/mf-global/.

226 **The bank was fined $410 million:** Federal Energy Regulatory Commission, "FERC, JP Morgan Unit Agree to $410 Million in Penalties, Disgorgement to Rate Payers," news release, July 30, 2013, http://www.ferc.gov/media/news-releases/2013/2013-3/07-30-13.asp#.Uunhg_lkSSo.

226 **possible criminal actions:** Emily Flitter, "JPMorgan Subject of Obstruction Probe in Energy Case," Reuters, September 4, 2013, http://www.reuters.com/article/2013/09/04/us-jpm-ferc-doj-idUSBRE9830QM20130904. By the end of 2013, JP Morgan had disclosed that they were in fact the subject of eight on-going investigations by the Department of Justice, including the investigation into criminal activity related to the case brought against them by

FERC. See Dawn Kopecki and Hugh Son, "JPMorgan Discloses Eight DOJ Probes From Asia to Madoff," Bloomberg, November 1, 2013, http://www.bloomberg.com/news/2013-11-01/jpmorgan-discloses-eight-doj-probes-from-asia-to-madoff.html.

226 **JP Morgan announced plans:** Kate Kelly, "Big Banks Are Looking to Dump Commodities Units," CNBC, November 1, 2013, http://www.cnbc.com/id/101160422.

227 **a private lawsuit accusing it of anticompetitive behavior:** On August 29, 2014, the antitrust claims were dismissed by a federal judge.

227 **in a scathing, 400-page report:** Permanent Subcommittee on Investigations, *Wall Street Bank Involvement with Physical Commodities*, November 20 and 21, 2014, http://www.hsgac.senate.gov/subcommittees/investigations.

227 **Levin was blunt in his depiction:** Kate Kelly, "Goldman Accused of Exploiting Aluminum Storage Rules," CNBC, November 19, 2014, http://www.cnbc.com/id/102201021.

228 **"The queues were the result":** Goldman Sachs, "Statement of Goldman Sachs: Background and Facts on Financial Intermediation, Certain Investments and Risk Management in the Commodities Markets," November 19, 2014, p. 2, http://www.goldmansachs.com/media-relations/in-the-news/current/commodities-markets-and-financial-intermediation.pdf.

229 **months before the Senate hearings:** Josephine Mason, "Goldman Puts Metro Metals Warehousing Unit up for Sale," Reuters, May 20, 2014, http://www.reuters.com/article/2014/05/21/us-goldman-metals-sale-idUSBREA-4J0NO20140521.

229 **"Stealing Africa":** *Stealing Africa*, a film directed by Christoffer Guldbrandsen (STEPS, 2013). http://www.whypoverty.net/en/all-about/stealing-africa/.

229 **BBC documentary:** John Sweeney, "Billionaires Behaving Badly?," *BBC Panorama*, April 23, 2012, in the absence of a working BBC link, the program can be found at http://www.youtube.com/watch?v=aSr_RgAPQ1M. Glencore's response can be found here: http://www.glencorexstrata.com/assets/uploads/201204160800-response-to-panorama.pdf.

231 **Arbalet Capital . . . She was thirty:** Barani Krishnan, "Former Head of Arbalet Commodities Fund Joins Millennium," Reuters, February 5, 2014, http://www.reuters.com/article/2014/02/05/us-hedgefund-commodities-fan-idUSBREA1421N20140205.

INDEX

INDEX

INDEX